THE FERN GUIDE

NORTHEASTERN AND
MIDLAND UNITED STATES
AND ADJACENT CANADA

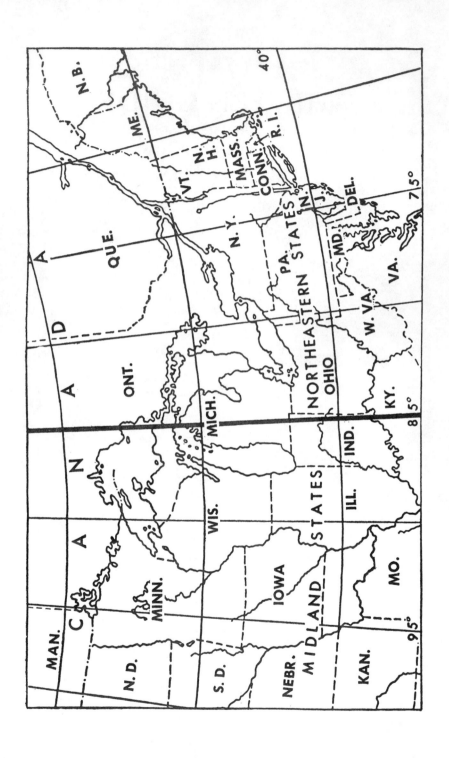

THE FERN GUIDE

NORTHEASTERN AND
MIDLAND UNITED STATES
AND ADJACENT CANADA

EDGAR T. WHERRY

ILLUSTRATED BY
JAMES C. W. CHEN

DOVER PUBLICATIONS, INC.
New York

Published in Canada by General Publishing Company, Ltd., 30 Lesmill Road, Don Mills, Toronto, Ontario.

Bibliographical Note

This Dover edition, first published in 1995, is an unabridged and unaltered republication of the work originally published by Doubleday & Company, Inc., Garden City, New York, 1961, as part of the Doubleday Nature Guides Series.

Library of Congress Cataloging-in-Publication Data

Wherry, Edgar Theodore, 1885–
    The fern guide : Northeastern and Midland United States and adjacent Canada / Edgar T. Wherry ; illustrated by James C.W. Chen.
        p.   cm.
    Originally published: Garden City, N.Y. : Doubleday, 1961, in series: Doubleday nature guides series ; 9).
    Includes bibliographical references (p.   ) and indexes.
    ISBN 0-486-28496-4 (pbk.)
    1. Ferns—Northeastern States—Identification. 2. Ferns—Middle West—Identification. 3. Ferns—Canada, Eastern—Identification. I. Title.
QK525.W59 1995
587'.3'0973—dc20
        94-39732
        CIP

Manufactured in the United States of America
Dover Publications, Inc., 31 East 2nd Street, Mineola, N.Y. 11501

DEDICATED TO AN UNKNOWN NATURALIST

W. I. BEECROFT

AUTHOR OF "WHO'S WHO AMONG THE FERNS"

WHICH IN 1915 AWAKENED MY INTEREST IN

THESE PLANTS AND SO MAY BE CONSIDERED

THE PROTHALLIUM OF THE PRESENT GUIDE

In the preparation of this book the author has received deeply appreciated friendly, helpful advice from many colleagues; they are not to be blamed, however, for the various unorthodox nomenclatorial plans adopted. The difficult task of bringing a complex mass of technical material into publishable form has been ably carried out by members of the staff of Doubleday and Company, notably DeElda Elwood, who put the manuscript into shape, Edwin Kaplin, who as book designer selected type and planned page arrangements, Sabra Mallett, who looked after the illustrations, and last but not least Clara Claasen, Nature Guide Series Editor, without whose encouragement, and aid in numerous directions, this book would never have appeared.

CONTENTS

INTRODUCTION

Over twenty years ago the writer published a *Guide to Eastern Ferns* as "an aid in the identification of the ferns and fern-allies of the region from Pennsylvania and New Jersey to Virginia"; a revised edition followed in 1942. Its popularity has encouraged the preparation of a similar work covering the whole of the northeastern and midland states, together with adjacent Canada. About 135 species are known to occur in this region; each of these is treated in a page of text (or for less important ones, half a page), facing a plate in which their significant characters are brought out. The drawings have been skillfully made by Mr. James C. W. Chen, a Formosan student of botany at the University of Pennsylvania.

Since technical botanical terms are in general simpler and more precise than colloquial expressions, they are used extensively in this *Guide*. To aid in their understanding, a Glossary is given immediately following this Introduction. To refer to the leafy structure of ferns, the time-honored term, frond, is here accepted, not in the sense of *Gray's Manual*, ed. 8, of merely a blade, but in that of *Britton & Brown's Flora*, ed. 3, of a blade plus a stalk (stipe). Some writers, to be sure, call this a leaf; but since true leaves (in flowering plants) never bear reproductive organs, while the corresponding structures in ferns do so, distinct terminology is deemed to be desirable. Measurements are given in the metric rather than the English system because the former is used in all scientific work, and is moreover becoming increasingly familiar to the general public. For simplicity, only the two units, millimeters (mm.) and centimeters (cm.) are actually employed. A diagram showing these in comparison with inches is furnished, with suggested arithmetical procedures for converting one to the other.

In planning the new *Guide,* helpful suggestions made by users of the previous one have been taken into account. One is concerned with the desirability of explaining how a key is constructed and how it is to be used, as well as making the keys easier to follow through. Accordingly when, preceding the text, keys are introduced, the plan on which they are based is discussed at the start. Then, instead of the inset type of key used in the previous *Guide,* the couplet type is adopted.

Another comment refers to the difficulty beginners have with nomenclature, in particular in understanding how it has come about that a given fern is often assigned different technical names from one "popular" fern book to another, and for that matter in two successive editions of the standard reference works, *Gray's Manual* (eds. 7 and 8) and *Britton & Brown's Flora* (eds. 2 and 3). This admittedly regrettable state of affairs has resulted from a number of causes, of which three of the more significant merit discussion.

(1) Rule changes. Technical names of plants are selected in accordance with rules which are assembled in *Codes of Botanical Nomenclature.* The first of these was published in 1867; in the nine subsequent decades the rules have undergone many changes, and every few years are revised again, some of the new ones being made retroactive.

(2) Unfamiliarity with literature. Especially in earlier days, when library facilities were poor, authors often proposed a new name for plants which had already received one, or applied to one plant a name previously assigned to another. When such duplications are discovered, the principle of priority, fundamental in all codes, comes into play: the only acceptable name for a given taxon (genus, species, etc.) is the earliest one published, (starting with the *Species Plantarum,* of Linnaeus, 1753) accompanied by sufficient data to establish its identity, later ones being discarded.

(3) Difference in viewpoint. Two taxa considered by one worker to belong to distinct genera or species may be placed by another in the same genus or species, and so on.

The plants treated in this *Guide* belong to the major group known as the Tracheophytes, in reference to their possession of a vascular system of long tubular cells; their conspicuous stage is the sporophyte, producing spores which germinate into a relatively small gametophyte, which gives rise to male and female gametes whose union forms a new sporophyte, thus completing the life-cycle. It is convenient (even though technically unsound) to subdivide this group into Pteridophytes (from Greek for fern plants) with independent gametophytes, and Anthophytes (from Greek for flower plants) with these organs developing within flowers.

Pteridophytes comprise Ferns and so-called Fern-allies, which since they are really not allied to ferns are here termed Lycosphens, a word formed by combining the initial syllables of the technical names of two of their divisions. All are assigned to families, genera, and species, a few to geographic varieties (or subspecies) and forms; there are also several interspecies hybrids.

For many years the Ferns proper have been placed in one comprehensive family, the Polypodiaceae; assignment to it is based on the possession of a unique type of sporangium, readily distinguished from that characterizing the other time-honored families. Recent workers have essayed to split this assemblage into several lesser ones, under individual family names; some of these comprise plants of such diverse character, however, as to defy any simple definition, and so to disfavor recognition here. The families, as well as the genera and species accepted, are mostly those to be found in one or the other of the two major reference works, *Gray's Manual*, ed. 8, and *Britton & Brown's Flora*, ed. 3.

The sequence here followed is, however, not that of either of the above works; instead, the taxa deemed to be the most highly specialized are treated first, followed by successively more primitive ones. This has the merit of locating the more commonly encountered ferns on early pages, and of ending with the rarer Clubmosses, the closest living relatives of the ancestral vascular plants.

Many modern taxonomists term the major species subdivision a subspecies. Thus far, however, only a few ferns have received names in this category, and as this *Guide* would not be an appropriate place to coin new combinations, subspecies are mentioned only incidentally. Instead the term, variety (abbreviated to v. or var.), is used for plants deemed not to merit species status, yet exhibiting some geographic or ecologic peculiarity of distribution.

When a species is divided into varieties, need may arise for indicating which of them includes the species-type. The once frequent plan of stating that "this variety differs from the species in such and such ways" involves contrasting a whole object with part of itself, so is illogical and unacceptable. The proper sort of statement is "this variety differs from the type variety of the species in . . ." Recent *Codes of Nomenclature* call for repeating the species epithet for type-including varieties; the resulting double talk seems, however, too confusing to introduce in a popular guide. Type (not "typical") variety is used here, in that the individual specimen which chanced to be selected as the basis of a taxon is not necessarily really typical of this as a whole.

The next lower category term form (abbreviated to f.) is here applied to mutants or sports which occur in the midst of populations of normal plants. Only a few of the more notable forms are included.

That hybridization can occur in ferns has long been recognized; while most frequent among species within one genus, hybrids between members of seemingly distinct genera are occasional. Hybrids are usually designated by placing the epithets of the parents in alphabetical order, separated by the symbol ✕. Some ferns originally named and often long classed as species have proved on detailed study to be really hybrids; their quasi-specific epithets are then preceded by the ✕. Since hybrids combine the characters of the parents, it has been deemed worth while to figure only a few. Simple hybrids are usually sterile, reproducing only vegetatively; however, chromosome-doubling sometimes occurs in them, resulting in normally reproducing polyploid species.

GLOSSARY OF TECHNICAL TERMS

acuminate: tapering to a sharp point.
acute: ending in a sharp point without tapering.
annulus: a ring of thick-walled cells on a sporangium.
apiculate: ending abruptly in a sharp point of blade tissue.
appressed: bent up against a stalk or margin.
areole: the space between veins which separate and rejoin.
auricle: an ear-like basal lobe.
axil: the notch between a stalk and anything arising from it.

basionym: the earliest name-combination including an epithet.
blade: the broad flat portion of a frond, leaf, or division.
bog: an open, wet, acid-soil area, with low-growing plants.

calcareous: containing lime in a form available to plants.
cilia: hairs extending from a margin.
circumneutral: from slightly acid to slightly alkaline.
code: the current set of rules for selecting technical names.
combination: the genus name plus the species epithet.
compound: made up of multiple parts.
cone: an ellipsoid to cylindric group of sporophyls.
cordate: having two large basal lobes, with broad notch.
coriaceous: of firm, dry texture.
crenate: shallowly cut into rounded teeth.

deciduous: withering at the close of a growing season.
dimorphic: having dissimilar fertile and sterile blades.
disjunct: occurring at points a considerable distance apart.

elliptic: rounded in outline and widened in the middle.
endemic: ranging over a limited area.
entire: having the margin uninterrupted by notches.
epithet: the technical name of a species or lower taxon.
erose: irregularly cut or frayed out at tip or margin.

falcate: obliquely curved like a scythe blade.
fertile: bearing reproductive organs, especially spores.
form (*forma;* abbrev., f.) : a minor variant of a species.
free: descriptive of separated vein tips and other objects.
frond: the "leaf" of a fern, comprising stipe and blade.

gametophyte: the sexual stage in a life-cycle.
genus (pl., genera): a group of closely related species.
glabrous: smooth; lacking hairs or scales.
gland: a waxy globule, often tipping a hair; may be fragrant.
glaucous: coated with a bluish gray film.

hirsute: bearing coarse hairs.
hybrid: the product of the union of sex-cells of two species.

incised: cut in a coarse, irregular manner.
indusium: a sheet of pale tissue covering a fern sorus.
internode: the portion of a stem between two nodes.

lanceolate: narrow-based, widening a bit, then tapering up.
lateral: lying at one side.
linear: long and narrow with essentially parallel sides.
lobe: a short, rounded division of a blade.
lunate: shaped like the quarter moon.
lycosphen: a novel term to replace the inapt "fern-ally."

meadow: an open, moist area, usually grass-covered.
medial: in the middle of; -sori, between margin and midrib.
megaspore: a relatively large female spore.
membranous: thinner in texture than ordinary blade-tissue.
microspore: a relatively small male spore.
midrib: a heavy vein medial in a blade or division.

node: the place on a stem at which branches or leaves arise.

oblong: parallel-sided and moderately longer than broad.
obsolete: lacking where expected to be present.
obtuse: blunt or rounded off at tip.
ovate: narrow-based, markedly widened, then short-tapering.

palmate: divided into a few diverging portions.
panicle: an open compound group of reproductive structures.
peduncle: the stalk supporting a cone or group of them.
peltate: supported by a central stalk, as in an umbrella.
petiole: a leaf stalk; in ferns often termed a stipe.
pilose: bearing long soft hairs.
pinna: a blade-division spaced on an axis, as in a feather.
pinnule: a pinna-division, similarly spaced on its axis.

pinnulet: proposed term for an analogous pinnule-division.
ploidy: number of chromosome-sets in a cell; see Cytology.
prothallium: the small sexual plant in a life-cycle.
pubescent: bearing hair of any sort.

rachis: the axis of a pinnate blade, bare between pinnae.
reflexed: bent backward or downward.
reniform: kidney-shaped; elliptic with a notch on one side.
revolute: turned under at a margin.
rhombic: conventionally diamond-shaped.
rootstock: an underground stem; may be erect or creeping.

scarious: thin, dry, lacking green color.
serrate: cut, like a saw, into acute forward-pointing teeth.
sessile: lacking a supporting stalk.
sheath: a sheet of tissue curved around a stalk.
simple: undivided; all in one piece.
sorus (pl., **sori**): a patch of spore-bearing tissue.
species (both sing. and pl.): a major plant group.
spike: an elongate compact group of reproductive structures.
spinulose: bearing small pointed structures.
sporangium (pl., **sporangia**): a container of spores.
spore: a minute thick-walled reproductive cell.
sporophyl: a leaf or blade supporting sporangia.
sporophyte: the spore-bearing stage in a life-cycle.
sterile: not producing spores; opposed to fertile.
stipe: the stalk supporting the blade in a fern frond.
subspecies: the major subdivision of a species.
subulate: awl-shaped, long-tapering from a narrow base.
superior: borne on the upper side of a structure.
swamp: a wet area grown up with trees or large shrubs.

talus: loose rocks sloping down and out from a cliff-base.
taxon (pl., **taxa**): group of plants which can be classified.
ternate: diverging into three equal or subequal parts.
truncate: ending abruptly and squarely.
type: the original representative of a taxon.
variety (*varietas;* abbrev. var. or v.) : a species subdivision.
vascular: traversed by elongate tubular cells or veins.

whorl: a radiating group of structures borne at a node.
woolly: bearing long matted kinky hairs.

ABBREVIATIONS : GEOGRAPHIC

adj.: adjacent
alt.: altitude
Amer.: America
arct.: arctic
Can.: Canada
c., centr.: central
Ct.: Connecticut
Del.: Delaware
e.: east, eastern
eastw.: eastward
Eu.: Europe
Gr. L.: Great Lakes
Greenl.: Greenland
I.: Island
Ia.: Iowa
Ill.: Illinois
Ind.: Indiana
Kans.: Kansas
Ky.: Kentucky
L.: Lake
lat.: latitude
Lab.: Labrador
L.I.: Long Island
L. Sup.: Lake Superior
long.: longitude
Man.: Manitoba
Mass.: Massachusetts
Md.: Maryland
Me.: Maine
Mex.: Mexico
Mich.: Michigan
Minn.: Minnesota
Miss.: Mississippi
Mo.: Missouri
mts.: mountains

n.: north, northern
northw.: northward
Neb.: Nebraska
Nf.: Newfoundland
N.A.: North America
N.B.: New Brunswick
N.C.: North Carolina
N.E.: New England
N.H.: New Hampshire
N.J.: New Jersey
N.S.: Nova Scotia
N.Y.: New York
O.: Ohio
Ont.: Ontario
Pa.: Pennsylvania
pen.: peninsula
pt.: point
Que.: Quebec
R.: River
R.I.: Rhode Island
s.: south, southern
southw.: southward
S.A.: South America
subarct.: subarctic
temp.: temperature
Tenn.: Tennessee
trop.: tropical
Va.: Virginia
Vt.: Vermont
vy.: valley
w.: west, western
westw.: westward
W. Va.: West Virginia
Wisc.: Wisconsin

ABBREVIATIONS : GENERAL

ca: (*circa*) : around or near a stated arithmetical value.
cm.: (centimeter) : a metric length-unit, *ca.* ⅖ inch.
diam.: diameter.
f.: (*forma*) : a minor variant of a species.
mm.: (millimeter) : a metric length-unit, *ca.* 1/25 inch.
pl.: plural.
sp.: (species) : a fundamental category of classification.
ssp.: (subspecies) : the major subdivision of a species.
sub-: a prefix meaning under, less than, or not quite.
t.: (taxon) : any plant group capable of classification.
v. or var.: (variety): a subdivision of a species.

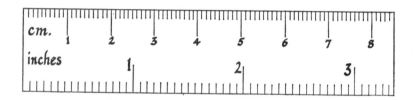

In this *Guide* measurements of plant parts are stated in millimeters (mm.) and centimeters (cm.). The above chart shows the equivalence of these metric units and inches. Users who find it difficult to visualize the values represented by metric data may find it comes easier through such calculations as the following:

To convert millimeters into inches, multiply by 4 and divide by 100. Thus, 25 mm. times $4 = 100$, divided by $100 = 1$ inch.

To convert centimeters into inches, multiply by 4 and divide by 10. Thus, 5 cm. times $4 = 20$, divided by $10 = 2$ inches.

To aid the beginner, the pronunciation of accepted technical names is indicated by the standard accents: grave (è) indicating the long English sound of the vowel and acute (´) the short sound. As to consonants, it may be noted that *ch* is pronounced like *k,* as is also *c,* except in *celsa* and *Cystopteris;* while the genus name *Matteuccia* is rendered mat-tee-ootch-ee-a.

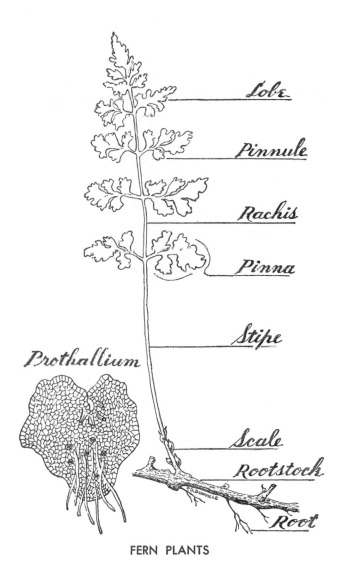

Lobe

Pinnule

Rachis

Pinna

Stipe

Prothallium

Scale

Rootstock

Root

FERN PLANTS

Left, Gametophyte, under side, enlarged   *Right,* Sporophyte

Drawn by Peter D. Domville

FERN CYTOLOGY

Since the cytologic ideas referred to at a number of places in this *Guide* will no doubt be unfamiliar to many of its users, a brief discussion of this field is in order. The branch of cytology concerned is caryology, the study of cell nuclei and their behavior.

Typical living cells of plants and animals contain a viscous liquid termed cytoplasm, suspended in which there is a globular body of denser make-up, known as the nucleus. From time to time they are stimulated to divide. Some of the nuclear material then forms a number of short threads, which thicken into rods; as these are capable of becoming colored when treated with appropriate dyes, they are called chromosomes. The number, size, shape, and features of these are characteristic of every species of organism.

The chromosomes now migrate to a medial plane which, since it intersects the cell wall in a line corresponding to the earth's equator, is termed the equatorial plane; they are then said to be in metaphase. They have meanwhile split lengthwise into two divisions, which float apart in such a way that ultimately one division of each chromosome remains above, and the other below, the equatorial plane.

One set of these divisions, now called daughter chromosomes, aggregates at what is termed by analogy the north pole, the other at the south pole, of the cell, condensing there into new nuclei. Material identical in composition to the cell wall then deposits in the position of the equatorial plane, dividing the cell into two half-size ones. Finally these double their dimensions and their content of cytoplasm, and so become full-fledged new entities—a single cell has divided into two. This process is known as mitosis. Normally one of the new cells is identical in character with the original, while the second may be the same and so increase the tissue involved, or dissimilar, leading to differentiation. The direction in which growth occurs—up, as in a frond, down, as in a root, or horizontally as in a running rootstock, is determined by the position of the equatorial plane.

The life-cycle of ferns, as of flowering plants, is characterized by alternation of generations: The conspicuous fern
or lycosphen, termed because of its producing spores the
sporophyte, is followed by a relatively small, inconspicuous
stage, which produces the gametes—sperms and eggs—and so
is known as the gametophyte.* The cells of the sporophyte
normally contain a pair of each of the chromosomes characterizing the species and it is accordingly said to be diploid;
those of the gametophyte only one of each kind, so it is
designated haploid or monoploid.

Monoploid sperms escape from the antheridium, the organ
in which they are produced, and swim in films of moisture
to the archegonium, enter it, and fertilize the enclosed egg,
which is likewise monoploid. In the resulting compound cell,
known as the zygote, the sets of chromosomes remain discrete, so that it is diploid. By a myriad of cell-divisions the
zygote develops into the sporophyte, every cell of which is
correspondingly diploid.

The sporangia, developing on the fronds or sporophyls,
become lined with what are termed spore-mother-cells; these
go through 2 successive divisions, in the course of which
the chromosomes from one parent pair off with those from
the other, the diploid number thereby becoming halved.
Correspondingly the 4 resulting cells, which mature into
the spores, contain only the basal, monoploid number. This
process is accordingly known as reduction-division, or technically as meiosis.

Through some little-understood physical or chemical influences, reduction-division may occasionally be prevented. In
this event, the spores, gametophyte cells, sperms, and eggs
remain, like the parent sporophyte, diploid. When such a
sperm fuses with the corresponding egg, the zygote and
resulting sporophyte have in their cells four times the basal
number for the species, and are said to be tetraploid. Some
workers hold that such plants should automatically be classed
as distinct species, while others favor this only if marked
morphologic divergence results.

* As shown in the illustration on page 21, the gametophyte of
typical ferns is a prothallium; archegonia develop near a notch
and antheridia at the base of thread-like appendages.

Several other possibilities can be visualized, and are indeed occasionally encountered. A tetraploid sperm may fuse with a diploid egg (or vice versa), whereupon a triploid should result; this has actually been observed to occur in certain fern hybrids. Because it leads to unbalance among the chromosomes, such triploids are usually infertile, their spores being shrunken and lifeless. Should reduction-division now fail, however, a plant with cells containing six sets of chromosomes—termed hexaploid—may result, constituting a new species, capable of normal spore development. Two tetraploid gametes may correspondingly yield an octoploid, and so on. For all plants with multiple chromosome numbers, there is a general term signifying manyfold—polyploid.

Whether a given polyploid has arisen from a single species or through hybridization between different ones can often be ascertained by study of chromosome behavior. Caryology has therefore become an important adjunct in the working out of relationships among the members of various groups of ferns.

To ascertain the number of chromosomes characterizing a given species, a group of actively dividing cells is treated with an appropriate dye, and a thin layer is placed on a microscope slide. Cells with the chromosomes spread out in metaphase figures can then be found by scanning under fairly high magnification. In plants with few chromosomes they can be counted directly, but in those like ferns with large numbers it is preferable to photograph the field, obtain enlarged prints, and make counts on them.

Diploid numbers can be observed on root-tips or other parts of sporophytes, but the more easily counted monoploid numbers can be readily obtained with ferns: a dormant rootstock is brought into the greenhouse and an uncoiling frond showing sori made use of. A thin slice from this is moistened with dye solution on a slide, a cover glass applied, and by pressing on this the tissue is "squashed." Counts can then be made on cells in which the chromosomes were in the course of meiosis. For further details, see *Problems of Cytology and Evolution in the Pteridophytes,* by Professor Irene Manton of the University of Leeds (1950).

A

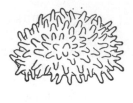

B

C

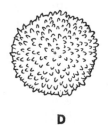

D

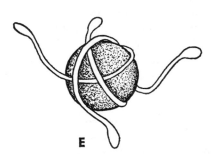

E

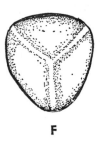

F

SPORES OF FERNS AND LYCOSPHENS

A. Polypodium   B. Cystopteris
C. Adiantum   D. Osmunda
E. Equisetum   F. Lycopodium

FERN SPORES

While the study of the spores of ferns and lycosphens is a rather specialized field, requiring a compound microscope, a brief discussion of it is deemed appropriate here. In the process of meiosis, each mother-cell forms a group of 4 spores, termed a tetrad. There are two principal ways in which this takes place. In the lycosphens and more primitive ferns, the division occurs in such a manner that each spore has an acute tip, down from which three ridges radiate, forming a triangular pyramid; this is technically termed a trilete pattern, while the surfaces between the ridges are known as commissural faces. Their bases form a subcircular girdle, below which is a convex so-called outer face, completing the tetrahedral solid.

In many of the more specialized ferns, on the other hand, the mother-cell splits into four spores, each with a single ridge. The latter leads to this pattern being termed monolete, although since three ridges extend a short distance from each end, it could also be considered doubly trilete. (A less apt term, bilateral, is sometimes applied.) At the start, spores formed in this way are bounded, then, by two flat faces and a convex surface representing a quarter of a sphere. In general they do not retain this outline, but become compressed-ellipsoidal, or colloquially, purse- or bean-shaped.

In maturing, the spore-surface takes on various sorts of sculpture, which may have considerable diagnostic value. Indeed, in the lycosphen family known as the Quillworts— technically, *Isoëtaceae*—many taxa can only be identified through observation of the surface features of their trilete female megaspores, which, fortunately, are relatively large as spores go. These are best studied in dry state; the spores of ferns, on the other hand, are preferably immersed in a mounting medium, a commercial preparation known as Permount being especially suitable. A few mature sporangia are scraped from a sorus onto a glass or plastic microscope slide, covered with a drop of the medium, and protected by a cover. Plastic mounts can be enclosed in small envelopes, glued to herbarium sheets, and so available for restudy.

EXPLORING FOR FERNS

Everyone who becomes interested in ferns is likely to want to make the acquaintance of more than the few common ones which chance to grow in his area. The first step is to gain some idea of the habitats in which to look, ranging from the driest of rock ledges to the wettest of bogs. Especially striking is the disjunct mode of occurrence of some species—their individual colonies may lie scores or even hundreds of miles apart. Fern spores, being very minute, are readily blown about by the wind; many of them fall in unfavorable places and come to naught, but when one lands in a suitable spot it starts a new colony.

LIMESTONE ROCKS. The calcium carbonate of which this rock is composed prevents the building up of acidity in accumulating humus, so that the reaction is neutral or even slightly alkaline. This suits the needs of several of the ferns treated in these pages, notably the Limestone Oak Fern, Bulblet Fern, Smooth Cliff Fern, Wall-rue, Black-stem, and Green Spleenworts, Walking Fern, Harts-tongue Fern, Southern Maidenhair Fern, Slender Rock-brake, Smooth and Hairy Cliff-brake, Smooth Lip Fern, and Limestone Adderstongue. These to be sure do not all grow side-by-side, for some require relatively warm and others cool climate. If, however, by consulting a geological map one locates an area of limestone, and is so fortunate as to find outcrops on which the vegetation has not been destroyed by man, scanning the ledges and crevices may well disclose the presence of one or more of them. Accompanying them may be other species, which thrive better on different rocks but, if in well-drained sites, can tolerate lime, such as Rock-cap Fern, Resurrection Fern, Brown-stem Spleenwort, and so on.

Sometimes, in the course of such a search, a fern student may have a "thrill that comes once in a lifetime," by discovering a species in an area where it had not previously been found. To mention an example from the writer's experience—the Slender Cliff-brake is a "northern" plant, widespread in limestone areas of Canada and adjoining states, but for many years believed to reach its southern limit in ravines of northern Pennsylvania.

One day I was looking for ferns in the upland valleys of West Virginia, and climbed over the fallen rocks to a limestone cliff that stood out on a hillside. Unexpectedly, there in a crevice so sheltered that the sun's rays never entered, and kept cool by evaporating moisture, was a colony of this tiny rock fern; its known range was thus extended some 200 miles southward. The point to be made is that the ranges of individual species given in the literature, including this *Guide,* represent only what is known about them to date, and is not the last word.

SANDSTONE AND GRANITE ROCKS. The siliceous minerals making up these rocks are so slowly soluble that the decay of humus in their crevices can build up a considerable degree of acidity. This favors the growth of another set of species, such as the Rusty Cliff Fern, the Lobed, Mountain, and Cliff Spleenworts and their hybrids, the Rock Spike-moss and the Rock Clubmoss. Those referred to above as merely tolerating lime, such as the Rock-cap Fern, are likely to be more luxuriant in the acid environment. Then, too, there are several which grow about equally well in either type of habitat, if moisture conditions are suitable—Brittle Fern, Blunt-lobe Cliff Fern, Maidenhair Spleenwort, Hairy and Woolly Lip Fern.

Under each of the species discussed in this *Guide* there is a paragraph on Habitat, in which further details are given, based on extensive firsthand observations. Discrepancies will at times appear between these and the statements in other writings, and it may be worth while to point out how this has come about in two instances.

Some years ago, the Cliff Spleenwort was discovered in southeastern New York state on rock ledges above a huge limestone quarry, and the statement that this fern grows on that rock was published. Copiers being more numerous than observers, ever since, in practically all amateur and indeed some professional fern books, this has been given as its rock preference. When one visits the spot, however, the rock on which the fern grew, high up the hillside, turns out to be sandstone instead, with humus just as acid as that satisfying this fern at its 50 or more other known stations.

A second case of misunderstanding involves Bartholomew's Cobble, a nature sanctuary in southwestern Massachusetts. This hill has a few limestone outcrops, on which several of the ferns listed above as favoring this rock are thriving. The great bulk of the area is, however, underlain by silica rock, which supports species, including the Rock Spike-moss, that do not grow on limestone a all. Articles which have been published about this interesting spot have, unfortunately, listed *all* the ferns and wild flowers observed to be growing there as limestone plants, which is misleading to naturalists and horticulturists alike.

SERPENTINE ROCKS. The curious name of this rock was given to it in the Alps, in reference to the occurrence on its areas of a snake of the same mottled green and gray color—a case of "protective resemblance." It is high in magnesium and other elements which are toxic to most plants, and so is occupied by characteristic "barrens," with sparse vegetation. Three northern ferns have, however, become adapted to growth upon it—the Mountain Holly Fern, the northwest variety of the Maidenhair Fern, and the Claw Fern. These occur on its outcrops at a few points in Quebec, a thousand miles or more from stations of the same taxa in western North America.

BOGS AND MARSHES. The growth and decay of Sphagnum moss yields peat with a high degree of acidity, in which relatively few higher plants thrive. In the open part of the bog formed by the filling in of a pond by such material, only Eastern Chain Fern, Cinnamon Fern, and Royal Fern are likely to be found. Where sandy flats adjoin the bog, however, they may support the Southern, Slender, Bog, Foxtail, and Meadow Clubmosses. In bordering swampland, if the shade is not too dense, one may look for the Bog or "Massachusetts" Fern, the Net-veined Chain Fern, the Curly-grass Fern, and its showier relative, the Climbing Fern, and the Ground Pine or perhaps other Clubmosses.

In marshes where the humus is formed from the remains of grasses and sedges, and so is less acid, the above list will be replaced by Marsh and Bead Ferns, Swamp Fern, and Water and Marsh Horsetails.

LAKES AND PONDS. The chief Pteridophytes one looks for in still waters are the Quillworts. These form rosettes of long slender leaves, firmly rooted in sand or mud, some species several feet down, where they are permanently submerged, others near shore, where they may be exposed to the air during periods of drought. They are usually accompanied by various grasses, sedges, and other plants, with disconcertingly similar foliage. Their leaves have a peculiar waxy luster, which once learned will aid in distinguishing them, but they can best be picked out by the "pinch test." Push a thumb and forefinger into the mud around a rosette, and bring them together; if the leaves prove to arise from a slender rootstock, try again. When the plant base turns out to be a firm globular mass, however, it is pretty certainly a Quillwort. It should be dug out, washed free of mud, dried between blotters and identified by observation of the sculpture of its megaspores, squeezed out from a sporangial leaf-base. A few sorts also grow in running water, where protected from being washed away by a sheltering rock or shrub, on tidal river shores, or in muddy temporary pools, ditches, and so on.

GENUS COMMUNITIES. In certain cases several members of a given genus may have similar habitat preferences, and so grow together. Notable are the various Grape Ferns, which favor damp wooded flats where the soil is moderately acid. When one of the tiny species turns up in such a spot, further search may well disclose some of the others; and the following autumn a return visit may lead to finding the evergreen sorts. Again, if one Clubmoss is encountered on a northern sand-barren, other species are likely to appear nearby. The notes on habitat supplied for individual taxa in the following pages will suggest additional places to explore.

GAMETOPHYTES. Finally, while searching for the conspicuous sporophytes, one should not forget that gametophytes are interesting too. Those of the typical ferns are heart-shaped green flakes, to be found on moist spots near adult colonies. What species they represent can be told when the young sporophyte pushes up through the notch. Those of Grape Ferns and Clubmosses, the latter the largest known, (big as peas) can be found by the "pinch test" at the base of tiny shoots.

FERNS IN THE GARDEN

The ornamental value of ferns being manifest, many users of this *Guide* are likely to bring some of the species they identify into their gardens. For success with all but the most vigorous ones, it is necessary to approximate the conditions under which each thrives in the wild. This, it is hoped, will be aided by the paragraphs on habitat and culture supplied for most of the taxa here included. The following general discussion may also prove helpful.

In the region here covered, the average garden has a loamy soil, which on testing with indicator dyes—available from dealers in horticultural supplies—will prove to be circum-neutral or slightly acid (technically, pH 7 or 6). For species observed to thrive in nature under conditions more acid than this, there should be added humus materials such as pine needles, hemlock bark, oak-leaf litter, decaying wood, well-rotted sawdust, or peat moss; for those which in contrast favor neutral to slightly alkaline conditions, crushed lime-stone or black (neutral) compost. Should the soil seem too heavy with clay, the addition of sand, gravel, or rock chips will be desirable. These should also be checked with the indicator dyes to make sure they correspond to the acidity desired (by rubbing bits of rock together, sufficient dust can be obtained to affect a drop of the dye solution).

For moisture-requiring species, the reaction of the water available will have to be considered. There is little use trying to grow the ones which need intense acidity in the outflow of a "hard-water," *i.e.* limy, alkaline spring. If water pumped from a well or obtained from a community supply is used, care should be taken that it does not flow through pipe lined with copper or coated with zinc ("galvanized"), as dissolved traces of these metals may poison delicate species.

Many ferns thrive in rather shady places, and if natural woodland is not available, they may be set out on the north side of garden trees or shrubs, of a wall, under a pergola, or in a slat house.

Horticulturists generally are well aware of the necessity of protecting "tender" plants against severe winter conditions, and so will not move ferns of southern range into exposed situations in more northern gardens. The reverse relationship is, however, less widely recognized. Species which in nature do not extend to very low latitudes or low altitudes also need protection, if moved south or down, to keep their soils from heating up considerably in summer. In some cases placing a "northern" fern so that the sunlight never falls directly on its soil may be sufficient; but if the change in climatic conditions is extreme, the cooling effect of running and especially of evaporating water can be turned to account.

The transplanting of ferns growing in loamy soils requires only usual horticultural procedures, but rock-dwellers pose special problems. These sorts often have numerous roots extending deep into crevices, which break off when the plant is taken up. Then, when the tuft is set in a rock-garden pocket, the fronds keep on transpiring, exhausting the water in the tissues, and death through drying out often results. To lessen the danger of this, it is advisable to trim off the bulk of the leafy tissue, as well as to surround the plant with transparent plastic in such a way as to enclose moist air and so keep the water loss at a minimum. Before long, roots will regenerate, proceed to absorb moisture from the substratum, and stimulate the development of new fronds. Members of the Lycosphen genus *Lycopodium*—the Club-mosses—are best treated in the same way as rock ferns.

Growing ferns from spores is a good way to obtain them in quantity for garden use, and is, moreover, a fascinating hobby. Anyone who wishes to take this up, or, for that matter, who becomes interested in any phase of fern study, should join the American Fern Society. He will then receive its quarterly publication, the *American Fern Journal,* and can correspond with members whose articles appear in its pages. As of spring 1961, when this *Guide* goes to press, the Secretary, to whom application should be made, is: Mr. Donald G. Huttleston, Longwood Gardens, Kennett Square, Pa.

RECENT FERN LITERATURE

1947. *Genera Filicum; the Genera of Ferns.* Edwin B. Copeland. Chronica Botanica, Waltham, Mass.

1950. *Problems of Cytology and Evolution in the Pteridophyta.* I[rene] Manton. Cambridge University Press.

1950. *Gray's Manual of Botany,* 8th edition. Merritt L. Fernald. (Pteridophytes, pages 3–51). American Book Co., N. Y.

1952. *New Britton & Brown Illustrated Flora.* Henry A. Gleason, with Pteridophytes by Conrad V. Morton, Vol. 1, pages 1 to 57. N. Y. Botanical Garden, N. Y.

Regional and State Fern Floras

Field Book of Common Ferns. Herbert Durand. G. P. Putnam Sons, New York, 1928 (and a subsequent reprint).

Field Guide to Ferns. Boughton Cobb. Houghton Mifflin & Co., New York, 1958.

Me.: *The Ferns of Maine.* Edith B. Ogden. Univ. Me. Stud., Ser. 2, No. 62. Orono, Me., 1948.

Md., Del., D.C.: *The Ferns and Fern Allies of Maryland and Delaware, incl. D.C.* Clyde F. Reed. Baltimore, 1953.

Mich.: *The Ferns of Michigan.* Cecil Billington. Cranbrook Inst. Sci. Bull. 32. Bloomfield Hills, Mich., 1952.

Minn.: *The Ferns and Fern Allies of Minnesota.* Rolla M. Tryon. University of Minnesota Press, Minneapolis, 1954.

N. H.: *Ferns and Fern Allies of New Hampshire.* Edith Scamman. N. H. Acad. Sci. Bull. 2. Durham, N. H., 1947.

N. J.: *The Ferns of New Jersey.* M. A. Chrysler and J. L. Edwards. Rutgers Univ., New Brunswick, N. J., 1947.

O.: *Ferns of Ohio.* Harry H. Vannorsdall. Curtis Book Store, Wilmington, Ohio, 1956.

Va.: *Ferns and Fern Allies of Virginia.* Arthur B. Massey. Va. Agr. Ext. Serv. Bull. 252. Blacksburg, Va., 1958.

W. Va.: *The Pteridophytes of West Virginia.* Maurice Brooks & A. L. Margolin. W. Va. Univ. Stud., Herb. Bull. 3, 1938.

Wisc.: *The Ferns and Fern Allies of Wisconsin.* Rolla M. Tryon *et al.* Ed. 2. Univ. Press, Madison, Wisc., 1953.

In the present *Guide* an effort has been made to straighten out discrepancies between data in these various works.

KEYS

While no doubt many users of this *Guide* will identify unknown Pteridophytes only by comparison with the figures and accompanying descriptions, some may wish to employ the helpful device known as an Analytical Key. The idea of this is to guide one in becoming a "nature detective," following clues to reach a conclusion. First, to ascertain which of the two major divisions is represented in a specimen at hand, one may apply this comparative couplet:

A. *If the* leaves *are* relatively large, *with a* blade borne on a stalk, *the plant is most probably a* **Fern.**

A'. *If the* leaves *are* relatively small, scale-like, lacking a stalk, *the plant is most probably a* **Lycosphen.**

In the interest of simplicity, botanists abbreviate such keys, omitting words like those above italicized, yielding:

A. Leaves relatively large; blade borne on a stalk: . . **Fern**

A'. Leaves relatively small, scale-like, lacking a stalk:
Lycosphen

Reversing the process, then, to use the keys which follow, mentally insert such words as *if, the, are, with, the plant is most probably,* etc. When a single family, genus, or species name cannot be reached by merely contrasting two lines in one couplet, the terminal conclusions are replaced by the additional letters B, C, and so on. The procedure is then repeated with the couplet lines headed by these and their primes, until ultimately single terms are reached.

While the general plan is the same, the keys furnished in other books may differ in detail: Initial letters may be omitted, or the second member of a pair may not be distinguished by a prime symbol, or numerals may be used instead of letters; successive couplets may be inset, or contrasted lines may be more or less widely separated, and so on. If expertly made, however, any such key should lead to the identification of most unknowns. Unfortunately, occasional anomalous individuals are capable of defying the best of keys.

Ferns : Key to Families

A. Plant terrestrial, or if growing in water, the fronds aerial: B, B'.

A'. Plant aquatic, in part or wholly floating: F, F'.

B. Sporangia small, stalked, consisting of a laterally flattened spheroidal capsule surrounded by a vertical annulus of thick-walled cells, grouped in sori on the under side of the frond-blade: . . . . **1. Fern Family** *

B'. Sporangia constructed and borne otherwise: C, C'.

C. Tissue translucent, only one cell thick; sporangia small, barely stalked, consisting of a globular capsule with an oblique annulus of thick-walled cells, grouped in sori borne part way up long bristles arising at blade-margins within tubular sheaths: . . . . **2. Filmy Fern Family**

C'. Tissue opaque, multicellular; sporangia not grouped in sori: D, D'.

D. Sporangia relatively large, ovoid, with a terminal annulus of thick-walled cells, in double rows partially imbedded beneath narrow blade divisions:

3. Climbing Fern Family

D.' Sporangia large, globular or ellipsoidal with little or no annulus, borne not in association with leafy tissue but openly in rows or clusters: E, E'.

E. Frond comprising only a stipe and blade; sporangial clusters highly compound: . . . **4. Royal Fern Family**

E'. Frond comprising a stipe bearing a sterile blade and a fertile segment; sporangia in compound to simple clusters, or in a double row: . . . **7. Adders-tongue Family**

F. Plant floating, consisting of a group of tiny fronds:

5. Water Fern Family

F'. Plant rooted in mud, the frond-blade floating:

6. Water-clover Family

---

* Divided by three eminent recent workers into highly discordant multiple subfamilies or so-called families, which defy separation by any simple key. Division into three major groups is all that is deemed practicable here; these groups are admittedly artificial, in that they at times bring together unrelated taxa, but this is less important than their ease of recognition by the nonspecialist.

1. Fern Family : Key to Major Groups

A. Sorus-shape round; sori lying back from margins, or if submarginal, not covered by marginal tissue; spores mostly monolete: . . . . . . I. Round-sorus Group
A′. Sorus-shape or position otherwise: B, B′.
B. Sori longer than broad, lying back from margins; spores mostly monolete: . . . . II. Long-sorus Group
B.′ Sori forming marginal bands, or if round and discrete, covered by marginal tissue; spores trilete:
III. Marginal-sorus Group

I. Round-sorus Group : Key to Genera

A. Indusium obsolete; rootstock cord-like: B, B′.
A′. Indusium present (sometimes early shriveling) : D, D′.
B. Rootstock superficial, the firm evergreen smallish fronds jointed to it; blade narrow, lobed: . . I. Polypodium
B′. Rootstock buried, the thin deciduous medium-sized fronds not jointed to it; blade triangular, divided into segments, in some taxa with also a few pinna-pairs: C, C′.
C. Pinnae 1 or 2 pairs, jointed at rachis; upper blade surface and margins glabrous: . . . . 2. Gymnocarpium
C′. Pinnae 1 pair or none, not jointed; upper blade-surface and margins fine-pubescent: . . . . 3. Phegopteris
D. Rootstock small and slender, or if stoutish, long-creeping; stipe with 2 vascular strands, which may unite upward; blade thinnish, mostly deciduous: E, E′.
D′. Rootstock stout, short-creeping to erect; stipe with 3 to 7 vascular strands; blade thickish, evergreen or tardily deciduous: I, I′.
E. Dimorphism of fronds extreme, the divisions of the fertile ones rolled up so that the sori are hidden: F, F′.
E′. Dimorphism of fronds slight or none, the divisions of the fertile ones never wholly hiding the sori: G, G′.
F. Sterile blade divided into opposite undulate segments; fertile divisions bead-like; veins areolate: . . 5. Onoclea
F′. Sterile blade pinnate, the pinnae round-lobed; fertile divisions worm-like; veins free: . . . . 6. Matteuccia
G. Indusium superior, reniform: . . . . 4. Thelypteris
G′. Indusium lateral or inferior: H, H′.

H. Young indusium hood-like, attached at inner side of sorus, early shriveling: . . . . **7.** *Cystopteris*
H'. Young indusium cup-like, attached beneath sorus, early splitting into segments: . . . . **8.** *Woodsia*
I. Indusium circular, peltate: . . . . . **9.** *Polystichum*
I'. Indusium reniform: . . . . **10.** *Dryopteris*

1. Fern Family: II. Long-sorus Group : Key to Genera

A. Sorus-position close to midribs: B, B'.
A'. Sorus-position away from midribs: C, C'.
B. Fronds dimorphic, the fertile with narrowed segments; margins finely serrate; veins areolate: . . **12.** *Lorinseria*
B'. Fronds uniform, pinnae lobed, the margins entire; veins free except along midribs: . . . . **13.** *Woodwardia*
C. Tissue deciduous; fronds large: . . . . **11.** *Athyrium*
C'. Tissue mostly evergreen; fronds small: D, D'.
D. Blade pinnate or pinnately lobed: . . **14.** *Asplenium*
D'. Blade simple, undulate: E, E'.
E. Blade-outline narrow-triangular, the tip prolonged into a "tail"; veins areolate; sori scattered: . **15.** *Camptosorus*
E'. Blade-outline oblong, the tip not prolonged; veins free; sori in regular rows: . . . . **16.** *Phyllitis*

1. : III. Marginal-sorus Group : Key to Genera

A. Sori discrete: B, B'.
A'. Sori forming bands just within margins: C, C'.
B. Protection of sori effected by a cup-shaped indusium and a recurved marginal tooth: . . . . **24.** *Dennstaedtia*
B'. Protection of sori effected by a reflexed scarious flap of marginal tissue, bearing them inside: . . **18.** *Adiantum*
C. Indusium present beneath reflexed margins: **17.** *Pteridium*
C'. Indusium lacking, but margins often indusioid: D, D'.
D. Dimorphism extreme: E, E'.
D'. Dimorphism slight or none: F, F'.
E. Stipe shining, much exceeding blade: . . **19.** *Onychium*
E'. Stipe dull, little exceeding blade: . . **21.** *Cryptogramma*
F. Margins not reflexed over sori; plant tiny: **20.** *Notholaena*
F.' Margins well-reflexed over sori: G, G'.
G. Frond-divisions joined to axes: . . . . **22.** *Pellaea*
G'. Frond-divisions not jointed to axes: . . **23.** *Cheilanthes*

Genera of Fern Family : Key to Species

1. *Polypodium*

A. Blade green and glabrous above, brownish and scaly beneath; rootstock-scales grayish: 1. *P. polypodioides* (p. 58)

A'. Blade green and glabrous on both sides; rootstock-scales shining brown: . . . . . . 2. *P. virginianum* (p. 60)

2. *Gymnocarpium*

A. Stipe and axes fine-glandular; 2 pinna-pairs developed, the lower moderately large: . . 1. *G. robertiana* (p. 62)

A'. Stipe and axes glabrous or obscurely glandular; only 1 large pinna-pair developed: . . 2. *G. dryopteris* (p. 64)

3. *Phegopteris*

A. Under blade-surface sparsely pubescent; only segments, separated by a winged midrib, developed, the lower markedly broadened medially: 1. *P. hexagonoptera* (p. 66)

A'. Under blade-surface bearing copious hairs and scales; 1 pinna-pair developed, separated from upper blade by bare rachis, little broadened: . . 2. *P. connectilis* (p. 68)

4. *Thelypteris*

A. Blade broadest above middle, the pinnae reduced downward to wings; veins simple: 1. *T. noveboracensis* (p. 70)

A'. Blade broadest below middle: B, B'.

B. Pinnae tending to be narrow-based; fertile lobes flat; veins of sterile ones simple: . . 2. *T. simulata* (p. 72)

B'. Pinnae tending to be broad-based; fertile lobes concave beneath; veins of sterile ones forked: 3. *T. palustris* (p. 74)

5. Onoclea : A single species, O. sensibilis (p. 76)

6. Matteuccia : A single species, M. pensylvanica (p. 78)

7. *Cystopteris*

A. Fronds well-spaced; stipe much longer than lacy-cut ternately 3-pinnate blade: . . . 1. *C. montana* (p. 80)

A'. Fronds close-set; stipe little longer than blade: B, B'.

B. Axes bulblet-bearing: . . . . 2. *C. bulbifera (p. 82)*
B'. Axes not bulblet-bearing: C, C'.
C. Rootstock tipped by fronds: . . 3. *C. fragilis (p. 84)*
C'. Rootstock extending beyond fronds: 4. *C. protrusa (p. 86)*

8. Woodsia

A. Stipe jointed above base, the stubble thus uniform: B, B'.
A'. Stipe not jointed, the stubble thus irregular: D, D'.
B. Fronds delicate, glabrous, the stipe green and blade scarcely 1.5 cm. broad, its lower pinnae mere wings; indusium splitting into short hairs: 1. *W. glabella (p. 88)*
B'. Fronds firm, the stipe and lower rachis brown; indusium splitting into numerous long hairs: C, C'.
C. Blade nearly glabrous, narrow: . . 2. *W. alpina (p. 88)*
C'. Blade copiously pubescent, broad: 3. *W. ilvensis (p. 90)*
D. Indusium splitting deeply into narrow segments: E, E'.
D'. Indusium splitting shallowly into broad segments: G, G'.
E. Pubescence of mixed gland-tipped and long white hairs; pinnae close-set: . . . . . . 6. *W. scopulina (p. 94)*
E'. Pubescence of only gland-tipped hairs or lacking; pinnae spaced: F, F'.
F. Segments of indusium resembling a string of beads; pinnules close-set: . . . . 4. *W. oregana (p. 92)*
F'. Segments of indusium resembling a ribbon frayed at tip; pinnules spaced: . . . . . 5. *W. cathcartiana (p. 92)*
G. Axis bearing hairs; indusium-segments few, broad, frayed, scarcely spreading: . . . . 7. *W. appalachiana (p. 94)*
G'. Axis bearing scales and hairs; indusium-segments fairly broad, not frayed, spreading: . . 8. *W. obtusa (p. 96)*

9. Polystichum

A. Pinnae dimorphic, the terminal fertile ones narrowed; tissue evergreen: . . . . 2. *P. acrostichoides (p. 100)*
A'. Pinnae uniform: B, B'.
B. Blade tardily deciduous, 2-pinnate, the pinnae spaced:
1. *P. braunii (p. 98)*
B'. Blade evergreen, pinnate, the pinnae close-set: C, C'.
C. Tissue firm, dark green, decidedly scaly; pinnae acute, auricled, barely lobed; teeth sharp: 3. *P. lonchitis (p. 102)*
C'. Tissue lax, pale green, sparsely scaly; pinnae obtuse, lobed; teeth incurved: . . . 4. *P. scopulinum (p. 102)*

10. Dryopteris

A. Scales copious on under side of 10 to 30 cm. long blade; pinnae and sori close-set: . . . 1. *D. fragrans (p. 104)*

A'. Scales few on under side of 30 to 100 cm. long blade; pinnae and sori spaced: B, B'.

B. Fronds somewhat dimorphic, the sterile the smaller; blade narrow-oblong, the lowest pinna-pair triangular; sori medial, the indusia glabrous: . . 2. *D. cristata (p. 106)*

B'. Fronds scarcely dimorphic; blade relatively broad: C, C'.

C. Blade pinnate, the pinnae cut into segments or at base into pinnules; indusium glabrous: D, D'.

C'. Blade 2-pinnate, the pinnules cut into lobes or at base into pinnulets; indusia various: H, H'.

D. Sori submarginal; blade leathery; divisions obtuse, entire, crenate, or round-lobed; lower stipe bearing copious long bright yellow-brown scales: . . 7. *D. marginalis (p. 116)*

D'. Sori close to midribs; blade, etc., otherwise: E, E'.

E. Tissue showing dark and light green color-play, tardily deciduous; blade massive, reduced abruptly to a short-acuminate tip; lowest pinna-pair undulate in outline; lower scales lustrous dark brown: 5. *D. goldiana (p. 112)*

E'. Tissue uniform dark green; blade reduced gradually to a long-tapering tip; pinnae, etc., otherwise: F, F'.

F. Lowest pinna-pair narrowed at base, somewhat undulate; tissue evergreen; stipe scales brown: 4. *D. celsa (p. 110)*

F'. Lowest pinna-pair broadest at or near base, tapering uniformly to a long-acuminate tip; scales pale: G, G'.

G. Stipe nearly as long as blade, sparse-scaly; sterile fronds evergreen, fertile subevergreen: 3. *D. clintoniana (p. 108)*

G'. Stipe much shorter than blade, dense-scaly; all fronds tardily deciduous: . . 6. *D. filix-mas,* relative *(p. 114)*

H. All fronds evergreen; lowest pinna-pair usually narrowed at base; pinnae oblong, short-acuminate, at right angle to rachis; indusia glandular: 10. *D. intermedia (p. 122)*

H'. All fronds tardily deciduous; lowest pinna-pair broad at base; many pinnae triangular-oblong, long-acuminate, sloping toward rachis; glandularity exceptional: I, I'.

I. Outline narrow-triangular; innermost bottom pinnule little broadened; teeth incurved: 9. *D. spinulosa (p. 120)*

I'. Outline broad-triangular; innermost bottom pinnule broad as 2 top ones; teeth spreading: 8. *D. dilatata (p. 118)*

11. *Athyrium*

A. Blade 1-pinnate; sori elongate: B, B′.
A′. Blade 2- or 3-pinnate; sori rather short: C, C′.
B. Pinnae long-tapering, undulate; stipe and rachis glabrous or sparse-hairy: . . . . . **2. A.** *pycnocarpon (p. 136)*
B′. Pinnae oblong, deeply lobed; stipe and rachis bearing copious narrow scales: . . **3. A.** *thelypterioides (p. 138)*
C. Sori submarginal; indusium none: **1. A.** *alpestre (p. 134)*
C′. Sori medial; indusium well-developed: D, D′.
D. Fronds produced in a vase-like group around rootstock tip; blade broadest in middle, markedly narrowed downward; sori roundish, spaced; indusium well-curved, fringed with long glandless cilia; spores yellow, bearing coarse dots: . . . **4. A.** *filix-femina* (vars.) (p. 140)
D′. Fronds produced on a row behind rootstock tip; sori longer than broad, the indusium moderately curved, fringed with short cilia: E, E′.
E. Stipe-base bearing persistent dark brown scales; blade broadest at *ca.* the 5th pinna-pair; indusium erose, with glandless cilia; spores yellow: **5. A.** *angustum (p. 142)*
E′. Stipe-base bearing loose pale brown scales; blade broadest at *ca.* the 2nd pinna-pair; indusium glandular ciliate; spores with a wrinkled blackish coat:
6. A. *asplenioides (p. 144)*

12. *Lorinseria* : A single species, **L.** *areolata* (p. 146)

13. *Woodwardia* : One species, **W.** *virginica* (p. 148)

14. *Asplenium*

A. Stipe brown below, green above, like rachis: B, B′.
A′. Stipe and part or all of rachis brown to black: E, E′.
B. Blade long-triangular, lobed: **1. A.** *pinnatifidum (p. 150)*
B′. Blade short-triangular or oblong, 1- to 3-pinnate: C, C′.
C. Outline oblong, 1-pinnate; tissue delicate, tardily deciduous: . . . . **8. A.** *viride (p. 164)*
C′. Outline rhombic to triangular-oblong, 2- or 3-pinnate; tissue firm, evergreen: D, D′.
D. Divisions few, alternate: . . **3. A.** *ruta-muraria (p. 154)*
D′. Divisions many, opposite: . . **2. A.** *montanum (p. 152)*

E. Rachis dark only ⅓ its length; pinnae with a superior auricle, lobed and sharp-toothed: 4. *A. bradleyi (p. 156)*

E′. Rachis dark throughout: F, F′.

F. Fronds dimorphic, the fertile tall and erect; axis shining brown; pinnae mostly alternate, the lower much reduced, the medial oblong with a superior auricle; margins finely or in variants coarsely toothed: 5. *A. platyneuron (p. 158)*

F′. Fronds uniform; pinnae opposite, the lower but little reduced: G, G′.

G. Axis-color black; pinnae oblong, with a low superior auricle, the margins undulate: . . *6. A. resiliens (p. 160)*

G′. Axis-color brown; pinnae oval, not auricled, the margins crenate: . . . . *7. A. trichomanes (p. 162)*

15. *Camptosorus* : One species, *C. rhizophyllus* (p. 168)

16. *Phyllitis* : One species, *P. scolopendrium* (p. 170)

17. *Pteridium* : A single species, *P. aquilinum* (p. 172)

18. *Adiantum*

A. Stipe arching, simple, sinuate; blade ovate, 1- to 3-pinnate; pinnules few, rhombic; reverse-indusioid flaps tending to be lunate: . . . . *1. A. capillus-veneris (p. 174)*

A′. Stipe erect, forking into 2 subequal curving rachises, from which arise *ca.* 5 to 7 oblong pinnae, producing a fan-shaped blade; pinnules numerous, obliquely oblong; reverse-indusioid flaps oblong: . . *2. A. pedatum (p. 176)*

19. *Onychium* : A single species, *O. densum* (p. 178)

20. *Notholaena* : A single species, *N. dealbata* (p. 178)

21. *Cryptogramma*

A. Rootstock short, erect; fronds tufted, firm, bright green:
1. C. acrostichoides (p. 180)

A′. Rootstock elongate, creeping; fronds in a row, delicate, pale green: . . . . *2. C. stelleri (p. 180)*

22. Pellaea

A. Rootstock-tip bearing red-brown hairs; stipe sparse-scaly, shining brown as is the glabrous rachis; blade bluish green, 1- or basally 2-pinnate, the pinna-stalks curving outward from rachis: . . . . . 1. *P. glabella (p. 182)*
A'. Rootstock-tip bearing gray hairs aging to brown; stipe and rachis blackish brown and rough-hairy; blade grayish green, often 2-pinnate well up, the pinna-stalks extending straight out from rachis: 2. *P. atropurpurea (p. 184)*

23. Cheilanthes

A. Fronds nearly glabrous; stipe and rachis blackish; indusioid marginal strips pale: 1. C. *alabamensis (p. 186)*
A'. Fronds densely pubescent; stipe and rachis brown: B, B'.
B. Blade mostly under 10 cm. long; pubescence sparse on stipe and upper side of blade, copious on under side, the hairs whitish, aging buff: . . . . 2. C. *feei (p. 186)*
B'. Blade mostly over 10 cm. long; pubescence various: C, C'.
C. Stipe hairy; blade densely hairy, the hairs brownish; division 2-pinnate, the pinnule-segments oblong; indusioid marginal strips greenish: . . . . 3. C. *lanosa (p. 188)*
C'. Stipe scaly and hairy; blade densely hairy, the hairs white, aging buff; division 3-pinnate, the pinnulets roundish; indusioid marginal strips pale: 4. C. *tomentosa (p. 190)*

24. Dennstaedtia : One sp., *D. punctilobula* (p. 192)

2. Filmy Fern Family : A single genus, *Trichomanes*

Trichomanes : A single species, *T. radicans* (p. 194)

3. Climbing Fern Family : Key to Genera

A. Plant mostly under 15 cm. high, unfernlike: 1. *Schizaea*

Schizaea : A single species, *S. pusilla* (p. 196)

A'. Plant over 50 cm. high; fronds twining: 2. *Lygodium*

Lygodium : A single species, *L. palmatum* (p. 198)

4. Royal Fern Family : A single genus, *Osmunda*
Osmunda : Key to Species

A. Dimorphism shown by whole fronds; sterile ones broad, pinnate, with woolly tufts at base of pinna-axes; fertile slender, lacking leafy tissue: 1. *O. cinnamomea (p. 200)*

A'. Dimorphism shown by frond-segments: B, B'.

B. Blade pinnate, lacking woolly tufts at base of pinna-axes; fertile fronds broad and pinnate; sporangia medial:
2. *O. claytoniana (p. 202)*

B'. Blade 2-pinnate, with simple oblong pinnules; fertile fronds broad and 2-pinnate; sporangia terminal:
3. *O. regalis (p. 204)*

5. Water Fern Family : A single genus, *Azolla*
Azolla : Key to Species

A. Blade-segments *ca.* 1 mm. long: 1. *A. mexicana (p. 206)*

A'. Blade-segments *ca* ⅗ mm. long: 2. *A. caroliniana (p. 206)*

6. Water-clover Family : A single genus, *Marsilea*
Marsilea : Key to Species

A. Floating blade *ca.* 13 to 25 mm. across, hairy; sporocarp borne at stipe-base, short-stalked: 1. *M. mucronata (p. 206)*

A'. Floating blade *ca.* 25 to 50 mm. across, nearly glabrous; sporocarp long-stalked: . . . 2. *M. quadrifolia (p. 206)*

7. Adders-tongue Family : Key to Genera

A. Sterile blade oval, simple; sporangia in 2 rows imbedded below tip of fertile stalk: . . . . . 1. *Ophioglossum*

A'. Sterile blade mostly compound; sporangia in mostly complex clusters at tip of fertile stalk: . . 2. *Botrychium*

1. *Ophioglossum* : Key to Species

A. Blade-tip abruptly pointed; veins in 2 series, polygonal areoles of thickish ones enclosing multiple areoles of finer ones: . . . . . . 1. *O. engelmannii (p. 208)*

A'. Blade-tip blunt; veins all alike, the polygonal areoles enclosing short free ones: . . 2. *O. vulgatum (p. 210)*

2. Botrychium : Key to Species

A. Tissue deciduous, the plant appearing in spring and spores soon maturing: B, B'.

A'. Tissue evergreen, the plant appearing in summer and spores maturing in autumn: G, G'.

B. Height up to 75 cm.; blade triangular, ternately divided and then dissected: . . . . **6. B. virginianum (p. 220)**

B'. Height mostly under 25 cm.; blade otherwise: C, C'.

C. Blade subsessile, broad triangular, pinnate with narrow-toothed pinnae, dark green, lasting to autumn; stalk of fertile segment very short: . . **5. B. lanceolatum (p. 218)**

C'. Blade stalked, oblong to narrow-triangular, or if broad-triangular, then ternate at base: D, D'.

D. Stalk ⅓ to ½ as long as blade, which is pinnately divided into rounded or fan-shaped segments, mostly broad-based and wing-like, the lowest pair sometimes remote and pinna-like, in luxuriant forms ternate at base, in reduced ones the whole blade of 3 lobes or even entire and spoon-shaped; tissue pale bluish green, often withering by early summer: . . . . **1. B. simplex (p. 212)**

D'. Stalk less than ⅕ as long as blade, which is pinnate or in extreme variants ternate: E, E'.

E. Outline of blade and lower pinnae triangular-oblong, the pinnae toothed, lobed, or the lower again pinnate, sharp-pointed; tissue bluish green, often lasting to midsummer:

4. B. matricariaefolium (p. 216)

E'. Outline of blade mostly oblong, rarely subternate at base; pinnae rhombic, fan-shaped, or lunate, blunt: F, F'.

F. Pinnae *ca.* 6 to 10 pairs, rhombic to fan-shaped, ascending toward rachis, uniformly reduced to blade-tip; tissue yellow-green: . . . . . . **3. B. minganense (p. 214)**

F'. Pinnae *ca.* 3 to 6 pairs, fan-shaped to lunate, standing straight out from rachis, abruptly reduced to irregular segments at blade-tip; tissue bluish green (or bright green in shade): . . . . . **2. B. lunaria (p. 214)**

NOTE: The above five taxa, treated in this key as species, known as the "Lesser Grape Ferns," are highly variable, and often seem to intergrade with one another; the contrasts given apply only to their typical or average forms.

G. Margins deeply dissected into bluntish subparallel-sided teeth; tissue bronzed in winter: **12. B. dissectum (p. 232)**

G'. Margins coarsely to finely toothed, but teeth not bluntish with subparallel sides: H, H'.

H. Pinnules few, only sparsely lobed; tissue not bronzed in winter: I, I'.

H'. Pinnules numerous: J, J'.

I Tip of divisions obtusish; divisions mostly about as long as broad: . . . . **9. B. oneidense (p. 226)**

I'. Tip of divisions acutish; divisions mostly much longer than broad: . . . . . . **10. B. tenuifolium (p. 228)**

J. Terminal segments much longer than broad; divisions moderately numerous; tissue bronzed in winter:

11. B. obliquum (p. 230)

J'. Terminal segments about as long as broad; divisions very numerous; tissue not bronzed in winter: K, K'.

K. Texture membranous; many divisions small, rhombic, acutish, fine-toothed: . . . . **8. B. ternatum (p. 224)**

K'. Texture succulent to leathery; many divisions coarse, roundish, obtusish, entire to jagged-toothed:

7. B. multifidum (p. 222)

Lycosphens : Keys to Families and Genera

A. Stem ridged and grooved, traversed by canals, simple or bearing whorled branches; leaves represented by scarious teeth on nodal sheaths; sporangia borne in short-lived terminal cones: . . . . **8. Horsetail Family : Equisetum**

A'. Stem, leaves, and sporangia otherwise: B, B'.

B. Plant sedge-like, its roundish stem sending up a rosette of quill-like leaves with minute male and larger female spores in sporangial bases: **9. Quillwort Family : Isoëtes**

B'. Plant moss-like, consisting of a running stem or a rootstock with erect simple or branching stems covered with scale-like leaves; sporangia borne at the base of specialized leaves, the sporophyls: C, C'.

C. Sporophyls borne in 4-sided terminal cones; sporangia containing either numerous minute male or few larger female spores: . . . **10. Spike-moss Family : Selaginella**

C'. Sporophyls borne in cylindric terminal cones or in zones on stems; sporangia containing only one kind of spore:

11. Clubmoss Family : Lycopodium

Horsetail Family : *Equisetaceae*
Genus *Equisetum* : Key to Species

A. Stems dimorphic, the sterile branched and green, the fertile at first simple and not green: B, B'.

A'. Stems uniform: D, D'.

B. Fertile stem stout, succulent, withering without developing green branches; sheaths bearing dark brown teeth; branches numerous, their first segment longer than the adjacent stem-sheath: . . . . . **1. E. arvense (p. 234)**

B'. Fertile stem somewhat stoutish and succulent, early developing green branches, at maturity distinguishable from the sterile only by truncated stem tip: C, C'.

C. Sterile stem slender and delicate; sheaths bearing whitish teeth with brown medial stripe; branches simple, their first segment shorter than the adjacent stem-sheath:
2. E. pratense (p. 236)

C'. Sterile stem stoutish and firm; sheaths bearing broad brown teeth fused in groups of 2 or 3; branches rebranched, their first segment as long as the adjacent stem-sheath: . . . . **3. E. sylvaticum (p. 238)**

D. Branches, when developed, in normal whorls; tissue herbaceous, the surface scarcely roughened: E, E'.

D'. Branches, when developed, irregular and solitary, resulting from injury: G, G'.

E. Ridges *ca.* 10 to 20; teeth of sheaths brown, with obscure pale margins; central canal occupying ⅘ of stem:
4. E. fluviatile (p. 240)

E'. Ridges fewer than 10; central canal less than ½ stem: F, F'.

F. Teeth of sheaths brown with obscure pale margins; central canal ⅓ to ½ stem diameter, much larger than outer ones; spores abortive: . . . . **5. E. × litorale (p. 240)**

F'. Teeth of sheaths dark brown with conspicuous pale margins; central canal only ⅕ stem diameter, smaller than outer ones; spores normal: **6. E. palustre (p. 242)**

G. Diameter of stem *ca.* 1.5 to 3 mm.: H, H'.

G'. Diameter of stem over 5 mm.: I, I'.

H. Plant *ca.* 5 to 10 cm. high, with intertwined stems *ca.* 1 mm. in diameter; ridges 3, deeply grooved so as to seem 6; central canal obsolete: . . **7. E. scirpoides (p. 244)**

H'. Plant *ca.* 15 to 30 cm. high, with spaced stems up to 3 mm. in diameter; ridges *ca.* 5 to 10; central canal present: . . . . **7. E. variegatum (p. 246)**

I. Cone rounded at tip; stem barely rough, deciduous; sheaths long, flaring: . . . . **8. E. laevigatum (p. 248)**

I'. Cone sharp-pointed; stem rough, mostly evergreen: J, J'.

J. Sheaths longer than broad, flaring; stem moderately rough, evergreen only in mild climates; spores mostly aborted: . . . . **9. E. × ferrissii (p. 248)**

J'. Sheaths about as long as broad, not flaring; stem very rough, evergreen; spores normal: **10. E. hyemale (p. 250)**

Quillwort Family : *Isoëtaceae*

Genus *Isoëtes* : Key to Species

A. Surface of megaspores marked by projections with circular outline, ranging from long spines to low granules: B, B'.

A'. Surface of megaspores marked by projections with long narrow outline, ranging from free to forming a net: E, E'.

B. Projections spiny: . . . . . . **1. I. muricata (p. 252)**

B'. Projections not spiny, merely dot-like: C, C'.

C. Leaves numerous, firm, up to 3 mm. thick; projections crowded: . . . . **2. I. melanopoda (p. 254)**

C'. Leaves few (*ca.* 10 to 20), lax, *ca.* 1 mm. thick: D, D'.

D. Leaf-base greenish, triangular: . . **3. I. butleri (p. 254)**

D'. Leaf-base brown, quadrangular: **4. I. virginica (p. 254)**

E. Ridges crest-like, discrete: F, F'.

E'. Ridges connected to form a network: H, H'.

F. Ridge-top with well-spaced teeth: **5. I. riparia (p. 256)**

F'. Ridge-top with many crowded teeth: G, G'.

G. Sporangia *ca.* 4 mm. long; megaspore-surface like granulated sugar; leaves few, slender: **6. I. saccharata (p. 256)**

G'. Sporangia *ca.* 8 mm. long; megaspore surface like alligator skin; leaves numerous, stout: **7. I. eatoni (p. 256)**

H. Megaspores nearly 1 mm. in diameter:
8. I. macrospora (p. 258)

H'. Megaspores mostly less than 0.5 mm. in diameter: I, I'.

I. Network only on outer face: . . **9. I. tuckermani p. 258)**

I'. Network on all faces: J, J'.

J. Ridges broad; areoles small, deep: **10. I. foveolata (p. 258)**

J'. Ridges narrow; areoles large: **11. I. engelmanni (p. 258)**

Spike-moss Family : *Selaginellaceae*
Genus *Selaginella* : Key to Species

A. Tissue firm and evergreen, the plants forming tufts *ca.* 2.5 to 5 cm. high; leaves crowded, very narrow, tipped with a bristle; cones quadrate: **2. S. rupestris (p. 262)**

A'. Tissue lax and subevergreen or deciduous, the plants forming low mats; cones subcylindric: B, B'.

B. Leaves all alike, in many rows, lanceolate and acute; cones *ca.* 2 to 4 cm. long: . . **1. S. selaginoides (p. 260)**

B'. Leaves in 4 rows, of 2 kinds, ovate-oblong, the lateral larger than the top and bottom ones; cones *ca.* 5 to 10 mm. long: . . . . **3. S. apus (p. 262)**

Club-moss Family : *Lycopodiaceae*
Genus *Lycopodium* : Key to Species

A. Sporangia borne in cones: B, B'.

A'. Sporangia borne in zones on leafy stems: O, O'.

B. Sterile branches erect, rebranched; tissue firm, evergreen (plants of dry or merely damp places) : C, C'.

B'. Sterile branches creeping; tissue lax, deciduous (plants of wet places) : K, K'.

C. Leaves in 4 or 5 rows: D, D'.

C'. Leaves in 6 to 10 rows: I, I'.

D. Plant compact, mostly under 15 cm. high: E, E'.

D'. Plant spreading, except in variants of bleak habitats 20 to 50 cm. high: F, F'.

E. Branchlets markedly flattened, the leaves in 4 rows, the under ones relatively short and free: **4. L. alpinum (p. 270)**

E'. Branchlets cylindric, the 5 rows of leaves all alike:
5. L. sitchense (p. 270)

F. Peduncles bearing *ca.* 6 rows of spreading uniform leaves, with solitary or paired cones: **6. L. sabinaefolium (p. 270)**

F'. Peduncles bearing scattered scale-like leaves: G, G'.

G. Flattening of branchlets slight, the under leaf-blades little shorter than the lateral; branchlets with annual constrictions; stem buried: . . **3. L. tristachyum (p. 268)**

G'. Flattening of branchlets marked, the under leaf-blades much shorter than the lateral: H, H'.

H. Annual constrictions of branchlets obscure; branchlets regularly arranged in fan-like groups; cones several, *ca.* 2.5 to 5 cm. long; stem surficial: 1. *L. flabelliforme (p. 264)*

H'. Annual constrictions of branchlets prominent; branchlets irregularly arranged; cones few, *ca.* 1.5 to 2.5 cm. long; stem usually a buried rootstock:

2. *L. complanatum (p. 266)*

I. Habit tree-like, the leaf-covered branches and branchlets slender; cones on short leafy peduncles:

7. *L. obscurum (p. 272)*

I'. Habit mat-forming, the leaf-covered branches and branchlets thickish: J, J'.

J. Cone sessile, solitary: . . . . 9. *L. annotinum (p. 276)*

J'. Cones peduncled, multiple or solitary in variants

8. *L. clavatum (p. 274)*

K. Lateral stem-leaves relatively broad; erect branches bearing scattered scale-like leaves: 10. *L. carolinianum (p. 278)*

K'. Lateral stem-leaves not broader than others; erect branches bearing crowded subulate leaves: L, L'.

L. Sporophyls and branch-leaves appressed, the cone only *ca.* 3 to 6 mm. in diameter: . . 11. *L. appressum (p. 278)*

L'. Sporophyls and branch-leaves spreading: M, M'.

M. Height mostly under 10 cm.; sporophyls broad-based, entire or with a basal pair of teeth, abruptly narrowed to a subulate tip: . . . . . 12. *L. inundatum (p. 280)*

M'. Height mostly well over 10 cm.; sporophyls narrow-based, usually ciliate below middle: N, N'.

N. Stem arching, rooting only at ends; erect branches *ca.* 8 to 15 and cone 13 to 25 mm. thick:

13. *L. alopecuroides (p. 282)*

N'. Stem prostrate, rooting all along; erect branches *ca.* 5 mm. and cone 10 mm. thick: 14. *t. elongatum (p. 282)*

O. Erect leafy stem uniformly cylindric; leaves swollen and concave at base: . . . . . . 17. *L. selago (p. 288)*

O'. Erect leafy stem knobby, the sporophyl zones narrow; leaves narrow and flat at base: P, P'.

P. Leaf-surface shining; stems forked upward; leaves broadest above middle, there conspicuously serrate-toothed

15. *L. lucidulum (p. 284)*

P'. Leaf-surface dull; stems forked at base and sparingly upward; leaves broadest below middle, obscurely toothed to entire: . . . . 16. *L. porophilum (p. 286)*

DESCRIPTIONS AND
ILLUSTRATIONS

PLAN OF TREATMENT

The account of each species is headed by a widely used vernacular or "common" name, at times followed by a second. Then comes a paragraph headed FEATURES. In it are furnished details which are not brought out in the drawings, but which may be of aid in identification. The dimensions given are normal or usual values; one must always bear in mind that in especially favorable situations considerably larger sizes may be attained, while in bleak or barren habitats the plants may be dwarfed. In discussing taxa which hybridize with one another, the results of cytologic study are noted.

A statement of RANGE is then given, indicating how each taxon is distributed over our region, and beyond.

In the paragraph headed HABITAT the sorts of places where the species grows are indicated. These are to be understood as only the most frequent situations, for some ferns are rather adaptable and may turn up in unexpected surroundings.

Under most species there follows a note on CULTURE, comprising remarks on their garden use.

To aid in interpreting the equivalence of multiple technical names, already discussed in the Introduction, the plan of giving only one combination, followed in many books, is departed from. After the one here favored, set in bold-face type, the "basionym" or epithet-source, if any, and the more frequently encountered synonyms are added; for all, author and date are given (L. = Linnaeus). The names used in *Gray's Manual,* edition 8, 1950 (by M. L. Fernald), are indicated by GM; those in *Britton & Brown's Flora,* edition 3, 1952 ("Pteridophytes" by C. V. Morton) by BB; and any still different usages in the writer's *Guide to Eastern Ferns,* edition 2, 1942, by GEF. When a novel choice of name is made in the present *Guide,* the reasons involved are discussed; in spite of the vast amount of research already carried out on the Pteridophytes, a number of conflicts of opinion remain to be settled by future workers.

1. Fern Family : *Polypodiàceae*

ROCK-CAP FERNS : *POLYPÒDIUM*

A member of this group of ferns was termed polypodium, from the Greek for many feet, by early botanists, in allusion to its rootstock branching into foot-like structures, and that was taken up as a genus name by Linnaeus in 1753.

The long cord-like superficial rootstock is densely covered with scales, and bears at intervals bulges, jointed to which firm evergreen fronds are produced. The stipe has three vascular strands which fuse toward the top. The moderate-sized blade, of general oblong outline, is divided nearly to the midrib into alternate oblong segments (sometimes inaptly termed pinnae). The round sori have no indusium. The basal chromosome number for the genus is 37.

Resurrection Fern

FEATURES: Rootstock scales narrow, dark brown with pale margins. Stipe nearly as long as blade, bearing, as does the under side of the latter, round peltate scales. Blade *ca.* 4 to 8 cm. long and 1.5 to 3 cm. broad. Sori 1 mm. across, obscured by the scales. Fronds curling up when dry but reviving after a rain, suggesting the colloquial name.

RANGE: Gulf states and locally up in our region to s. Del., s.-centr. Md., s. O., Mo. and e. Kans.

HABITAT: Mostly perched on trees, but at times spreading over rocky cliffs. Soon dies when it falls to the ground.

CULTURE: Possible in a mild-climate rock garden.

NOMENCLATURE:

Polypòdium polypodioìdes Watt, 1866 (GM, BB).
(*Acrostichum polypodioides* L., 1753, basionym).
Marginaria polypodioides Tidestrom, 1905.
P. polypodioides v. *michauxianum* Weatherby, 1929 (GM, BB).

The type variety of the species grows in tropical America, and when that of our region is being distinguished from it, the varietal epithet above listed is available.

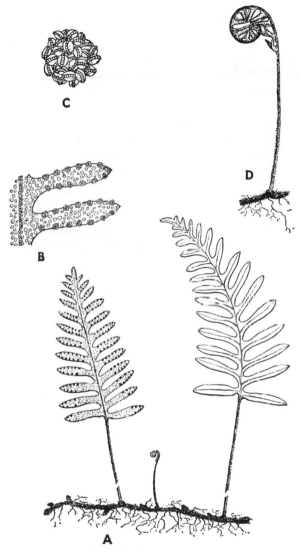

RESURRECTION FERN

A. *Plant, reduced.* B. *Segments.* C. *Sorus, enlarged.*
D. *Frond in dry weather.*

Rock-cap Fern—Polypody

FEATURES: Rootstock-scales brown, broad-based with hair-like tip. Stipe *ca.* ⅔ as long as blade, both scaleless. Blade thick-textured, bright green, in one phase *ca.* 5 to 10 cm. long and 2 to 4 cm. broad, in another respectively 10 to 20 and 3 to 6 cm.; perhaps these are diploid and tetraploid states. Segments blunt to acutish. Sori 1 to 2 mm. across, yellow, aging brown; sporangia accompanied by sterile knobs. The plate opposite shows the extremes of the type form, together with portions of three variants deemed especially noteworthy:

Tapering: *P. virginiànum* f. *acuminàtum* Fernald, 1922 (GM; *P. vulgare acuminatum* Gilbert, 1902, basionym).
Broad-based: *P. virginiànum* f. *deltoìdeum* Fernald, 1922 (GM; *P. vulgare* f. *deltoideum* Gilbert, 1906, basionym).
Frilled: *P. virginiànum* f. *bipinnatìfidum* Fernald, 1922. The variant named f. *cambricoides* by F. W. Gray, 1924, seems too similar to deserve a separate name; both are sterile.

RANGE: Over most of our region, rare toward e. and w. sides; also in uplands further s.

HABITAT: In partial shade, on dry rocks and talus slopes, often capping boulders and ledges, rarely on clay banks and tree trunks. Soil reaction mostly subacid.

CULTURE: Can be grown in a shaded rock garden, though difficult to get started, as the soil must be rich in humus but poor in nutrients, and be kept both moist and well-drained.

NOMENCLATURE:

Polypòdium virginiànum L., 1753 (GM).
Polypodium vulgare v. *virginianum* A. Eaton, 1818 (BB).

An alternative colloquial name, Golden Polypody, refers to the color of the sori, not the blade. While Linnaeus distinguished a common European member of the genus from this east-American one, and subsequent workers have pointed out many differences, their specific distinctness is still sometimes questioned; it is, however, here accepted.

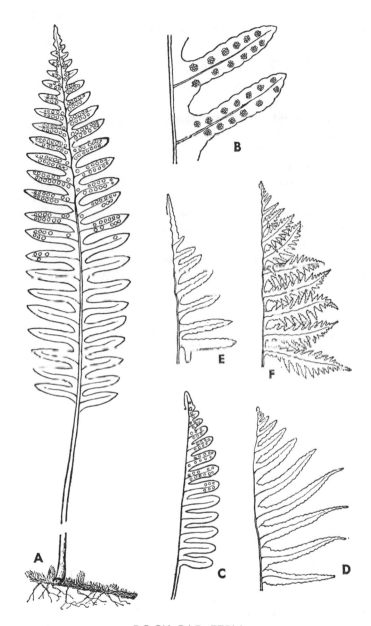

ROCK-CAP FERN

A. Plant, reduced.   B. Segments, large phase. Half blades
of forms: C. Small.   D. Tapering.   E. Broad-based.
F. Frilled.

OAK FERNS : GYMNOCÁRPIUM

This genus name, from Greek for naked fruit, was proposed by Newman in 1851 for a series of ferns lacking an indusium; he indicated his choice of what we now term the type by spelling out in full only one basionym (a Beech Fern). Ignoring this, Ching in 1933 redefined it as pertaining to the Oak Ferns alone. The earliest name restricted to thelypteroid ferns with joints along the rachis, *Currania*, Copeland, 1909, was taken up in the *Guide to Eastern Ferns*, ed. 2, 1942; as *Gymnocarpium* is widely used in current literature, however, it is accepted in the present work.

The cord-like rootstock sends up a row of fronds, their stipe with two vascular strands, blade triangular, and small round sori without indusium. Basal chromosome number 80.

Limestone Oak Fern

FEATURES: Fronds aromatic-glandular. Stipe somewhat longer than the triangular blade, which is *ca.* 10 to 20 cm. long and broad, usually with 2 pinna-pairs at base, their stalk jointed at the rachis. Sori near lobe-margins.

RANGE: From subarct. e. Can. to N.B., Que. and the n. Gr. L., with one disjunct station each in Pa. and Ia.; also nw. N.A. and Eurasia.

HABITAT: Shaded limestone slopes and calcareous swamps, the circumneutral soil remaining cool through summer.

CULTURE: Can be grown in a cool shady rock garden.

NOMENCLATURE:

Gymnocárpium robertiànum Newman, 1851 (BB).
(*Polypodium robertianum* Hoffmann, 1795, basionym).
Phegopteris robertiana A. Braun, 1859.
Dryopteris robertiana Christensen, 1905 (GM); withdrawn, 1938.
Currania robertiana Wherry, 1942 (GEF).

The species epithet refers to a fancied resemblance to the leaves of St. Robert's Geranium. Further discussion of the nomenclatorial situation appears under the following taxon.

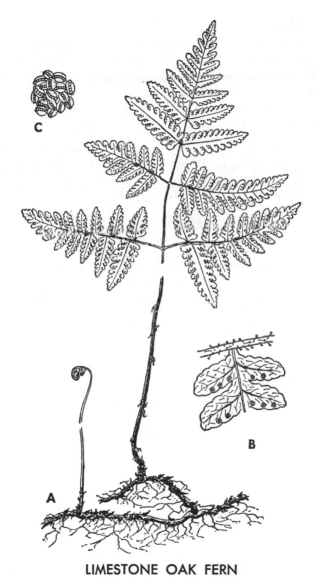

LIMESTONE OAK FERN

A. *Plant, reduced.* B. *Pinna-base.* C. *Sorus, enlarged.*

Oak Fern

FEATURES: Fronds glabrous or bearing a few scattered glands. Stipe ⅓ longer than the triangular blade, which is *ca.* 10 to 20 cm. long and 13 to 25 cm. broad. Paired pinnae on long stalks, jointed at the rachis, much larger than the lowest blade-segments, indeed approaching in size the whole upper blade. Sori near lobe-margins.

RANGE: From arct. e. Can. down over our region, becoming rare southw., though locally reaching lat. 40° at low alt., and 38° in the mts. of Va. and W. Va.; also in w. N.A., well down the mts., and in Eurasia.

HABITAT: Cool rocky woods, shaded talus slopes, and swamp margins; soil rich in humus and mostly subacid.

CULTURE: Desirable for a shady rock- or woodland garden, where the soil is cool and damp yet well-drained. The unrolling buds of the 3 blade-divisions suggest the emblem of a fairy pawnbroker, and the delicate bright green tri-angular blades, which may continue to arise through the growing season, are very attractive.

NOMENCLATURE:

Gymnocárpium dryópteris Newman, 1851 (BB).
(Polypodium dryopteris L., 1753, basionym).
Phegopteris dryopteris Fée, "1850–52."
Dryopteris linnaeana Christensen, 1905; withdrawn, 1938.
Thelypteris dryopteris Slosson, 1917.
Dryopteris disjuncta Morton, 1941 (GM).
(Polypodium dryopteris γ *disjunctum* Ruprecht, 1845, basi-onym).
Currania dryopteris Wherry, 1942 (GEF).

The above long series of combinations, to which at least five more could be added, further emphasizes the complexity of the nomenclatorial problem in the Oak Fern group. There is now general agreement, however, that these ferns do not belong to any of the genera to which they were assigned prior to 1942 except for *Gymnocarpium* as redefined by Ching in 1933. Although the validity of that redefinition is open to question, it is here accepted for simplicity.

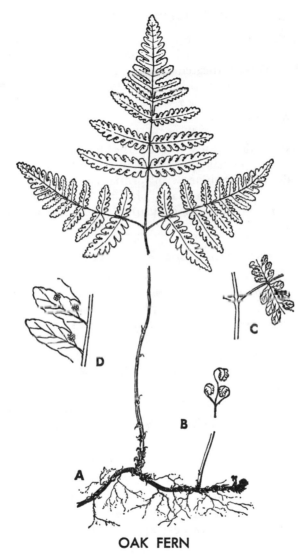

OAK FERN

A. *Plant, reduced.*   B. *Triple bud.*   C. *Jointing.*
D. *Segments, enlarged.*

BEECH FERNS : *PHEGÓPTERIS*

While this genus name, proposed by Fée from the Greek for Beech Fern, has been little used in recent writings, it is here favored. As indicated under the Oak Ferns, the name *Gymnocarpium,* which covered the same taxa, seems to have been published first; Fée's work, dated "1850–52," appeared only in the latter.

The rootstock is cord-like and scaly and bears a row of medium-sized deciduous fronds, the fertile later than the sterile. The stipe has two vascular strands, fusing upward. The blade is triangular with pinna-like segments, in one taxon plus a basal pinna-pair. The small round sori lie near lobe-margins and lack an indusium. The basal chromosome number is 30.

Southern Beech Fern—Broad Beech Fern

FEATURES: Stipe ¼ longer than blade, which is *ca.* 18 to 35 cm. long and 20 to 40 cm. broad, with hexagonal wings at segment base, the under surface bearing fine hairs and a few narrow scales, especially on midribs. Lowest pair of divisions pinna-like (although the rachis is rarely wholly wingless above them), widened in the middle, and cut into lobed segments; blade above these with narrow divisions along a broadly winged midrib.

RANGE: Gulf states and up over our region, becoming rare n. of lat. 43°, though locally reaching s. Que., n. Mich., and se. Minn.

HABITAT: Wooded slopes, less commonly on rocks or at swamp margins, in moderately acid humus-rich soil.

CULTURE: Readily grown in a woodland garden, the strikingly triangular blades yielding an attractive effect. The rootstocks lengthen rather rapidly, however, so its spreading far and wide is to be anticipated.

NOMENCLATURE:

Phegópteris hexagonóptera Fée, "1850–52" (GEF).
(*Polypodium hexagonopterum* Michaux, 1803, basionym).
Dryopteris hexagonoptera Christensen, 1905 (GM); withdrawn.
Thelypteris hexagonoptera Weatherby, 1919 (BB).

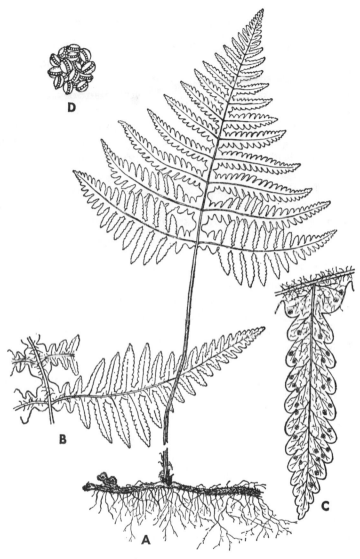

SOUTHERN BEECH FERN

A. *Plant, reduced.*   B. *Basal division.*   C. *Segment, enlarged.*
D. *Sorus, enlarged.*

Northern Beech Fern—Long or Narrow Beech Fern

FEATURES: Stipe ⅛ longer than blade, bearing long narrow
brownish scales. Blade *ca.* 10 to 20 cm. long and broad,
with copious scales and hairs on the under side, in contrast to the preceding species. Lowest blade-divisions true
pinnae, set off from those above by a bit of wingless rachis,
widened somewhat in the middle, cut into subentire lobes.
Midrib-wings not hexagonal. This species has been found
to be triploid, with anomalous reproduction.

RANGE: From arct. e. Can. down over our region, becoming
rare southw., though reaching lat. 40° at low alt. and
extending down the mts. to Va.; also in N.C., w. N.A.,
and Eurasia.

HABITAT: Cool woods, damp thickets, and shaded rock
crevices, in moderately to strongly acid soil, the latter
when it spreads into sphagnum moss hummocks. In America shows no preference for beech woods, which the technical and colloquial names imply it does in Europe.

CULTURE: Can be grown in a shady rock- or woods-garden,
if the soil is kept acid, cool, and moist, the fronds being
ornamental.

NOMENCLATURE:

Phegópteris connéctilis Watt, 1866 (GEF) .
(*Polypodium connectile* Michaux, 1803, basionym) .
Gymnocarpium phegopteris Newman, 1851.
(*Polypodium phegopteris* L., 1753, basionym) .
Phegopteris polypodioides Fée, "1850–52."
Dryopteris phegopteris Christensen, 1905 (GM) ; withdrawn.
Thelypteris phegopteris Slosson, 1917 (BB) .

This species was selected as the type of the two genera,
Gymnocarpium of Newman, 1851, and *Phegopteris* of Fée,
1852; these comprised both Oak Ferns and Beech Ferns.
While strict application of the principle of priority would
therefore lead to assignment of the name *Gymnocarpium* to
this and other Beech Ferns, current usage, which is here
followed, is to place these in *Phegopteris* instead.

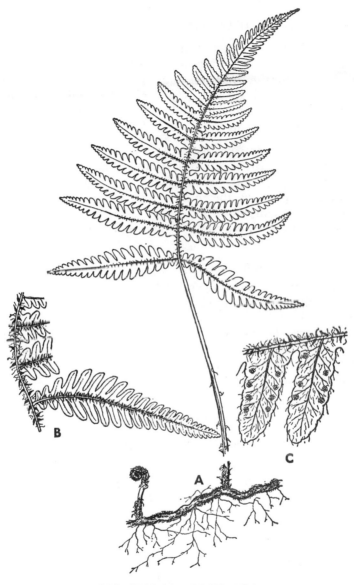

NORTHERN BEECH FERN

A. *Plant, reduced*.   B. *Pinna*.   C. *Segments, enlarged*.

MARSH FERNS : *THELÝPTERIS*

The earliest valid name for this genus was *Lastrea*, proposed by Bory de St. Vincent in 1824 in honor of a contemporary botanist, Delastre. The alternative name *Thelypteris*, signifying female fern, was used by Schmidel in 1762;
his publication is deemed invalid, and it is rejected in the
current *Code*, but is nevertheless widely accepted.

The rootstock is cord-like and bears a row of moderate-
sized deciduous fronds, the fertile later than the sterile. The
stipe has two vascular strands, fused upward. The blade is
broadest at or above the middle, and cut into round-lobed
pinnae. The small round submarginal to medial sori have a
delicate reniform indusium. Chromosome number variable.

Tapering Fern—New York Fern

FEATURES: Fronds short-stiped, yellow-green, the fertile somewhat taller and narrower than the sterile. Blade *ca.* 25 to
50 cm. long and 8 to 15 cm. broad, tapering gradually
downward, the lowest pinnae being reduced to mere wings.
Pinnae cut into bluntish oblong entire segments. Rachis,
midribs, and veins—which are simple—pubescent beneath.
Indusium ciliate.

RANGE: Common throughout the e. part of our region, but
w. of long. 88° only scattered; also s. uplands.

HABITAT: Woods, thickets, and swamps, in moderately acid
humus-rich soil.

CULTURE: Readily grown in a woodland garden, its odd blade
shape producing an attractive effect.

NOMENCLATURE:

Thelýpteris noveboracénsis Nieuwland, 1910 (BB).
(*Polypodium noveboracense* L., 1753, basionym).
Aspidium noveboracense Swartz, 1801.
Lastrea noveboracensis Presl, 1836.
Dryopteris noveboracensis Gray, 1848 (GM).

Linnaeus received this fern from Canada, and never explained why he used for its epithet a latinization of New
York.

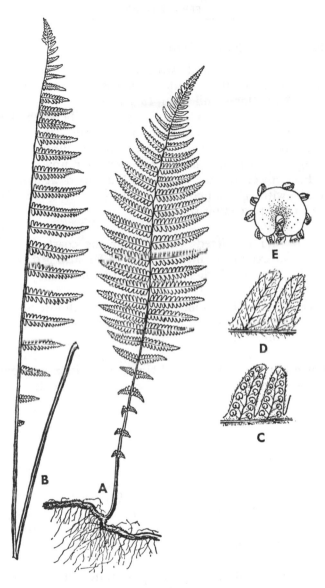

TAPERING FERN

A. *Plant with sterile frond, reduced.* B. *Half fertile frond,*
reduced. C. *Fertile and* D. *Sterile segments.*
E. *Sorus, enlarged.*

Bog Fern—Massachusetts Fern

FEATURES: Rootstock and stipe-base sparsely scaly. Stipe somewhat longer than blade, which is yellowish green, *ca.* 18 to 35 cm. long and 8 to 15 cm. broad, tapering only slightly downward, moderately pubescent beneath. Fertile fronds somewhat taller than the sterile, the margins scarcely recurved, the veins in both simple. Pinnae cut into oblong lobes which tend to fold together upward in dry weather; lower pinnae markedly narrowed at base. Sori spaced, with gland-margined reniform indusium larger than in the preceding species.

RANGE: Rather restricted: chiefly near the coast, from N.S. to Va., but extending into the mts. in Pa. and Md. Reports from W. Va. and Ind. are regarded as mistaken.

HABITAT: Bogs and hummocks in swamps, almost always in association with sphagnum moss, the soil being correspondingly intensely acid.

CULTURE: Can be expected to thrive only in a bog garden supplied with lime-free water, so that high acidity can be maintained in the humus.

NOMENCLATURE:

Thelýpteris simulàta Nieuwland, 1910 (BB).
(*Aspidium simulatum* Davenport, 1894, basionym).
Dryopteris simulata Davenport, 1894, as synonym (GM).
Nephrodium simulatum Davenport, 1894, as synonym.
Lastrea simulata Davenport, 1894, as synonym.

In describing this fern, Davenport stated that his species epithet referred to its resemblance to two others of the same genus (those on our next-preceding and next-following text pages) and especially to some forms of Lady Fern. As the chief occurrences he noted were in Massachusetts, this state is often used in a colloquial name, but as the fern is not more frequent there than in several others, a term referring to its usual habitat is here preferred.

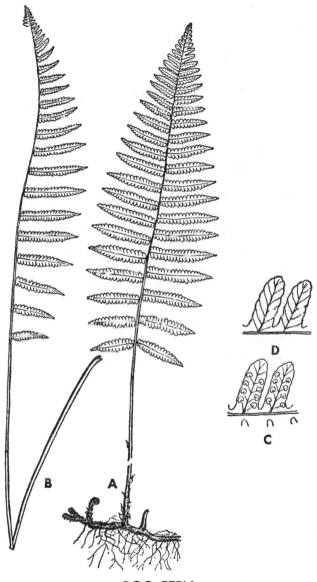

BOG FERN

A. *Plant with sterile frond, reduced.* B. *Half fertile frond, reduced.* C. *Fertile and* D. *Sterile segments.*

Marsh Fern

FEATURES: Rootstock nearly scaleless. Stipe dark-based, ca. 1½ times as long as the thin-textured bluish green blade, which (in t. *pubescens*) is *ca.* 18 to 35 cm. long and 8 to 15 cm. broad, slightly tapering downward, moderately pubescent beneath. Fertile fronds longer and narrower than sterile. Veins of sterile blades forked, of fertile partly so. Pinnae mostly broad-based and somewhat auricled, cut into oblong acutish segments. Sori medial, crowded, with a sparsely ciliate indusium, often hidden by reflexed margins. The southern "var.," t. *haleana* differs in being *ca.* ⅓ larger, somewhat scaly beneath, and in having the pinnae cut into definitely spaced pinnules, at least below.

RANGE: Of t. *pubescens,* from Nf. to Man. and down over our region, rare w. of the Miss. R. and in s. states. Of t. *haleana,* lower Miss. v. sporadically up in our region to *ca.* lat. 41° from Pa. to Ind.

HABITAT: Marshes, meadows, bog-margins, and clayey banks, most luxuriant when the soil acidity is low.

CULTURE: Spreads rapidly and crowds out smaller plants, so not satisfactory as a garden subject.

NOMENCLATURE:

Thelýpteris palústris Schott, 1834 (BB).
Lastrea thelypteris Bory de St. Vincent, 1824.
(*Acrostichum thelypteris* L., 1753, basionym).
Dryopteris thelypteris Gray, 1848 (GM).

AMERICAN VARIANTS:

Thelýpteris palústris v. *pubéscens* Fernald, 1929 (BB).
(*Lastrea thelypteris* f. α *pubescens* Lawson, 1864, basionym).
Dryopteris thelypteris v. *pubescens* Nakai, 1931 (GM).
Thelýpteris palústris v. *haleàna* Fernald, 1929.
Dryopteris thelypteris v. *haleana* Broun, 1936 (GM).

The chief representative of this world-wide species in our region is currently assigned Lawson's inapt epithet. Both of them need further study and are referred to above merely as taxa without category designation.

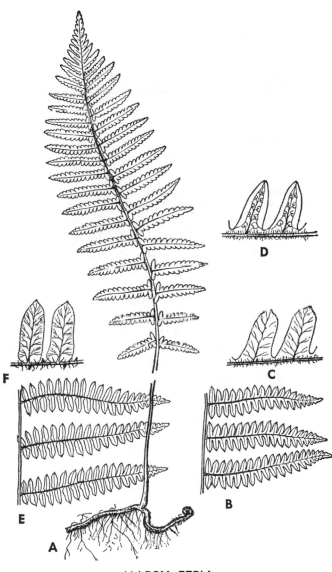

MARSH FERN

Widespread variety: A. *Plant, reduced.* B. *Pinnae.*
C. *Sterile and* D. *Fertile segments.*
Southern variety: E. *Pinnae.* F. *Pinnules.*

BEAD FERN : *ONOCLEA*

This word was used by the ancients for some now unknown plant, and was taken up as a genus name by Linnaeus in 1753. There is only one species.

Bead Fern—Sensitive Fern

FEATURES: Rootstock thickish, long-creeping, and branching, holding old stipe-bases, sending up a row of fronds. Stipe slightly scaly at the brown base, *ca.* ⅓ longer than blade. Fronds markedly dimorphic: Sterile ones with thickish but deciduous leafy blades *ca.* 20 to 40 cm. long and broad, cut almost to midrib into nearly or quite opposite areolate-veined shallowly undulate to deeply lobed segments (which, unlike the similar-looking Net-veined Chain Fern, lack marginal teeth). Fertile fronds autumnal, somewhat shorter than the sterile ones, becoming blackish brown and firm in texture, persisting for 2 or 3 years, pinnate with erect pinnae divided into roundish pinnules which roll up into bead-like structures. Sori round, with a delicate basally attached indusium, hidden in the pinnules. Occasional fronds intermediate between fertile and sterile, appearing chiefly after injury to the rootstock, are classed as f. *obtusilobàta* Gilbert, 1901 (GM, BB; *Onoclea obtusilobata* Schkuhr, 1809, basionym).

RANGE: S. states and nearly throughout our region, up to Lab. and to se. Man.

HABITAT: Marshes, swamps, and muddy banks, the soil most often subacid.

CULTURE: Not recommended, since its rapidly spreading growth will choke out more delicate ferns.

NOMENCLATURE:

Onoclèa sensìbilis L., 1753 (GM, BB).

The species epithet is a misnomer, as the plant is not really sensitive, merely wilting rather rapidly when injured. The colloquial name here preferred refers, then, to the bead-like fertile pinnules.

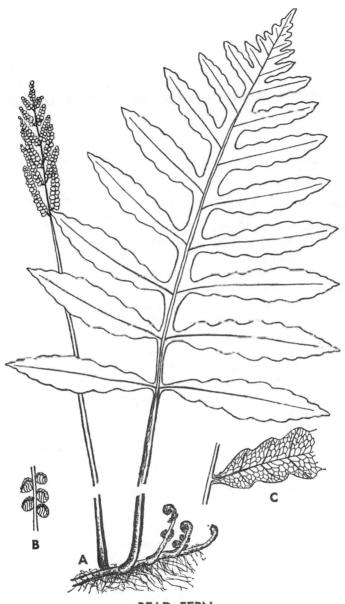

BEAD FERN

A. *Plant with fertile and sterile fronds, reduced.*
B. *Fertile pinnules.*   C. *Base of sterile segment.*

OSTRICH FERNS : MATTEÙCCIA

The European representative of this group was named *Osmunda struthiopteris* by Linnaeus in 1753. It was provisionally assigned to an independent genus *Pteretis* by Rafinesque in 1818, and his name has been rather widely used, but is not valid under the current Code of Nomenclature. Accordingly the name *Matteuccia,* given to it in honor of an Italian naturalist by Todaro in 1866, is now accepted.

(American) Ostrich Fern

FEATURES: Rootstock long-creeping, sending up at intervals short scaly erect branches holding old stipe-bases, in the midst of which arises in spring a vase-like group of sterile fronds. Stipe of these ¼ as long as blade, angled and grooved, dark brown and scaly at base. Blade firm but deciduous, *ca.* 50 to 100 cm. long and 18 to 35 cm. broad, or in luxuriant colonies twice as large, tapering gradually to base but narrowed abruptly to tip, its pinnae cut into entire segments. Fertile fronds appearing in summer, much shorter than sterile, their stipe about equaling blade, crescent-shaped in section, shining brown; blade *ca.* 15 to 30 cm. long and ¼ as broad, becoming dark brown, with crowded pinnae resembling segmented worms, in which the sori are hidden.

RANGE: From Nf. to Man., and down to n. Va., c. W. Va., s. Ind. and n. Mo., though becoming rare s. of lat. 41°.

HABITAT: Moist wooded slopes, alluvial flats and swamps, the soil usually circumneutral.

CULTURE: An attractive subject for an ample garden, though spreading too rapidly for a small one.

NOMENCLATURE:

Matteùccia pensylvánica Raymond, 1950.
(*Struthiopteris pensylvanica* Willdenow, 1810, basionym).
Pteretis nodulosa Nieuwland, 1916 (GEF).
(*Onoclea nodulosa* Michaux, 1803, basionym).
Pteretis pensylvanica Fernald, 1945 (GM).
Matteuccia struthiopteris v. *pensylvanica* Morton, 1950 (BB).

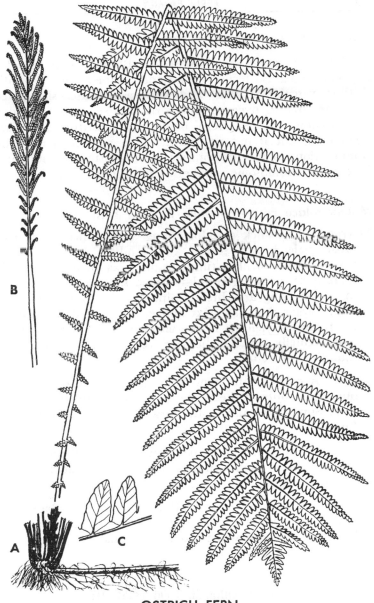

OSTRICH FERN

A. Plant with sterile frond, reduced.   B. Fertile frond.
C. Sterile segments.

BLADDER FERNS : *CYSTÓPTERIS*

This genus name was proposed by Bernhardi in 1806 for a group of smallish ferns with a slender stipe having 2 wholly distinct vascular strands, and with a delicate, short-lived indusium arching over a round sorus in a somewhat bladder-like fashion. In some fern books the substitute *Filix* has been used, but it has no validity as a generic name, and combinations of it with epithets are not listed for our taxa. The basal chromosome number of the genus is 42.

Mountain-lace Fern—Mountain Bladder Fern

FEATURES: Rootstock cord-like, long and branched, bearing broad pale brown scales, and sending up well-spaced fronds. Stipe *ca.* 1½ times as long as blade, brownish, sparsely scaly, and glandular. Blade subpentagonal, *ca.* 10 to 20 cm. long and broad, pinnate with the lowest pair much larger than the next above, all divided into deeply cut pinnules, yielding a lacy effect. Under surface sparsely hairy, chiefly on the heavier veins. Sori medial, with roundish indusium.

RANGE: A cold-climate fern, from subarct. e. Can. down in our region only to the Gaspé pen., Que., and the n. shore of L. Sup., Ont.; also in the mts. of w. N.A., Greenl., and Eurasia.

HABITAT: Shaded stream banks, talus slopes, and rock ledges, at moderate to high altitudes; soil mostly subacid, remaining cool and moist through summer.

CULTURE: In view of the attractive pattern of its blades, this should be a desirable fern garden subject, but it can only be grown in permanently cool situations.

NOMENCLATURE:

Cystópteris montàna Bernhardi, 1806 (GM, BB).
(*Polypodium montanum* Lamarck & DeCandolle, 1778, basionym).

This fern has been placed in several other genera, but only that here accepted is widely used. The species epithet refers to its most frequent occurence.

MOUNTAIN-LACE FERN

A. Plant, reduced.   B. Pinnules and   C. Sorus, enlarged.

Bulblet Fern

FEATURES: Rootstock short, brown-scaly, holding old stipe-bases. Stipe short, pinkish. Blade long-triangular, usually *ca.* 23 to 45 cm. long and 8 to 15 cm. broad at base, lax, the pinnae cut into toothed pinnules and segments. Rachis and pinna-axes bearing scattered globular bulblets on under side. Indusium truncate at tip, sparse-glandular.

RANGE: From Nf. to Minn., down to sw. Va. and w. Mo.; also sparingly in s. uplands and the s. Rocky mts.

HABITAT: Cliffs and ledges of limestone and calcareous shale, also in limy swamps northw., the fronds there becoming 2 or 3 times the usual length of rock-dwelling forms.

CULTURE: Grows readily in a shady rock garden, soon spreading by the rooting of fallen bulblets.

NOMENCLATURE:

Cystópteris bulbífera Bernhardi, 1806 (GM, BB).
(*Polypodium bulbiferum* L., 1753, basionym)

HYBRID BULBLET FERNS. Apparent hybrids between the above taxon and that described on the following text page are occasionally encountered; they combine the characters of the two in various ways. When they bear bulblets, these are chiefly along the rachis, and instead of being rounded and loosely attached are low and mound-like, and irregularly shaped with anomalous appendages. Such plants may occur along with both presumptive parents, with but one, or, especially when they invade masonry, remote from either. Their interrelationships remain to be worked out. Three which have received names are:
Cystopteris fragilis v. *laurentiana* Weatherby, 1926 (GM, BB). Bulblets rare; indusium pointed, glandular. Que. to Pa.
C. fragilis f. *simulans* Weatherby, 1926 (GM, BB). Bulblets rare; frond-divisions about as broad as long; indusium pointed, glabrous. Pa. to Kans., also s. uplands.
C. tennesseensis Shaver, 1950. Bulblets frequent; indusium truncate, sparsely glandular. Mich. to Tenn. and Kans.

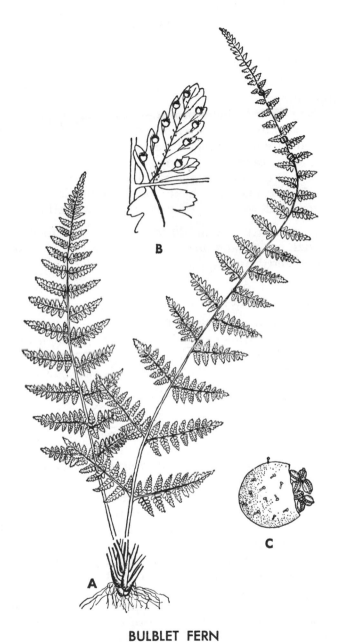

BULBLET FERN

A. *Plant, reduced.*   B. *Pinnule and*   C. *Sorus, enlarged.*

Brittle Fern—Bladder Fern

FEATURES: Rootstock ascending, short to moderately long, simple or few-branched, holding old stipe-bases, bearing at tip long narrow light brown scales, and sending up at intervals through the season clustered delicate fronds. Stipe slightly shorter than blade, brownish, sometimes with a few loose scales. Blade light green, *ca.* 10 to 20 cm. long and 4 to 8 cm. broad, mostly 2-pinnate, the lowest pinna-pair shorter than the next above. Indusium ovate and pointed, with some jagged teeth at tip, withering early.

RANGE: From arct. e. Can. down in our region to moderate altitudes in Pa. and in mts. to Va. and Mo.; also over w. N.A. and Eurasia.

HABITAT: Cool rock crevices and talus slopes, in circum-neutral to subacid soil.

CULTURE: Can be grown in a shady rock garden, and notable in sending up fronds in earliest spring, although the delicate tissue tends to become dilapidated by summer.

NOMENCLATURE:

Cystópteris frágilis Bernhardi, 1806 (GM, BB).
(*Polypodium F. fragile* L., 1753; *P. fragile* L., 1755, basionym).
Cystopteris fragilis v. *fragilis* BB; typical [v.], GM. -type var.

———————

The above description covers only the species type; several variants, relatives, or hybrids occur over our region. Most widespread is C. *frágilis* [v.] β *mackàyi* Lawson, 1889 (GM, BB). This differs in having the lower pinnules of major pinnae narrower and taper-based, and especially in the indusia being nearly circular and truncate at tip. It ranges from s. Que. to Minn. and down well over our region, also in s. uplands. Plants with both types of indusium on the same blade occur where the ranges of this and the type overlap, and are probably hybrids. In addition there is apparent intergradation with another member of the genus, a *Cystopteris fragilis* relative named *Polypodium diaphanum* Bory de St. Vincent, 1804, an especially thin-textured plant with narrow pinnules and likewise roundish indusium.

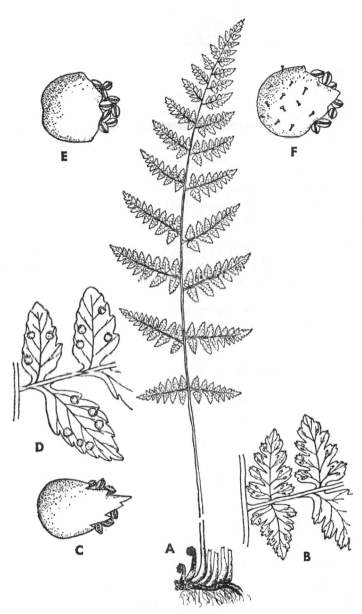

BRITTLE FERN

Type variety: A. *Plant, reduced.*   B. *Pinnules.*
C. *Sorus, enlarged.*
Widespread variety: D. *Pinnules.*   E. *Sorus, enlarged.*
Hybrid with Bulblet Fern: F. *Sorus, enlarged.*

Lowland Brittle Fern

FEATURES: Rootstock slender, extensively creeping and branching, sparsely scaly but copiously hairy, in the course of the season lengthening at the tip until it extends 2 to 4 cm. beyond the row of fronds. Stipe somewhat shorter than blade, green to light brown, glabrous. Blade bright green, *ca.* 13 to 25 cm. long and 5 to 10 cm. broad, narrowed at base, 2-pinnate. Lower pinnules tapering to stalk-like bases, deeply cut-lobed. Indusium round with truncate tip (as in t. *mackayi*).

RANGE: Best developed in midland areas, up to n. Wisc., but extending locally e. to N.J. and Va.; also in s. Miss. vy. lowlands and adj. uplands.

HABITAT: Unlike the other varieties: wooded alluvial flats, only exceptionally extending up hillsides, in humus-rich circumneutral soil.

CULTURE: Readily grown in a woodland garden; its rapid spread may be disconcerting, but the beauty of its fronds especially in spring makes it worth having.

NOMENCLATURE:

Cystópteris protrùsa Blasdell, 1960.
C. fragilis v. *protrusa* Weatherby, 1935 (basionym; GM, BB).
   This taxon is now regarded as deserving species status, as it differs from *C. fragilis* not only in morphology but also in cytology, being diploid instead of polyploid.

Wavy-spored Brittle Fern—*Cystópteris dickieàna* Sim, 1848.

This fern is not illustrated as it looks exactly like *C. fragilis.* Under the microscope its spore-coat is seen to be wavy-wrinkled, whereas that in *C. fragilis* is studded with coarse spines. Discovered in England many years ago, it was first recognized as occurring in w. N.A. in 1951, and soon thereafter was found to enter our region, from Minn. to Mich. The relationships between these taxa remain to be worked out; it seems unlikely that they are really specifically distinct.

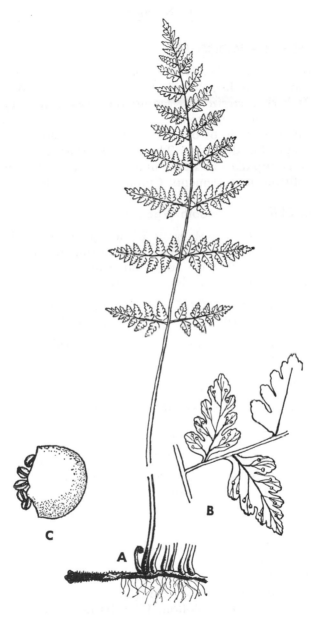

LOWLAND BRITTLE FERN

A. Plant, reduced.   B. Pinnules.   C. Sorus, enlarged.

CLIFF FERNS : WOÒDSIA

This genus was first validly named in honor of a contemporary naturalist, Joseph Woods, by Robert Brown in 1813. It is characterized by a short rootstock which sends up a tuft of rather small fronds at the scaly tip, in the midst of a persistent stubble of old stipe-bases. The blade is pinnate with deeply lobed pinnae. The sori are round, and the indusium is cup-like, attached under the mass of sporangia, early splitting into segments. Chromosome number 41.

Smooth Cliff Fern—Smooth Woodsia

FEATURES: Stipe ⅓ as long as blade, green, jointed below middle so that the stubble is uniform. Blade thinnish, glabrous, *ca.* 4 to 8 cm. long and 6 to 12 mm. broad. Indusium forming a few short threads.

RANGE: From arct. e. Can. down in our region at scattered stations to Catskill mts., N.Y., sw. Ont., and ne. Minn.

HABITAT: Crevices in cliffs of limestone and calcareous shale, the soil circumneutral. Not cultivated.

NOMENCLATURE:

Woòdsia glabélla R. Brown, 1823 (GM, BB).

Alpine Cliff Fern—Alpine Woodsia

FEATURES: Differing from *W. glabella* in: Stipe shining brown; blade thickish, somewhat scaly, *ca.* 8 to 15 cm. long and 1 to 2 cm. broad; indusial threads numerous.

RANGE AND HABITAT: Essentially the same as for the preceding taxon, except for sometimes growing on rocks other than limestone, in slightly acid soil.

NOMENCLATURE:

Woodsia alpina S. F. Gray, 1821 (GM).
(*Acrostichum alpinum* Bolton, 1790, basionym).

AMERICAN VARIANT:

Woòdsia alpìna v. *béllii* Morton, 1952 (BB).
(*W. glabella* [v.] β *bellii* Lawson, 1864, basionym).
W. bellii Porsild, 1945.

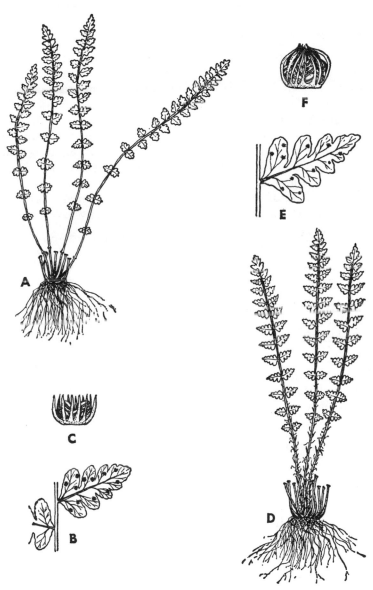

TWO CLIFF FERNS

Smooth: A. *Plant.*   B. *Pinna, enlarged.*   C. *Sorus, enlarged.*
Alpine: D. *Plant.*   E. *Pinna, enlarged.*   F. *Sorus, enlarged.*

Rusty Cliff Fern—Rusty Woodsia

FEATURES: Rootstock short and thick, often branched. Stipe
ca. ⅔ as long as blade, brown, bearing hair-tipped scales,
jointed at or below middle, the subuniform stubble copious. Blade dark green, somewhat hairy above, densely (or
in moist habitat forms sparsely, covered beneath with
mixed hairs and scales, which as indicated in the vernacular name become rusty brown, *ca.* 6 to 12 cm. long and
1.5 to 3 cm. broad. Pinnae cut into obtuse entire or crenate-
toothed segments with somewhat reflexed margins. Sori
close-set; indusium split into numerous thread-like segments much longer than the mass of sporangia.

RANGE: From arct. e. Can. over our region at moderate alt.
to R.I., Pa., n. Ill., and sw. Minn., also down the mts. to
sw. Va.; s. of our region on but one mt. in N.C., also in
nw. N.A. and Eurasia.

HABITAT: Dry or less often moist crevices in cliffs, ledges,
and talus slopes, frequently in sunny situations; known
on almost all kinds of rock except limestone, the soil subacid.

CULTURE: Suitable for a non-calcareous rock garden, the
tufts of fonds with their glistening rusty coating yielding a
striking effect.

NOMENCLATURE:

Woòdsia ilvénsis R. Brown, 1813 (GM, BB).
(*Acrostichum ilvense* L., 1753, basionym).

How this fern came to be assigned the epithet *ilvense* is a
mystery, for Linnaeus gave its locality as "Europe, frigid-
issime," and there is nothing frigid about the Island of Elba,
of which that epithet is a latinization.

Lawson's Cliff Fern

Woòdsia × *grácilis* : *W. alpìna* × *ilvénsis* Butters, 1941, (BB).
(*W. ilvensis* [v.] β *gracilis* Lawson, 1864, basionym).

This hybrid, intermediate in aspect, has been observed
with the parents from Que. and Vt. to Minn.

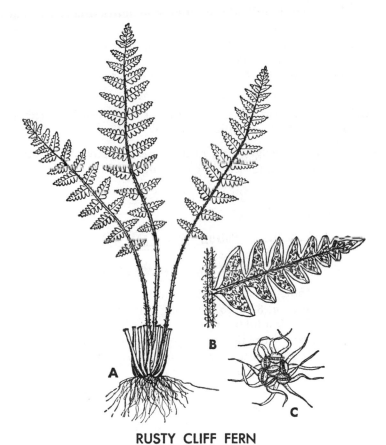

RUSTY CLIFF FERN

A. Plant, reduced.   B. Pinna.   C. Sorus, enlarged.

Western Cliff Fern—Oregon Woodsia

FEATURES: Rootstock stoutish, bearing narrow light brown scales. Stipe *ca.* ¾ as long as blade, without a joint, the stubble correspondingly of uneven lengths. Blade *ca.* 6 to 12 cm. long and 2 to 4 cm. broad, minutely glandular, grading to glabrous. Pinnules close, blunt, their rounded lobes somewhat reflexed. Indusial segments resembling chains of minute beads, about as long as the mass of sporangia.

RANGE: Widespread in w. N.A., in our region only scattered, e. Que., w. N.Y., n. Wisc., and nw. Ia.

HABITAT: Cliffs, ledges, and talus slopes, mostly of limestone or calcareous shale, the soil circumneutral.

CULTURE: Might be grown in a shady rock garden.

NOMENCLATURE:

Woòdsia oregàna D. C. Eaton, 1865 (GM, BB).

Midland Cliff Fern—Miss Cathcart's Woodsia

FEATURES: Rootstock, stipe, and stubble as in the preceding taxon. Blade *ca.* 8 to 15 cm. long and 2.5 to 5 cm. broad, consistently glandular. Pinnae and pinnules well-spaced, the margins distinctly thickened, sharp-toothed. Indusial segments linear, with long thread-like tip, much exceeding the mass of sporangia.

RANGE: Endemic w. of the Gr. L., from nw. Mich. to nw. Wisc., ne. and s. Minn. Reports from further e. and w. are here considered to represent glandular extremes of *W. oregana.*

HABITAT: Ledges and talus slopes, chiefly of shale, the soil mostly subacid. Not cultivated.

NOMENCLATURE:

Woòdsia cathcartiàna Robinson, 1908 (GM).
Woodsia oregana v. *cathcartiana* Morton, 1950 (BB).
Woodsia pusilla Fournier, 1880, v. *cathcartiana* Taylor, 1947.

The view that this taxon is a distinct species is here accepted because of its marked morphologic divergences.

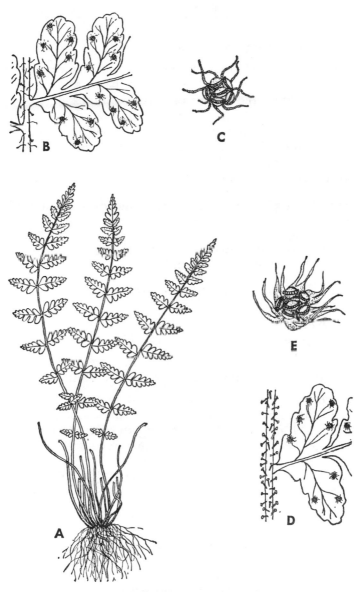

TWO CLIFF FERNS

Western: A. *Plant, reduced.*   B. *Pinna-base.*
C. *Sorus, enlarged.*
Midland: D. *Pinna-base.*   E. *Sorus, enlarged.*

Mountain Cliff Fern—Mountain Woodsia

FEATURES: Rootstock stout, bearing narrow somewhat toothed brown scales. Stipe *ca.* ⅔ as long as blade, shining brown, scaly at base and hairy upward, without a joint, the stubble uneven. Blade *ca.* 8 to 15 cm. long and 2.5 to 5 cm. broad, bearing both hairs and tiny glands. Pinnae well-spaced; pinnules divided into obtuse crenate-toothed segments. Indusia deeply cut into 3 to 6 ribbon-like segments with frayed tips, about as long as the sporangial cluster.

RANGE: Widespread in w. N.A., rare and disjunct in e. Que., e. Ont., ne. Minn., and n. Wisc.

HABITAT: Cliffs and ledges of various rocks, rarely limestone, the soil reaction mostly subacid.

CULTURE: No doubt possible in northern rock gardens.

NOMENCLATURE:

Woòdsia scopulìna D. C. Eaton, 1865 (GM, BB).

Appalachian Cliff Fern—Appalachian Woodsia

FEATURES: Like the preceding, except that the rootstock-tip and stipe bear hair-like scales, and the indusium forms a cup which may be only jagged-edged, or at most split halfway down into a few broad erose tipped segments.

RANGE: Endemic in the Appalachians and Interior Plateau, s. W. Va. and sw. Va.; also scattered further s. and w.

HABITAT: Cliffs of shale and gneiss, in subacid soil.

CULTURE: A promising rock garden subject.

NOMENCLATURE:

Woòdsia appalachiàna Taylor, 1947 (GM).
Woodsia scopulina v. *appalachiana* Morton, 1950 (BB).

While this and the closely related preceding taxon can scarcely be told apart except by examining their indusia under magnification, they are so disjunct in range that their species independence is here accepted.

TWO CLIFF FERNS

Mountain: A. *Plant, reduced.* B. *Pinna-base.*
C. *Sorus, enlarged.*
Appalachian: D. *Pinna-base.* E. *Sorus, enlarged.*

Blunt-lobe Cliff Fern—Obtuse Woodsia

FEATURES: Rootstock stoutish, often branched, bearing sparse narrow brown scales. Stipe *ca.* ¾ as long as blade, brown at base, straw-color upward, bearing minute glands and whitish brown scales, lacking a joint, the stubble very uneven. Blade pale green, with small glands and scales on axes and veins beneath (therein differing from the Brittle Fern, with which sometimes confused); *ca.* 13 to 25 cm. long and 5 to 10 cm. broad, slightly dimorphic: the sterile ones subevergreen, with obtuse pinnules and lobes and fertile deciduous with the margins of the divisions sub-reflexed, seeming acutish. Indusial segments broad, few, at first covering the sorus, then spreading in star-like fashion.

RANGE: S. states and up over our region to sw. Me., c. O., w. Mich., s. Minn., and e. Neb.

HABITAT: More varied than in other Cliff Ferns: shaded crevices in various rocks, talus slopes, and sandy banks, often invading masonry, the soil circumneutral to subacid.

CULTURE: Readily grown in a rock garden or in open woods.

NOMENCLATURE:

Woòdsia obtùsa Torrey, 1840 (GM, BB).
(*Polypodium obtusum* Sprengel, 1804, basionym).

Hybrid Cliff Ferns

Besides the one mentioned above, the following are known:

(*Woodsia cathcartiana* × *ilvensis* Butters, 1941; discredited).

W. cathcartiàna × *scopulìna* = *W.* × *maxònii* Tryon, 1948 (BB). Mingled with the parents in sw. Ont.

W. glabélla × *ilvénsis* Tryon, 1948. With parents in sw. Ont.

W. ilvénsis × *scopulìna* Tryon 1948 = *W.* × *abbèae* Butters, 1941, & = *W. confusa* Taylor, 1947, according to Tryon, 1948 (BB). With parents from sw. Ont. to ne. Minn.

BLUNT-LOBE CLIFF FERN

A. Plant, reduced.   B. Pinna-base.   C. Sorus, enlarged.

HOLLY FERNS : POLÝSTICHUM

This genus was proposed by Roth in 1799 for a fern which had been placed by Linnaeus in his too inclusive *"Polypodium."* The name is from Greek for many rows, in allusion to the regularity of the sorus pattern.

The rootstock is short, stout, and covered with old stipe-bases and scales; it sends up a cluster of moderate-sized firm-textured fronds. Their stipe is short and scaly, with several free vascular strands, and blade pinnate or 2-pinnate, with bristle-tipped teeth. The round sori, borne astride forks of free veins, are covered by a firm discoid centrally attached indusium.

Eastern Holly Fern—Braun's Holly Fern

FEATURES: Fronds thick-textured but only subevergreen. Stipe *ca.* ¼ as long as blade, bearing, as does the rachis, light brown mixed broad and narrow scales. Blade dark green above, paler and scaly beneath, *ca.* 38 to 75 cm. long and 10 to 20 cm. broad, tapering downward, 2-pinnate with spaced divisions. Sori borne well down blade, spaced, the indusium *ca.* 1 mm. across. A hybrid with *P. acrostichoides,* first reported by Thompson and Coffin in 1940, is occasional where the parents mingle; its blades are less cut, and sori developed only toward the tip.

RANGE: From Nf. to ne. Wisc. and down to the mts. of w. Mass. and ne. Pa.; also nw. N.A. and Eurasia.

HABITAT: Slopes and flats in cool, humus-rich woods, the soil usually circumneutral.

CULTURE: A beautiful subject for the woodland garden, wherever the soil does not heat up much in summer.

NOMENCLATURE:

Polÿstichum braùnii Fée, 1852 (GM, BB).
(*Aspidium braunii* Spenner, 1825, basionym).
Polystichum braunii v. *purshii* Fernald, 1928 (GM; BB?).

The differences of the east-American taxon from the European species-type seem too slight for varietal segregation.

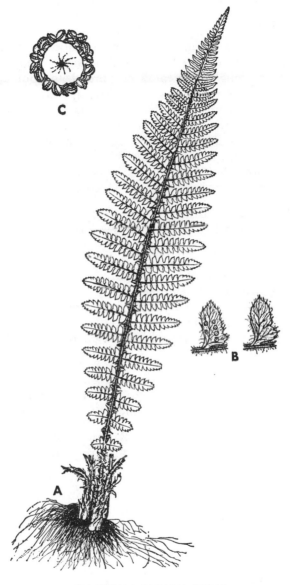

EASTERN HOLLY FERN

A. Plant, reduced.   B. Pinnules.   C. Sorus, enlarged.

Christmas Fern

FEATURES: Stipe *ca.* ⅓ to ½ as long as blade, bearing both broad and narrow light brown scales. Blade evergreen, *ca.* 25 to 50 cm. long and 6 to 12 cm. broad, the pinnae with minute (or in variants coarse) bristle-tipped teeth, and a conspicuous superior auricle. Fronds dimorphic, the smaller ones sterile and larger fertile toward the tip, the sorus-bearing pinnae gradually or often abruptly reduced. Sori crowded, the indusium *ca.* 1 mm. across. Besides the common form, shown in the main figure, there are many variants, the more significant of which are:

Frilled: f. *crispum* Broun, 1938 (GM). (*P. a.* v. *crispum* Clute, 1901, basionym). Even narrow upper pinnae sterile.

Bristle-tipped: f. *gràvesii* Clute, 1912 (GM). Pinnae truncate, with trough-like tip and projecting midvein.

Incised: f. *incìsum* Gilbert, 1901 (GM, BB). (*P. a.* v. *incisum* Gray, 1848, basionym). Pinnae coarsely serrate to jagged-lobed, some of the medial ones sorus-bearing.

Twice-pinnate: f. *multifidum* Clute, 1907 (GM, BB). Pinnae cut into pinnules or pinna-like segments with toothed margins.

RANGE: Gulf states and up over our region to a line from s. Que. to se. Wisc. and thence to e. Kans.; also disjunct in far n. Mich. One of the commonest of e. U.S. ferns.

HABITAT: Shaded slopes and well-drained flats, chiefly in rather infertile subacid to circumneutral soil.

CULTURE: A most useful plant, both the normal form and the striking variants deserving a place in every woodland garden. On barren slopes it retards erosion and helps rebuild soil. In rich loam, however, it becomes flabby, less evergreen, and short-lived.

NOMENCLATURE:

Polýstichum acrostichoìdes Schott, 1834 (GM, BB).
(*Nephrodium acrostichoides* Michaux, 1803, basionym).

The colloquial name of this fern refers to its having been used for Christmas decoration by early New England settlers.

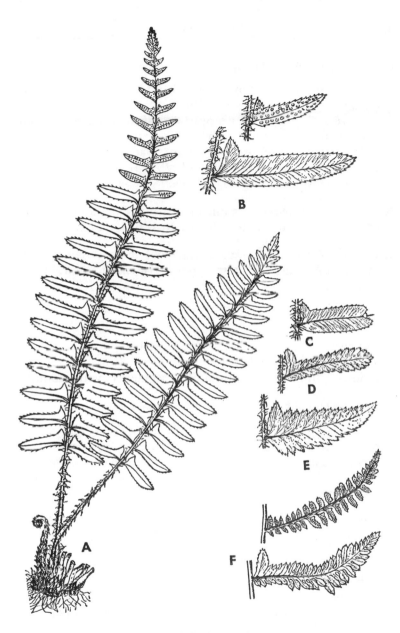

CHRISTMAS FERN

A. Plant, reduced.   Pinnae of forms: B. Type.
C. Bristle tipped.   D. Frilled.   E. Incised.   F. Twice-pinnate.

Narrow Holly Fern—Northern Holly Fern

FEATURES: Stipe very short, blackish and scaly below. Blade *ca.* 20 to 40 cm. long and 3 to 6 cm. broad with close-set spiny-serrate pinnae, the upper subfalcate with a superior auricle, the lower gradually reduced to mere wings. Sori crowded, chiefly on upper half of blade, the indusium 1 to 2 mm. across. A hybrid with *P. acrostichoides* was reported by W. H. Wagner in 1954.

RANGE: From subarct. e. Can. down to s. Que. and Ont., in e. U.S. only in n. Mich.; also w. N.A. mts. and Eurasia.

HABITAT: North-facing ledges and cool talus slopes, chiefly of limestone, the soil correspondingly circumneutral. Not cultivated.

NOMENCLATURE:

Polýstichum lonchìtis Roth, 1799 (GM, BB).
(*Polypodium lonchitis* L., 1753, basionym).

Mountain Holly Fern—Western Holly Fern

FEATURES: Stipe *ca.* ⅓ as long as blade, bearing light brown scales and hairs. Blade *ca.* 13 to 25 cm. long and 2.5 to 5 cm. broad, the rachis pubescent and pinnae close-set and lobe-auricled, their teeth obscure and only short-bristled. Sori large, numerous, crowded.

RANGE: In our region known only on serpentine rock on Mt. Albert, Que.; also mts. of nw. N.A. Not cultivated.

NOMENCLATURE:

Polýstichum scopulìnum Maxon, 1900 (BB).
(*Aspidium aculeatum* v. *scopulinum* D. C. Eaton, 1880, basionym).
P. mohrioides Presl, 1836, v. *scopulinum* Fernald, 1924 (GM).

In the interest of simplicity the species rank of this taxon is accepted here. The relative to which it can be assigned as a variety is remotely disjunct in the South American Andes.

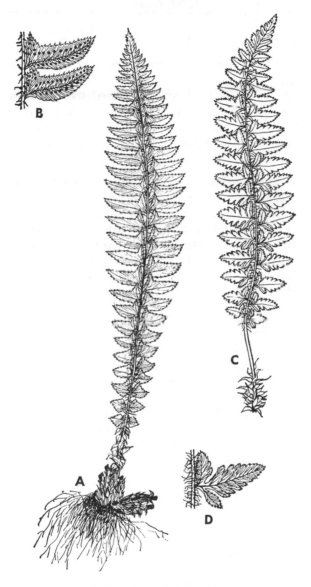

TWO HOLLY FERNS

Narrow: A. *Plant, reduced.*   B. *Pinnae.*
Mountain: C. *Blade, reduced.*   D. *Pinna.*

WOOD FERNS : DRYÓPTERIS

The term dryopteris, from the Greek for Oak Fern, used by Linnaeus only as a species epithet, was made a genus name by Adanson in 1763, and redefined by Schott in 1834. From time to time it has been replaced by *Aspidium, Nephrodium,* etc., but is now generally accepted. It is the largest genus in our region; the basal chromosome number is 41.

In this genus as here restricted by the removal, as independent genera, of *Gymnocarpium, Phegopteris,* and *Thelypteris,* there is a stout, scaly rootstock, holding old stipe-bases. The fronds, borne in a tuft or short row, are of firm texture, with scaly stipe having a number of free vascular strands, and mostly rather large-sized pinnate or 2-pinnate blade. The veins fork repeatedly and bear round sori with firm reniform indusium.

Fragrant Wood Fern

FEATURES: Rootstock retaining a conspicuous mat of brown withered fronds. Stipe *ca.* ⅛ as long as blade, bearing both broad and narrow light brown scales. Blade in type variety *ca.* 6 to 12 cm. long and 1.5 to 3 cm. broad, in v. *remotiuscula* 12 to 25 and 3 to 6 cm. respectively; under side bearing copious scales and fragrantly aromatic glandular hairs. Pinnae deeply cut into crenately toothed lobes. Sori closeset; indusium 1 to 2 mm. across.

RANGE: Type variety arct., down to bleak situations in n. Can.; var. *remotiuscula,* from subarct. e. Can. to e. Minn., down to mts. of Vt. and se. N.Y.; both also in Eurasia.

HABITAT: Crevices in north-facing cliffs and shaded talus slopes, in subacid to circumneutral soil. Not cultivated.

NOMENCLATURE:

Dryópteris fràgrans Schott, 1834 (GM, BB).
(*Polypodium fragrans* L., 1753, basionym).

MILD-CLIMATE VARIANT:

D. fràgrans v. remotiúscula Komarov, 1934 (GM, BB).
(*Nephrodium f.* v. *remotiusculum* Komarov, 1911, basionym).

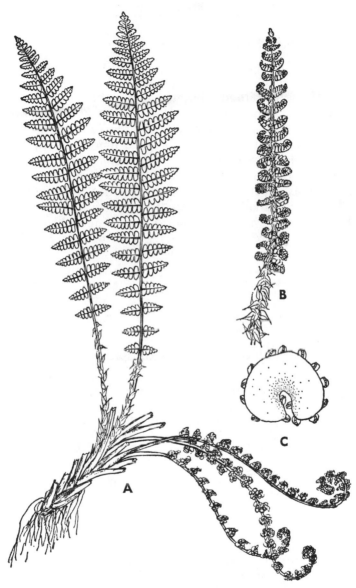

FRAGRANT WOOD FERN

Mild-climate variety: A. *Plant, reduced.*
Type (arctic) variety: B. *Frond, reduced.*
C. *Sorus, enlarged.*

Narrow Swamp Fern—Crested Wood Fern

FEATURES: Rootstock-tip bearing broad pale brown scales. Stipe *ca.* ⅓ to ⅔ as long as the strikingly narrow blade, sparsely scaly. Fronds dimorphic, the blade of the evergreen sterile ones *ca.* 15 to 30 cm. long and 6 to 12 cm. broad, of the tardily deciduous fertile ones 25 to 50 cm. long and 8 to 15 cm. broad. Pinnae tending to twist to a horizontal position, the lower triangular and upper oblong, all (except in variants) short-tapering to a bluntish tip, deeply cut into pinnule-like segments, which are somewhat serrate-toothed, especially toward upper part of blade. Sori medial, the glabrous indusium 1 to 2 mm. across. The existence of variants with relatively broad blades and some with pinnae long-tapering to a sharper point, as well as of hybrids approaching other species in aspect, has led to a false impression that this taxon grades into the following one. Cytologic study has shown *D. cristata* to be tetraploid, so it is to be classed as distinct from taxa with other degrees of ploidy.

RANGE: Throughout our region, and though becoming rarer southw. and westw., occurs disjunctly far in both directions; also in Eu. but seemingly not in Asia.

HABITAT: Swamps, wet thickets, marshes, and springy slopes, the soil mostly subacid.

CULTURE: Suitable for growing in a moist spot, the narrow blades with the pinnae tending to turn like the slats of an open venetian blind producing a striking effect.

NOMENCLATURE:

Dryópteris cristàta Gray, 1848 (GM, BB).
(*Polypodium cristatum* L., 1753, basionym).
Aspidium cristatum Swartz, 1801.
Nephrodium cristatum Michaux, 1803.

Linnaeus never explained the significance of his species epithet, so instead of using a translation of this as a colloquial name, one descriptive of its aspect and habitat is here given as first choice.

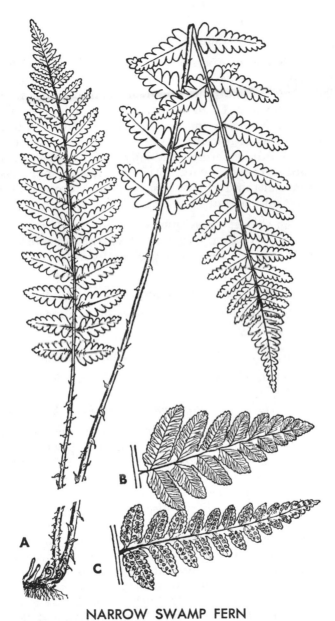

NARROW SWAMP FERN

A. *Plant, reduced.*   B. *Sterile and*   C. *Fertile pinna.*

Broad Swamp Fern—Clinton's Wood Fern

FEATURES: Scales of rootstock-tip pale with darker brown base. Stipe over ½ as long as blade, moderately scaly. Blades barely dimorphic, evergreen or nearly so, *ca.* 30 to 60 cm. long and 13 to 25 cm. broad, slightly narrowed below and long-tapering to tip. Lower pinnae elongate-triangular or in variants ovate-oblong, and upper ones oblong, mostly tapering gradually to a sharp tip, with appressed-serrate segments. Sori lying close to midveins, or rarely medial toward blade base, with a glabrous indusium *ca.* 1 to 2 mm. across.

RANGE: From w. Me. across Que., Ont., and Mich. to s. Wisc., and down to ne. Va. and se. W. Va. Most reports from further s. and w. seem to represent hybrids (except one in N.C.).

HABITAT: Swamps and damp woods, mostly in subacid soil.

CULTURE: A desirable fern for a moist shady garden.

NOMENCLATURE:

Dryópteris clintoniàna Dowell, 1906 (BB).
(*Aspidium cristatum* v. *clintonianum* D. C. Eaton, 1867, basionym).
Dryopteris cristata v. *clintoniana* Underwood, 1893 (GM).

Again a descriptive colloquial name is favored. This fern has been assigned to other genera both as a species and as a variety, but the combinations are little used. The different usage in the two major reference works might lead to the inference that the question as to its deserving species or only varietal rank is still in dispute; cytological study has shown, however, that it is hexaploid, and so wholly distinct from *D. cristata.* The alleged intermediates, on the existence of which denial of its species independence has been based, seem to represent either variant individuals or hybrids. A supposedly related taxon was named *"D. clintoniana* var. *australis"* by the writer in 1937 (included in *Guide E. Ferns*), but it has proved to be a hybrid, so should be designated *D.* × *australis* (Small, 1938, as species). The hexaploid *D. clintoniana* presumably originates when tetraploid *D. cristata* crosses with diploid *D. goldiana,* and the resulting triploid doubles its chromosome number.

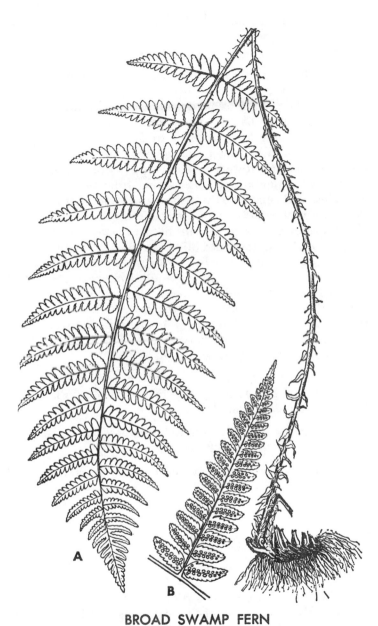

BROAD SWAMP FERN

A. *Plant, reduced.*   B. *Fertile pinna.*

Log Fern

FEATURES: Rootstock creeping shallowly through moist humus, its tip covered by shiny brown to blackish scales. Stipe over ½ as long as blade, light green, bearing mixed broad and narrow pale brown scales. Blade firm, evergreen, *ca.* 38 to 75 cm. long and 15 to 30 cm. broad, slightly narrowed at base and tapering very gradually to tip. Lower pinnae narrowed at base, upper oblong, all fairly uniformly long-tapering. Sori varying from medial to near midveins, with glabrous indusium *ca.* 1 mm. across. Cytologic study shows *D. celsa* to be tetraploid, and it no doubt originated as a hybrid between two diploids, followed by chromosome-doubling. It has frequently been interpreted as a simple hybrid between *D. clintoniana* and *D. goldiana* (treated on the next-following text page), and was so listed in *Guide E. Ferns.* The cytologic evidence, however, shows this not to be the case, its seemingly close resemblance to *D. clintoniana* being fortuitous. Its ultimate ancestor was most likely *D. goldiana* × *ludoviciana*, the latter native only south of our region.

RANGE: A rare plant, scattered over the s. states, and thus far known in our region only in the Coastal Plain and Piedmont Plateau from Va. to se. Pa.

HABITAT: Rotting logs and humus-hummocks in swamps, the soil moderately to strongly acid.

CULTURE: Readily grown in a moist woodland garden, and very attractive.

NOMENCLATURE:

Dryópteris célsa Small, 1938 (GM).
(*Dryopteris goldiana* ssp. *celsa* W. Palmer, 1899, basionym).
"Probable hybrid" (BB).

The above species epithet signifies held high, in reference to the plant's growing perched up on logs or humus hummocks above water level in swamps. The taxon has been variously interpreted as a species, subspecies, variety, form, and hybrid, but cytologic study indicates that the first view is the correct one, although its spores show unexplained anomalies.

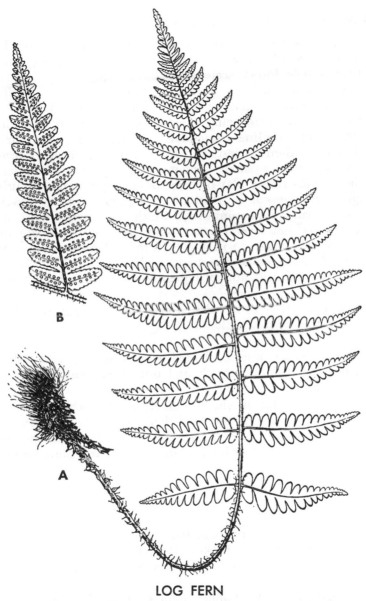

LOG FERN

A. *Plant, reduced.*   B. *Fertile pinna.*

Giant Wood Fern—Goldie's Wood Fern

FEATURES: Scales of rootstock-tip shining brown to black. Stipe brownish, slightly shorter than blade, bearing long narrow pale brown scales, the lower with a medial dark stripe. Blade *ca*. 30 to 60 cm. long and 20 to 40 cm. wide, firm but tardily deciduous, the claim made in some books that it is evergreen being based on observation of misidentified ferns; outline triangular to ovate (the 2nd or 3rd pinna-pair then longest) and the upper part abruptly contracted, with a small long-tapering tip. Surface often showing a striking play of color from bright to dull bluish green. Pinnae cut into subfalcate segments (or the lower ones basally into pinnules), which vary irregularly in length, so that several lower pinna-pairs are undulate in outline. Sori close to midveins, with a glabrous indusium 1 to 2 mm. across. Cytologic study shows this to be a diploid species; it not infrequently hybridizes with others.

RANGE: From N.B. to n. Mich. and se. Minn., down to s. Va. and c. Ill.; also s. uplands.

HABITAT: Damp woods, shaded stream banks, and talus slopes, the soil humus-rich and usually circumneutral.

CULTURE: Desirable in the woodland garden, where it may grow larger than in the wild, heights to 200 cm. having reportedly been attained. Its hybrids with other species are especially worth while, tending to be even more vigorous as well as evergreen.

NOMENCLATURE:

Dryópteris goldiàna Gray, 1848 (GM, BB).
(*Aspidium goldianum* Hooker, 1822, basionym).
Nephrodium goldianum Hooker & Greville, 1829.

The species epithet honors John Goldie, who discovered this fern at Montreal, Canada, and the widely used colloquial name refers to him; the preference in this *Guide* being for descriptive names, however, the one here placed first emphasizes that this is our most massive Wood Fern.

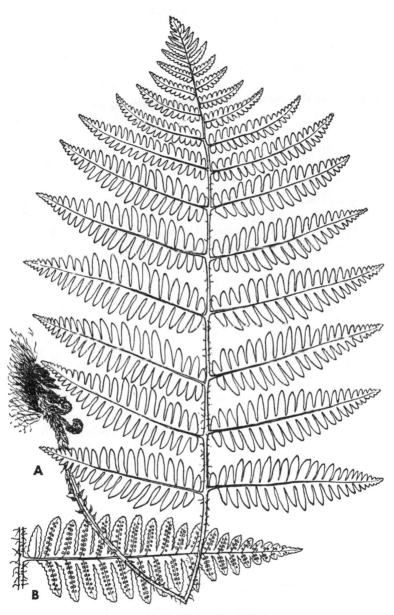

GIANT WOOD FERN

A. *Plant, reduced.*   B. *Fertile pinna.*

Male Fern

FEATURES: Rootstock-tip covered with long brown scales, the short stipe bearing both broad and narrow scales. Blade firm but deciduous, *ca.* 38 to 75 cm. long and 15 to 30 cm. broad, tapering gradually to both base and tip. Pinnae deeply cut into blunt, somewhat serrate segments. Sori near midribs, with a glabrous indusium 1 to 2 mm. across. Hybrids with both next-preceding and next-following species known.

RANGE: The e. North American taxon is rare, extending only from Nf. across Que. to nw. Vt. and n. Mich.; another, commonly treated under the same name but believed to be distinct, is widespread in the w. mts.

HABITAT: Woodlands and shaded talus slopes, usually of limestone or calcareous shale, the soil correspondingly circumneutral.

CULTURE: In Europe members of this species-complex are extensively cultivated; if a British garden includes but a single fern, it is likely to be *Dryopteris filix-mas*. In the U.S., stock from the Rocky Mountains is sold by dealers, who have nearly exterminated it from many a valley; it often grows well in eastern woodland gardens. The taxon of our region thrives only in areas of very cool summer climates, and in view of its rarity, it should not be dug wholesale for attempted culture where it is unlikely to succeed, as this could result in its near extinction.

NOMENCLATURE:

Dryopteris filix-mas Schott, 1834 (GM, BB).
(*Polypodium filix-mas* L., 1753, basionym).
Aspidium filix-mas Swartz, 1801.

EAST-AMERICAN VARIANT:

Dryópteris filix-más Schott, 1834, unnamed relative.

Cytologic study has shown that the supposed unitary taxon to which the Schott name was applied really comprises three or more species in Europe, and the east-American one may well constitute still another. At any rate its spores differ markedly in sculpture from those of the European, as well as the west-American, taxa.

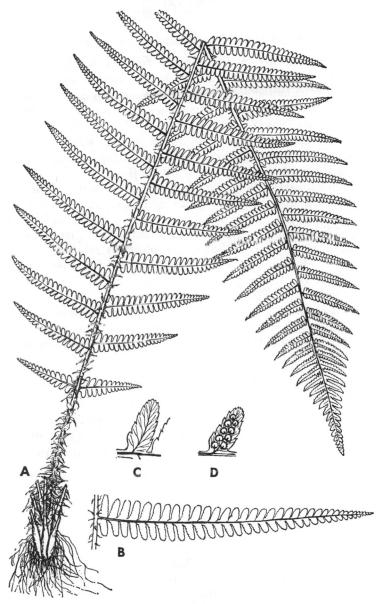

MALE FERN

A. *Plant, reduced.*   B. *Pinna.*   C. *Sterile and*
D. *Fertile segments.*

Marginal Wood Fern—Evergreen or Leather Wood Fern

FEATURES: Rootstock-tip densely covered by long yellow-brown scales, which extend up the rather short stipe in a conspicuous shaggy cone. Blade grayish green, leathery in texture especially when growing in the sun, evergreen, *ca.* 25 to 50 cm. long, and 13 to 25 cm. broad. Pinnae deeply cut into obtuse segments, which differ from most of our other wood ferns in their margins being but very obscurely toothed, and instead shallowly or exceptionally deeply round-lobed. Sori lying close to though not quite touching the margins, or near the base of segments, with a glabrous indusium *ca.* 1.5 mm. across. Two variants are worth noting: f. *tripinnatifida* Weatherby, 1936 (*Nephrodium marginale* f. *"bipinnatifidum"* Clute, 1911 [misprint], basionym) with deeply lobed pinnules; and f. *élegans* F. W. Gray, 1924 (*Aspidium marginale* v. *elegans* J. Robinson, 1875, basionym) in which the pinnules are so long as to overlap those on adjacent pinnae, and still more deeply lobed. The first is occasional and the second rare, as especially vigorous individuals in colonies of the type form.

RANGE: From e. Que. to n. Mich., down over our region to sw. Va. and s. Kans.; also s. uplands.

HABITAT: Rock ledges, talus slopes, clay banks, and rarely hummocks in swamps, in both sun and shade, the soil sterile and subacid or less commonly circumneutral.

CULTURE: Desirable and easily grown in any well-drained situation, like the Christmas Fern useful as a slope holder.

NOMENCLATURE:

Dryópteris marginàlis Gray, 1848 (GM, BB).
(*Polypodium marginale* L., 1753, basionym).
Aspidium marginale Swartz, 1801.
Nephrodium marginale Michaux, 1803.

The species epithet and the colloquial translation here favored refer to the position of the sori; at first sight this appears marginal, although on close observation is seen to be really submarginal. The other names listed are not uniquely characteristic of this taxon.

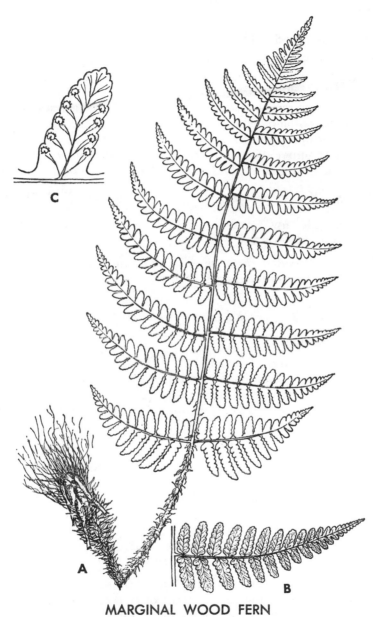

MARGINAL WOOD FERN

A. Plant, reduced.   B. Pinna.   C. Fertile segment.

Mountain Wood Fern—Spreading Wood Fern

FEATURES: Stipe *ca.* ⅔ as long as blade, bearing broad brown scales, in part medially dark-striped. Blade early deciduous, *ca.* 30 to 60 cm. long and 20 to 40 cm. broad, 2-pinnate with the pinnules deeply cut into sharply serrate segments. Lowest pinna-pair obliquely triangular, the elongate innermost lower pinnule so broad as to match the width of 2 short upper ones. Sori medial, the indusium *ca.* 1 mm. across, glabrous or rarely glandular.

RANGE: From subarct. e. Can. down to n. N.E. and e. Minn., further s. rare, in widely disjunct areas, and at increasingly higher alt., nw. Conn. to nw. N.Y. and to sw. Va.; also in highest mts. southw.

HABITAT: Wooded rocky slopes and swamp-margins, in cool humus-rich mostly subacid soil.

CULTURE: Can be grown in a woodland garden where the soil does not heat up much in summer; very ornamental.

NOMENCLATURE:

Dryopteris dilatata Gray, 1848.
(*Polypodium dilatatum* Hoffmann, 1795, basionym).
Dryopteris austriaca Woynar, 1915 (BB).
(*Polypodium austriacum* Jacquin, 1765, basionym). Another genus.

EAST-AMERICAN VARIANT:

Aspidium spinulosum v. d. f. *anadenium* B. L. Robinson, 1907.
Dryopteris spinulosa v. *americana* Fernald, 1915 (GM).
(*Aspidium s.* v. *americanum* Fischer, 1848, basionym).
Dryopteris campyloptera Clarkson, 1930 (GEF).
(*Aspidium campylopterum* Kunze, 1848, basionym, invalid).
Dryópteris dilatàta Gray, 1848, unnamed relative.

The nomenclature of this taxon represents the worst comedy of errors among the ferns of our region: under the current *Code* neither species epithet for the east-American taxon is valid, since they were proposed only provisionally. Also inacceptable is *"austriaca,"* in that Jacquin's detailed diagnosis does not fit any *Dryopteris* at all. Further study of both the taxonomy and nomenclature is called for.

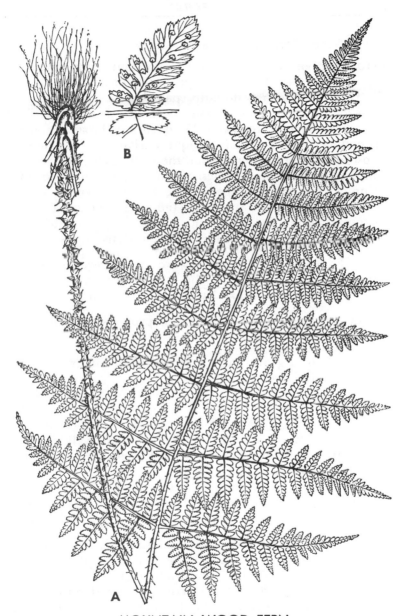

MOUNTAIN WOOD FERN

A. *Plant, reduced.* B. *Pinnule.*

Toothed Wood Fern—Spinulose Wood Fern

FEATURES: Rootstock tending to lie horizontal and to send up a short row of fronds. Stipe nearly as long as blade, bearing, like the rootstock-tip, pale brown scales. Blades subevergreen, the sterile persisting longer than the fertile, *ca.* 23 to 45 cm. long and 13 to 25 cm. broad. Pinnae ascending, the lowest pair obliquely triangular, the innermost lower pinnule longer than the next outer one, matching 1 to 1½ short upper ones; all tapering gradually to tip. Pinnules cut into appressed-serrate segments. Sori in regular rows at base of segments, the indusium *ca.* 1 mm. across, glabrous. Cytologic study shows this taxon to be a tetraploid species; it hybridizes with various others.

RANGE: From subarct. e. Can. down over our region, becoming rare s. of lat. 38° in the e. and 42° in midlands; sporadic in s. uplands, and nw. N.A., common in Eurasia.

HABITAT: Swamps, damp woods, and springy slopes, the soil mostly subacid.

CULTURE: Can be grown in a moist woodland garden, though less attractive than its relatives.

NOMENCLATURE:

Dryópteris spinulòsa Watt, 1867 (GM); not really valid.
(*Polypodium spinulosum* O. F. Mueller, 1767–77, basionym).
Aspidium spinulosum Swartz, 1801.
D. lanceolatocristata Alston, 1957; strictly the prior epithet.
(*Polypodium lanceolatocristatum* Hoffmann, 1790, basionym).
D. austriaca v. *spinulosa* Fiori, 1943 (BB); *cf.* preceding t.

Another nomenclatorial mix-up occurs here. The epithet *spinulosa* is valid only if the *Code* is liberalized to admit that it dates from Mueller's publication of a drawing of a frond, even though he did not actually name it until later. It having been accepted without question for nearly 200 years, however, replacement by Hoffmann's 8-syllable one (as has been done at the British Museum) would lead to endless complications. The epithet *"austriaca"* is here considered not to represent the preceding *Dryopteris,* and still less the present one.

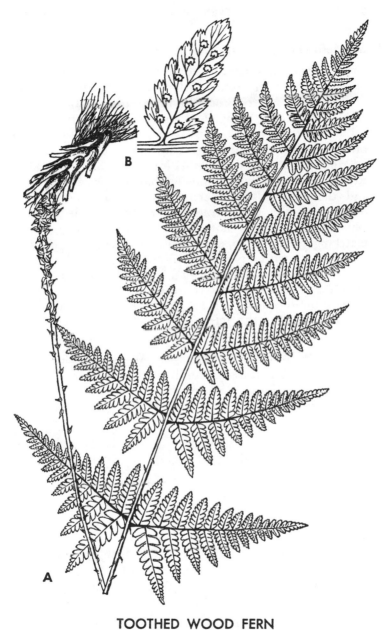

TOOTHED WOOD FERN

A. *Plant, reduced,*   B. *Pinnule.*

Fancy Fern—Evergreen or Intermediate Wood Fern

FEATURES: Rootstock tending to grow erect and to send up a vase-like group of fronds. Stipe *ca.* ⅔ as long as blade, bearing like the rootstock-tip light brown scales in part with a medial dark stripe. Both sterile and fertile blades fully evergreen, *ca.* 25 to 50 cm. long, and 13 to 25 cm. broad, the rachis and pinna-axes above middle of blade bearing gland-tipped hairs. Pinnae tending to extend straight out from rachis, mostly oblong to beyond middle, and then thereafter tapering to tip; lowest pinna-pair obliquely ovate, their innermost lower pinnule normally (though in variants not) shorter than the next outer, matching 1½ short upper ones. Pinnules cut into pinnulets or segments with diverging serrate teeth. Sori lying near base of segments, the indusium *ca.* 1 mm. across, bearing manifest stalked glands. Cytologic study has shown this to be a diploid species; it hybridizes not only with other diploids but also with tetraploids, and especially frequently with *D. spinulosa,* falsely suggesting intergradation.

RANGE: From subarct. e. Can. to e. Minn. and down over our region, but rare in midlands; also in s. uplands. Though traditionally absent from Eu., some specimens classed there as *"D. dilatata"* seem identical with our taxon.

HABITAT: Wooded rocky slopes and hummocks in swamps, the soil rich in humus and subacid to circumneutral.

CULTURE: A most desirable fern for the woodland garden.

NOMENCLATURE:

Dryópteris intermèdia Gray, 1848.
(*Polypodium intermedium* Muhlenberg, 1810, a synonym of:
   Aspidium intermedium Willdenow, 1810, basionyms).
D. spinulosa v. *intermedia* Underwood, 1893 (GM).
D. austriaca v. *intermedia* Morton, 1950 (BB); *cf.* prec. taxa.

   The favored colloquial name is that used by florists who employ the fronds by the million for ornamental purposes. Morphologically and cytologically this taxon is too distinct for "varietal" classification; supposed intermediates are now known to be hybrids. Its species rank is therefore accepted.

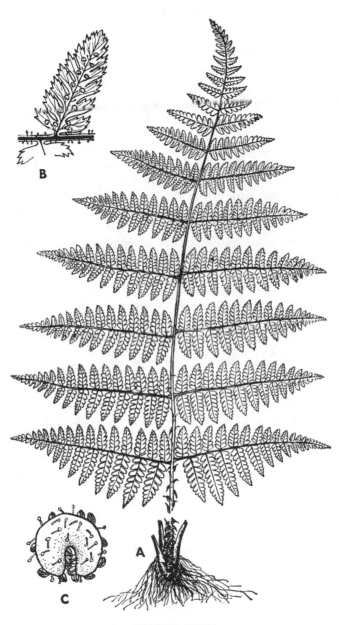

FANCY FERN

A. Plant, reduced.   B. Pinnule.   C. Sorus, enlarged.

DRYÓPTERIS HYBRIDS

Some of the confusion which exists in the classification of the wood ferns by different workers is due to the frequency with which they hybridize. Although hybrids were early recognized in Europe, none were interpreted as such in this country until 1894. They usually occur mingled with the parents, combine the features of these in a striking way, and grow larger than either. Their sporangia contain mostly shrunken, nonviable spores, along with a few extra large ones (presumably unreduced mother-cells) which can develop into normal plants. Their chromosomes show various irregularities in behavior, although it is often possible to obtain some indication of parentage by noting the ploidy, or multiples of basal chromosome number, which in *Dryopteris* is 41.

The 20 of these thus far reported are here listed with the parents in alphabetical order, along with the quasi-specific epithets they have received, if any. Few of them have any colloquial names, although these can be coined. Search for hybrids is an interesting phase of fern study.

Dismal Swamp Fern

Dryópteris célsa × *cristàta* Wherry, suggested herewith.
D. × *atropalústris* Small, 1938, as species (BB).

When he proposed the epithet, from Latin for dark swamp, Small did not indicate its hybrid character; it was suggested to represent *D. cristata* × *goldiana* in *Guide E. Ferns,* 1937; more likely it is the hybrid of the two above listed, with which it grew. It seems to have disappeared from the type locality in the Dismal Swamp of Va., and reports elsewhere are doubtful.

Spaced Wood Fern

Dryópteris célsa × *intermèdia* Wherry, suggested herewith.
D. × *separábilis* Small, 1938, as species.

The colloquial name and epithet refer to the widely spaced blade-divisions. In *Guide E. Ferns,* 1937, it was classed as *D. goldiana* × *intermedia,* but is manifestly the hybrid of the parents above stated, among which it grows. Its spores and chromosomes confirm this interpretation.

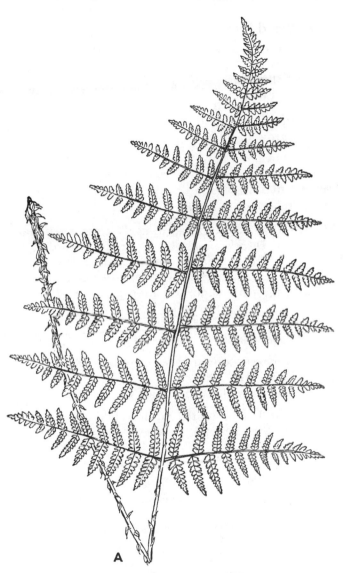

A

SPACED WOOD FERN

A. Frond, reduced.

Deceptive Wood Fern

Dryópteris clintoniàna × *cristàta* Wherry, 1961.

The existence of this hybrid, seemingly intergradational between the parents, is the basis for the widely held but erroneous view (GM) that *D. clintoniana* is a mere variety of *D. cristata*. This hybrid occurs over our region wherever the parents grow together.

Simulated Log Fern

Dryópteris clintoniàna × *goldiàna* Dowell, 1908.

This hybrid bears an extraordinarily close resemblance to the Log Fern, *D. celsa,* and the latter has accordingly been widely interpreted as representing it (GEF, BB). The spore and chromosome characters, however, disprove this view. It is rare since the parents do not often grow nearby.

Dowell's Wood Fern

Dryópteris clintoniàna × *intermèdia* Dowell, 1908.
D. × *dowéllii* Wherry, 1961.
(*Filix dowellii* Farwell, 1923, basionym).

A rare hybrid, represented in few herbaria, and not recently reported in the wild. It is very glandular.

[Hybrid Wood Fern]

Dryópteris clintoniàna × *marginàlis* Slosson, 1910.

Rarely collected since this original report.

Benedict's Wood Fern

Dryópteris clintoniàna × *spinulòsa* Benedict, 1909.
D. × *benedictii* Wherry, 1961.
(*Filix benedictii* Farwell, 1923, basionym).

As the parents grow in similar swampy habitats, this hybrid is occasionally found among them.

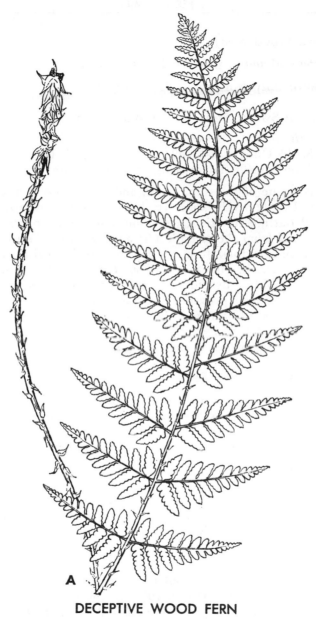

DECEPTIVE WOOD FERN

A. Frond, reduced.

[Hybrid Wood Fern]

Dryópteris cristàta × *goldiàna* Benedict, 1909.

Known only from this original report.

Glandular Swamp Fern—Boott's Wood Fern

Dryópteris cristàta × *intermèdia* Dowell, 1908.
D. × *boòttii* Underwood, 1893, as species; GM, BB, as hybrid.
(*Aspidium boottii* Tuckerman, 1843, basionym).

This is one of the commonest, and by far the best known of the *Dryopteris* hybrids. Its blade shows a narrow sub-parallel outline inherited from the first named parent, and sharp teeth from the second. The axes and indusia are often even more glandular than the first, while the sori lie nearer midveins than in either. The first being tetraploid and the second diploid, a hybrid between them should be triploid, which has indeed proved to be the case here. This hybrid commonly occurs in wet habitats alongside the *cristata* parent, from Nf. to nw. Wisc., down to sw. Va. and e. Ind., its other one growing at the swamp-margin not far away.

Miss Slosson's Wood Fern

Dryópteris cristàta × *marginàlis* Davenport, 1894.
Aspidium cristatum × *marginale* Davenport, 1894.
Dryópteris × *slossònae* Wherry, 1942.
(*Nephrodium slossonae* Hahne, 1904, basionym).

This was the first *Dryopteris* hybrid to be recognized as such in this country. Its blades are sometimes symmetrical and can be told from *D. marginalis* only by noting the medial sori, but again may be unsymmetrical or distorted. It occurs at scattered localities from Que. to ne. Va.

Braun's Wood Fern

Dryópteris cristàta × *spinulòsa* Christensen, 1905.
Dryópteris × *uliginòsa* Druce, 1909 (as species).
(*Aspidium spinulosum* v. *uliginosum* A. Braun, 1843, basionym).

The discovery and naming of this hybrid occurred in Europe, but it is now known as a rarity in our region. It resembles *D.* × *boottii,* but differs in the lack of glands.

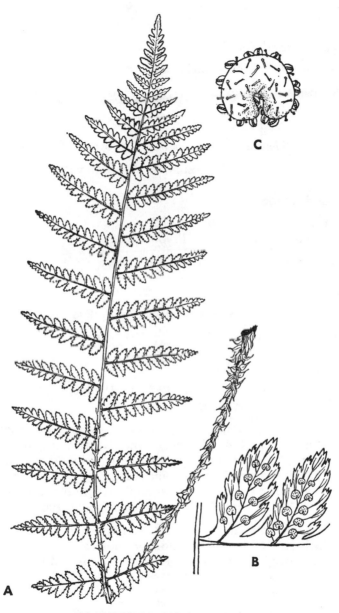

GLANDULAR SWAMP FERN

A. *Frond, reduced.*   B. *Pinnules.*   C. *Sorus, enlarged.*

[Hybrid Wood Fern]

Dryópteris "filix-más" × *goldiàna* Rugg, 1950.

Known only from this original report.

Vermont Wood Fern

Dryópteris "filix-más" × *marginàlis* Winslow, 1910.

This striking hybrid occurs in Vermont with the parents.

[Hybrid Wood Fern]

Dryópteris fràgrans × *intermèdia: D. fragrans* v. *remotiuscula* × *spinulosa* v. *intermedia* Tryon, 1942.

Known only from this original report.

[Hybrid Wood Fern]

Dryópteris goldiàna × *intermèdia* Dowell, 1908.

Rarely found since this original report.

Susquehanna Wood Fern

Dryópteris goldiàna × *marginàlis* Dowell, 1908.
D. × *leèdsii* Wherry, 1942.

This striking evergreen hybrid was given a quasi-specific name in honor of A. N. Leeds, who discovered a colony in northern Maryland. Both parents being diploid, the hybrid is likewise. A few plants in that colony proved, however, to have spores normal for a species and tetraploid chromosomes: Wherry's Wood Fern, *Dryópteris whérryi* Crane, 1961.

This resembles its hybrid ancestor so closely that it must be distinguished by observation of spores; it is known only from the original locality in Harford County, Md.

Poyser's Wood Fern

Nephrodium cristatum clintonianum f. *silvaticum* Poyser, 1908.
Dryópteris goldiàna × *spinulòsa* Benedict, 1909.
D. × *poỳseri* Wherry, 1960.

Very rare with parents in N.Y. and Pa.

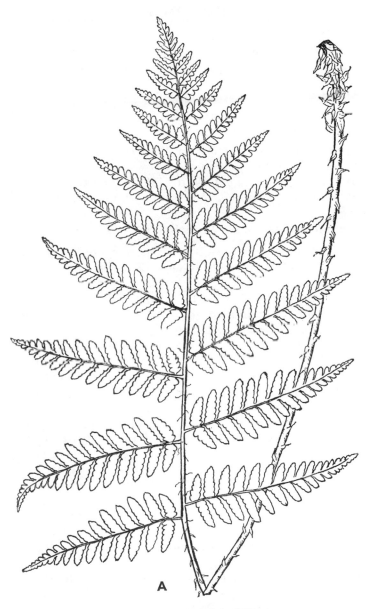

A

WHERRY'S WOOD FERN

A. Frond, reduced.

[Hybrid Wood Fern]

Dryópteris intermèdia × *marginàlis* Benedict, 1909.

A rare occurrence where the parents grow together.

Triploid Wood Fern

Dryópteris intermèdia × *spinulòsa* Wherry, 1960.
D. × *triploìdea* Wherry, 1960.
D. intermedia f. *fructuosa* Clute, 1938, in part.
(*Nephrodium spinulosum fructuosum* Gilbert, 1901, basionym).
D. spinulosa v. *fructuosa* Trudell, 1930 (GM).

The colloquial name and quasi-specific epithet proposed for this hybrid refer to its having been the first unnamed American *Dryopteris* demonstrated to be a triploid by Manton and Walker in 1955. The epithet *fructuosum,* in subspecies status, was applied to a mere vigorous extreme of *D. intermedia* bearing, as the term implies, unusually large and numerous sori. As specimens of this hybrid also frequently have such sori, they are so-labeled in many herbaria; the description in GM covers both species and hybrid. In species status this epithet is unavailable, having previously been used for an Asian fern.

Dryopteris intermedia and *D. spinulosa* are actually markedly distinct taxa, and the supposed intermediates between them, on the basis of which they are commonly classed as only varieties of one another (GM, BB), represent this, by far the most frequent, Wood Fern hybrid. The finding that the first-named parent is diploid and the second tetraploid accounts for its being a triploid. It occurs wherever the two grow together and is often larger than either; it has the blade and pinna outline of *D. spinulosa,* but is copiously glandular. Though developed in large number, the sporangia contain mostly abortive spores, observation of which will settle its identity.

Pittsford Wood Fern

Dryópteris marginàlis × *spinulòsa* Slosson, 1904.
D. × *pittsfordénsis* Slosson, 1904.

Very rare in company with the parents.

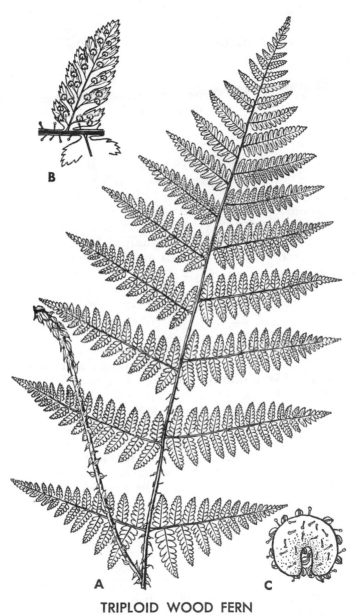

TRIPLOID WOOD FERN

A. *Frond, reduced.* B. *Pinnule.* C. *Sorus, enlarged.*

GLADE FERNS AND LADY FERNS : ATHÝRIUM

A common European fern, termed *Polypodium filix-femina* by Linnaeus in 1753, was made the basis of the genus *Athyrium* by Roth in 1799; this name is from the Greek for lacking a door, in reference to the tardily opening indusium. Though once included in *Asplenium,* it is now deemed wholly distinct.

The rootstock is moderately stout, and bears broad thin scales. The rather large fronds are delicate and deciduous, having a U-shaped vascular strand in the upper stipe, and a 1- to 3-pinnate blade; the fertile ones usually appear only late in the season. The forking veins are free at tip. The sori vary from round-oblong to linear, and may follow a veinlet or curve across it; an indusium is usually present, but in the first listed species is obsolete. This genus differs markedly from *Asplenium* in rootstock, scales, and especially vascular system. The basal chromosome number is 40.

Alpine Lady Fern

FEATURES: Rootstock erect, holding old stipe-bases, sending up a vase-like group of short-stiped fronds. Blade *ca.* 30 to 60 cm. long and 13 to 25 cm. broad, *ca.* 3-pinnate, with well-spaced pinnae, pinnules, and lobes. Sori roundish, submarginal, without indusium. The type variety, native in Greenland and subarctic Eurasia, is a smaller, more compact plant with less divided blades and medial sori; a relative in nw. N. Amer.—var. *americanum*—seems intermediate between them, as does also a variant in Nf.

RANGE: Tabletop Mt., Gaspé pen., Que.

HABITAT: Exposed cliffs and rock slides, in bleak situations, the soil moderately acid. Not cultivated.

NOMENCLATURE:

Athyrium alpéstrè Rylands, 1857 (BB).
(*Aspidium alpestre* Hoppe, 1805, basionym).
Phegopteris alpestris Mettenius, 1856.

GEOGRAPHIC VARIANT:

Athýrium alpéstrè v. *gaspénsè* Fernald, 1928 (GM).

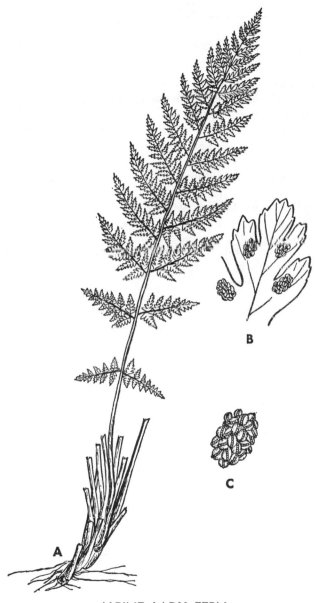

ALPINE LADY FERN

A. *Plant, reduced.*   B. *Pinnule-tip, enlarged.*
C. *Sorus, enlarged.*

Glade Fern—Narrow-leaved Athyrium (not Spleenwort)

FEATURES: Rootstock creeping, sending up a short row of fronds. Stipe pale, *ca.* ½ as long as blade, bearing scattered scales and hairs. Blade *ca.* 38 to 75 cm. long and 13 to 25 cm. broad, its pinnae subentire, lacking auricles, the lower 1 or 2 pairs short. Fertile narrower and more widely spaced than sterile. Sori long and narrow, lying along a series of upward-sloping veins. Remotely resembling the Christmas Fern, but different in numerous respects.

RANGE: From the Gulf coast up over our region to a line from s. Que. to se. Minn.

HABITAT: Woodland glades, alluvial thickets, and rocky slopes, frequently over limestone, the soil rich in nutrients and mostly circumneutral.

CULTURE: An attractive fern, readily grown in a woodland garden, where it will slowly spread.

NOMENCLATURE:

Athýrium pycnocárpon Tidestrom, 1906 (GM, BB).
(*Asplenium pycnocarpon* Sprengel, 1804, basionym).
Asplenium angustifolium Michaux, 1803, name preoccupied.
Diplazium angustifolium Butters, 1917, combination invalid.
Diplazium pycnocarpon Broun, 1938.
Homalosorus pycnocarpus Small, 1935.

The colloquial name used for this taxon in many fern books is a translation of Michaux's invalid technical one; the plant is now known not to be a Spleenwort. Were translation deemed desirable, the accepted Latin name would yield "Crowded-fruited Doorless Fern." In preference to such ponderosities a graceful, habitat-indicating name, Glade Fern, is here favored.

Some workers class this and the next-treated taxon as belonging to the genus *Diplazium,* but the features on the whole favor retention in *Athyrium.* There is no need for "*Homalosorus,*" the regularity of the sori to which this name refers not being significant.

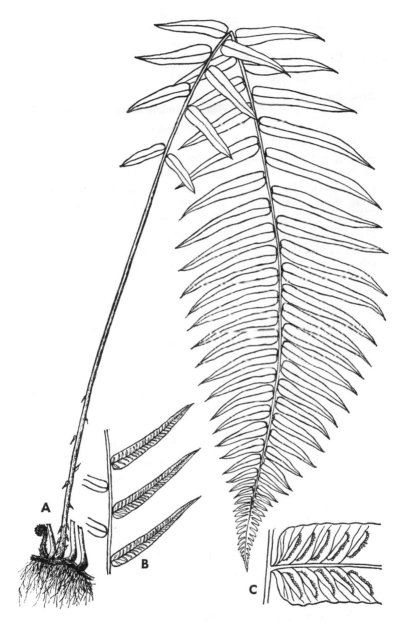

GLADE FERN

A. *Plant, reduced.*   B. *Fertile pinnae.*
C. *Base of a fertile pinna, enlarged.*

Silvery Glade Fern—Silvery Athyrium (not Spleenwort)

FEATURES: Rootstock creeping, sending up a row of rather firm-textured fronds. Stipe dark below, ½ to ⅔ as long as blade, bearing copious fragile narrow scales. Blade fine-scaly beneath, *ca.* 35 to 70 cm. long and 13 to 25 cm. wide, decidedly narrowed downward. Pinnae deeply cut into oblong segments, the basal ones tending to form auricles. Segments in the type form subentire and strikingly truncate at tip; in the toothed form, f. acrostichoìdes Gilbert, 1901 (basionym *Asplenium a.* Swartz, 1801) (GM, BB) they are toothed and acute instead. Fertile fronds somewhat longer and with narrower pinnae than sterile. Sori short and narrow, lying along close-spaced upward-sloping veins, with an indusium which at partial maturity is strikingly silvery, as indicated in the colloquial names.

RANGE: S. uplands, and up over our region to a line from N.S. to se. Minn.; also mts. of se. Asia. The f. *acrostichoides* occurs mingled with the type form, more frequently toward the n. side of the range.

HABITAT: Damp woods, shaded slopes, and occasionally open thickets, the soil rich in humus and subacid or less often circumneutral.

CULTURE: Readily grown in a woodland garden. Though not unattractive, it tends to spread rapidly and crowd out more delicate plants, so not especially desirable.

NOMENCLATURE:

Athýrium thelypterioìdes Desvaux, 1827 (GM, BB).
(*Asplenium thelypterioides* Michaux, 1803, basionym).
Diplazium thelypterioides Presl, 1836.
Asplenium acrostichoides Swartz, 1801; epithet not validly transferable to *Athyrium* in species status.
Diplazium acrostichoides Butters, 1917.

As in the preceding taxon, a widely used colloquial name refers to a now discredited genus assignment, so a descriptive alternative is preferred here. The situation as to technical naming corresponds also.

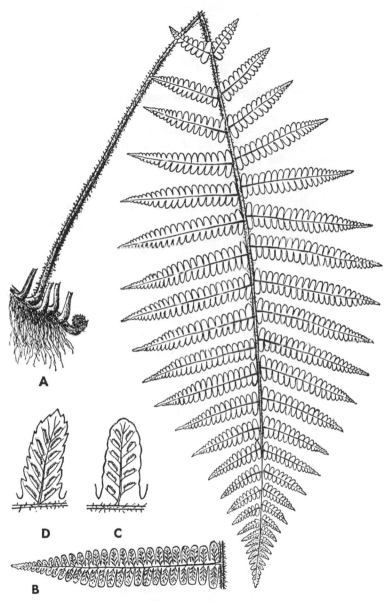

SILVERY GLADE FERN

A. *Plant, reduced.*   B. *Pinna.*
Segments of: C. *Type form and*   D. *Toothed form.*

LADY FERNS

Athyrium filix-femina Roth, 1799 (GM, BB).
(*Polypodium filix-femina* L., 1753, basionym).
Asplenium filix-femina Bernhardi, 1806.

Why Linnaeus chose this epithet is a mystery, for the ancients had applied the term Lady Fern to an entirely different plant. The independent genus *Athyrium* was based on this taxon by Roth in 1799.

The Lady Ferns of our region are exceedingly variable, and intergrade to such an extent as to defy any simple classification; three major taxa are recognized here.

Subarctic Lady Fern

FEATURES: Rootstock erect, sending up a vase-like group of rather heavy-textured fronds. Stipe *ca.* ⅓ as long as blade, bearing long pale brown scales. Blade *ca.* 75 to 150 cm. long and 15 to 30 cm. broad, conspicuously narrowed toward base, 2-pinnate with lobed pinnules, glandular beneath. Sori at most twice as long as broad, the indusium curved, from merely hooked at upper end to c-shaped, fringed with long glandless cilia. Spores yellow.

RANGE: Disjunct in our region, from Nf. to the Gaspé pen., Que.; chiefly in nw. N.A.

HABITAT: Swamps and moist thickets, in which the moderately acid soil remains cool in summer.

CULTURE: This striking plant can scarcely be expected to thrive in mild-climate gardens.

NOMENCLATURE:

Athýrium filix-fémina v. *sitchénsè* Ruprecht, 1860 (GM).
Athyrium filix-femina v. *cyclosorum* Ruprecht, 1860 (BB).

The varietal epithet favored here refers to the plant's having been discovered at Sitka, Alaska; the alternative one to the sori being markedly curved. Whether the two really differ enough for nomenclatorial segregation is undecided.

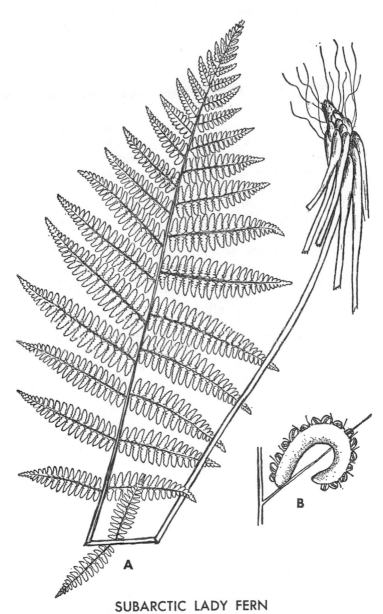

SUBARCTIC LADY FERN

A. *Plant, reduced.*   B. *Sorus, enlarged.*

Northeastern Lady Fern

FEATURES: Rootstock creeping, sending up a short row of fronds. Stipe from ½ to nearly as long as blade, bearing deep brown scales with narrow thick-walled cells. Blade *ca.* 30 to 60 cm. long, broadest at *ca.* the 5th pinna-pair up, tapering downward, 2-pinnate with lobed pinnules. Breadth in type var. under 20 cm., the sterile pinnules broad but fertile narrow, the mature sporangia coalescing; in var. *elatius* up to 40 cm., the pinnules similar, the indusia more curved; and in var. *rubellum* ca. 13 to 25 cm., both kinds of pinnules broad, the sori discrete, the stipe-hue either red (*cf.* epithet) or green. Sori much longer than broad, the indusium straight to curved, ciliate with glandless hairs. Spores yellow, dotted.

RANGE: From Que. to w. Minn. and down over our region, eastw. rare s. of lat. 39°, in Miss. vy. s. of lat. 37°; also occasional further s. and w.

HABITAT: Damp woods, swamps, and thickets, the soil mostly subacid; var. *rubellum* occupies the shadier places.

CULTURE: Spreads too rapidly for a small garden.

NOMENCLATURE:

Athýrium angústum Presl, 1825 (GEF).
(*Aspidium angustum* Willdenow, 1810, basionym).
Athyrium filix-femina v. *michauxii* Farwell, 1916 (GM, BB).
(*Asplenium michauxii* Sprengel, 1827, basionym).

MAJOR VARIANTS:

Athýrium angústum v. elàtius Butters, 1917.
A. filix-femina v. *michauxii* f. *elatius* Clute, 1938 (GM).
(*Asplenium elatius* Link, 1841, basionym).
Athýrium angústum v. rubéllum Butters, 1917.
A. filix-femina v. *michauxii* f. *rubellum* Farwell, 1916 (GM).
(*A. filix-femina* v. *rubellum* Gilbert, 1901, basionym).

While there is merit in the view that this taxon is a variety of the widespread Lady Fern (GM, BB), its species status is here maintained in the interest of simplicity. Taxon *rubellum* is the most widespread.

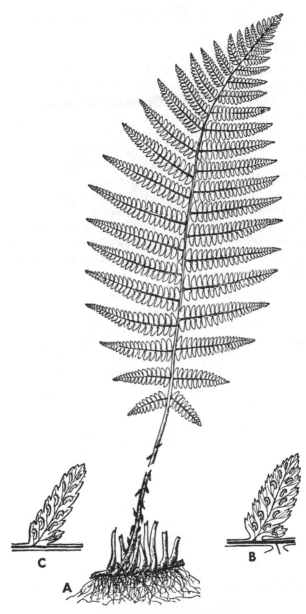

NORTHERN LADY FERN

A. Plant, reduced.   Pinnules of: B. Widespread and
C. Type variety.

Southern Lady Fern

FEATURES: Rootstock horizontal, sending up a row of fronds.
Stipe nearly equaling blade in length, bearing sparse pale
brown scales with broad thin-walled cells. Blade *ca.* 25 to
50 cm. long and 18 to 35 cm. broad at the 2nd pinna-pair
up, 2- to 3-pinnate, the pinnules having a small superior
auricle. Sori longer than broad, the indusium ciliate with
gland-tipped hairs. Spores having a wrinkled blackish outer
coat. The Lacy form, f. *subtripinnatum* is the largest and
most dissected extreme with the blade up to 40 cm. broad
and pinnules to 2 cm. long. Forma *ellipticum* is the
smallest and least dissected, its blade *ca.* 10 to 20 cm. broad
at the 4th pinna-pair up, thus resembling *A. angusium* but
differing from that in its pale stipe-scales and dark-hued
spores.

RANGE: Gulf States and up over our region, becoming rare
northw., though locally reaching Mass., s. Vt., se. N.Y.,
n. Ind., and c. Mo. The f. *subtripinnatum* attains its max-
imum development in the s. Appalachians, up to s.-centr.
Pa., with small phases to se. Mass. The f. *ellipticum* is
occasional up to N.J. lowlands, chiefly in shady situations.

HABITAT: Swamps, damp thickets, and wooded ravines, the
soil mostly subacid.

CULTURE: Another rapid spreader to be wary of, although
the beauty of the Lacy form encourages its admission to
woodland gardens.

NOMENCLATURE:

Athýrium asplenioìdes A. Eaton, 1817 (GEF).
(*Nephrodium asplenioides* Michaux, 1803, basionym).
A. filix-femina v. *asplenioides* Farwell, 1923 (GM, BB).

MAJOR VARIANTS:

A. asplenioìdes f. *subtripinnàtum* Butters, 1917 (GEF).
A. asplenioìdes f. *ellipticum* Wherry, 1948.

The colloquial name Lowland Lady Fern used in some
books is wholly inapt, in that this taxon occurs in southern
mountains 2000 feet higher than any other Lady Fern. The
distinctive features and geography favor its maintenance as
a species.

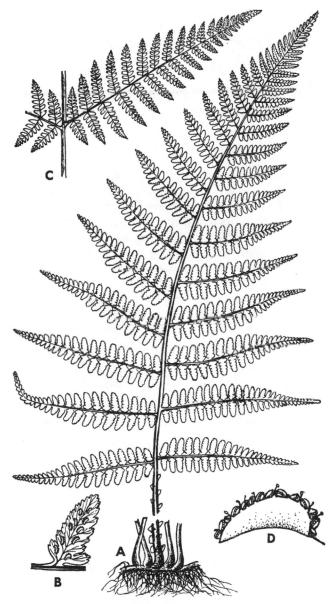

SOUTHERN LADY FERN

A. *Plant of type form, reduced.*   B. *Pinnule of type form.*
C. *Pinna of lacy form.*   D. *Sorus, enlarged.*

NET-VEINED CHAIN FERN : *LORINSÈRIA*

This genus was named in honor of G. Lorinser, an early fern student, by Presl in 1851. Being closely related to the world-wide genus *Woodwardia,* it is often included under that (GM, BB). Its features are those of its single species.

Net-veined Chain Fern

FEATURES: Rootstock long-creeping and branching, sending up scattered markedly dimorphic deciduous fronds. Stipe of sterile ones dark at base, of fertile ones becoming lustrous blackish brown throughout, *ca.* as long as blade. Sterile blade *ca.* 15 to 30 cm. long and 10 to 20 cm. broad, cut into alternate divisions, the shortened lower ones, spaced and simulating pinnae, their undulate or rarely lobed margins finely but manifestly serrate. Fertile blade arising in autumn, sometimes overtopping the sterile, cut into narrow wide-spaced alternate pinnae and pinna-like segments. Veins all areolate. Sori elongate, borne in chain-like rows along midvein.

RANGE: Widespread in the s., in our region chiefly in Atlantic lowlands up to N.S., but also in scattered upland stations from Va. to Mo. and Mich.

HABITAT: Bogs and swamps, in moist intensely acid humus.

CULTURE: Readily grown in a shady garden where the soil is fairly moist and acid. The blade is pinkish when young, and at maturity becomes bronzy green and glossy, producing an attractive effect.

NOMENCLATURE:

Lorinsèria areolàta Presl, 1851 (GEF).
(*Acrostichum areolatum* L., 1753, basionym).
Woodwardia angustifolia J. E. Smith, 1793; not valid.
Woodwardia areolata Moore, 1857 (GM, BB).

Whether the genus *Lorinseria* should be regarded as distinct from *Woodwardia* or not is a matter of opinion. In view of their marked morphological differences, they are here separated, even though there is a seeming intermediate between them in Asia.

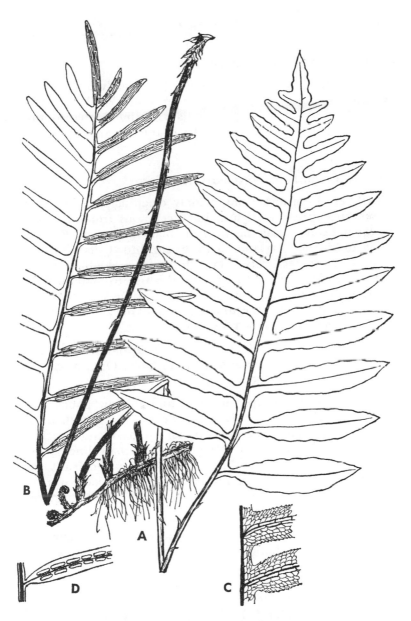

NET-VEINED CHAIN FERN

A. *Plant with sterile frond, reduced.*
B. *Fertile frond, reduced.* Base of: C. *Sterile and*
D. *Fertile segments.*

CHAIN FERNS : WOODWÁRDIA

This genus was named for T. J. Woodward, an early English botanist, by J. E. Smith in 1793. While the taxon treated on the preceding page is sometimes assigned to it, only another is here included. Its characters appear below.

Eastern Chain Fern—Virginia Chain Fern

FEATURES: Rootstock stout, widely creeping and branching, sending up a row of firm but deciduous fronds. Stipe *ca.* equal blade, becoming lustrous blackish brown. Blade *ca.* 35 to 70 cm. long and 15 to 30 cm. broad, its pinnae cut into entire segments. Veins forming a double chain of areoles along midrib, free from this out to margin. Fertile fronds produced in summer, similar to the sterile ones, the long narrow sori forming chain-like rows along midribs of pinnae and of larger segments.

RANGE: Gulf states and up over coastal lowlands to N.S., and in rather disjunct upland areas to Que., Ont., Mich., and ne. Ill.; also Bermuda.

HABITAT: Bogs, swamps, marshes, and shallow ponds, often rooted in mud which is too toxic for the growth of any other fern. Soil reaction varying from intensely acid to neutral, or even, near the ocean, to subalkaline. This is one of the few ferns which thrives better and fruits more freely in the sun than in the shade. It is, moreover, one classed as a weed, in that it may invade and damage commercial cranberry bogs.

CULTURE: In view of its invasive tendencies, recommended only for muddy hollows too barren for anything else.

NOMENCLATURE:

Woodwárdia virgínica J. E. Smith, 1793 (GM, BB).
(*Blechnum virginicum* L., 1771, basionym).
Anchistea virginica Presl, 1851.

This fern is so much like members of the genus *Woodwardia* from other regions that the placing of it in the segregate genus proposed by Presl is not acceptable.

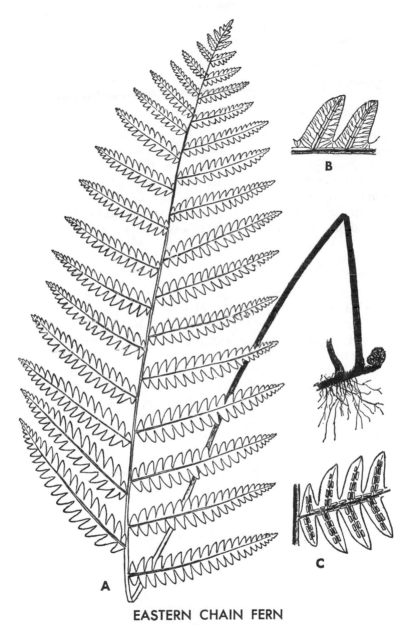

EASTERN CHAIN FERN

A. Plant, reduced.   *B. Sterile and*   *C. Fertile segments.*

SPLEENWORTS : *ASPLÈNIUM*

The genus *Asplenium* was founded by Linnaeus in 1753, its name being an ancient one for some plant supposed to cure disease of the spleen. It is a vast, world-wide group, and the second largest in our region.

In our species a short rootstock covered by old stipe-bases and narrow scales sends up a rosette or tuft of small to moderate-sized fronds. The stipe is short with a slender rounded vascular strand inside, and the blade simple to 3-pinnate, often evergreen. Linear sori diverge along vein-branches, and have a narrow glabrous indusium. The basal chromosome number in the genus is 36.

Lobed Spleenwort—Pinnatifid Spleenwort

FEATURES: Fronds few, evergreen. Stipe ⅔ as long as blade, brown below. Blade simple, elongate-triangular, bilaterally rather unsymmetrical, *ca.* 6 to 12 cm. long and 1.5 to 3 cm. broad, with a tail-like extension, rarely rooting at tip. Margins lobed, often subpinnate below, the lobes obtuse to acutish or even acuminate. Veins chiefly free, or a few areolate. Cytologic study indicates that this taxon, a tetraploid species, originated as a hybrid between *A. montanum* and *A. rhizophyllum* (*Camptosorus*), in which the chromosomes doubled.

RANGE: S. uplands and over our region to a line from n. N.J. to s. Ill.; seemingly nowhere very common.

HABITAT: Dry shaded crevices of hard rocks, especially sandstone and gneiss. Soil subacid or rarely circumneutral.

CULTURE: Practically impossible, since the habitat it requires can scarcely be constructed artificially.

NOMENCLATURE:

Asplènium pinnatifidum Nuttall, 1818 (GM, BB).
(*A. rhizophyllum* β *pinnatifidum* Muhlenberg, 1813, basionym).

Both of the colloquial as well as the technical names of this taxon refer to the cutting of the simple blade.

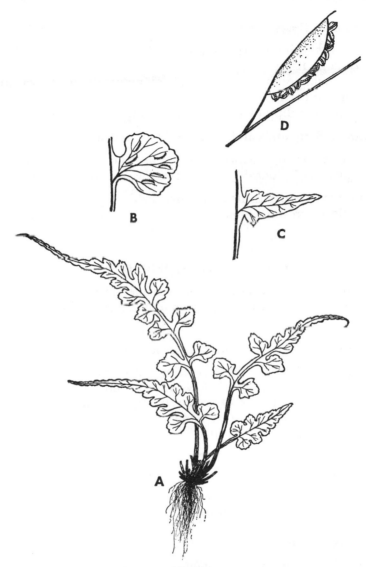

LOBED SPLEENWORT

A. Plant. Segments of: B. *Blunt and* C. *Tapering variants.*
D. *Sorus, enlarged.*

Mountain Spleenwort

FEATURES: Stipe nearly as long as blade, brown below. Blade *ca.* 5 to 10 cm. long and 3 to 6 cm. broad, 1- to 2-pinnate, the subopposite pinnae and pinnules rhombic, serrate, varying from barely cut to dissected into slender segments. A normal diploid species, which hybridizes with others.

RANGE: S. uplands and up to w. Mass. and ne. Ohio.

HABITAT: Damp shaded crevices in sandstone, gneiss, and other hard, noncalcareous rocks, the soil strongly acid.

CULTURE: Owing to its specialized habitat, practically impossible to grow in a garden.

NOMENCLATURE:

Asplènium montànum Willdenow, 1810 (GM, BB).

Both colloquial and technical names refer to this fern's having been sent to Europe from our eastern mountains.

Trudell's Spleenwort—Pinnate Spleenwort

FEATURES: More closely resembling the second-named parent, but the blade divided below into 2 or more pairs of serrate or somewhat lobate obliquely triangular pinnae, to which the preferred colloquial name refers; also more symmetrical, and shorter-tailed at tip.

RANGE: Occasional wherever the parents grow near together, w. N.J. to c. Ohio, sw. Va. and Ky.; also s. uplands.

HABITAT: Crevices of non-calcareous rocks, the soil mostly decidedly acid. Not cultivated.

NOMENCLATURE:

Asplènium montànum × pinnatifidum (GM) =
Asplènium × trudéllii Wherry, 1925 (GM).
A. pinnatifidum v. *trudellii* Clute, 1938 (BB).

The hybrid nature of this taxon was suggested when it was originally described, and has been confirmed by cytologic study: As predicted from the parents being respectively diploid and tetraploid, it has proved to be a triploid hybrid.

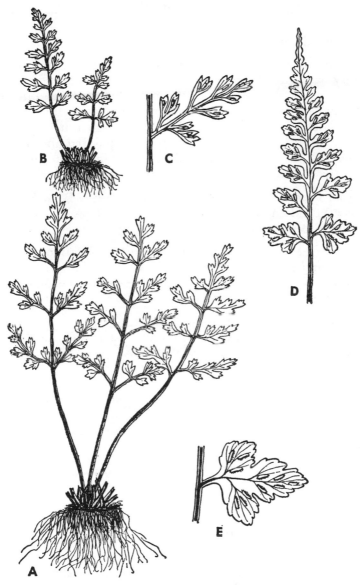

TWO SPLEENWORTS

Mountain: *Plants of:* A. *Average and* B. *Dwarf forms.*
C. *Pinna.*
Trudell's: D. *Frond and* E. *Basal pinna.*

Wall-rue Spleenwort

FEATURES: Stipe somewhat longer than blade, brown only at very base. Blade evergreen, *ca.* 3 to 6 cm. long and 2 to 4 cm. broad, divided into alternate long-stalked pinnae, composed of a few rhombic pinnules. In the type form the latter are rounded and shallowly toothed at tip, while in taxon *subtenuifolium* they are taper-pointed and deeply jaggedly cut. Sori few, spaced in shade-forms but crowded on the narrower divisions of plants in sunny situations.

RANGE: From n. Vt. and s. Ont. along the Gr. L. to Keweenaw Pt., Mich., down limestone valleys to sw. Va. and sw. Mo.; also s. uplands.

HABITAT: Ledges and talus of limestone and calcareous shale, most luxuriant where moderately shaded, the soil neutral to subalkaline. Contrary to book statements, the American taxon does invade masonry, then resembling the European.

CULTURE: Can be grown in a limestone rock garden, though difficult to get started, since it must be kept from drying out until a new root system develops.

NOMENCLATURE:

Asplenium ruta-muraria L., 1753 (BB).

AMERICAN VARIANTS:

Asplènium rùta-murària v. *cryptólepis* Wherry, 1942 (BB).
(*A. cryptolepis* Fernald, 1928, basionym). (GM).
A. rùta-murària v. **subtenuifòlium** Christ, 1903.
A. ruta-muraria v. *ohionis* Wherry, 1942 (GEF, BB).
(*A. cryptolepis* v. *ohionis* Fernald, 1928, basionym). (GM).

Since the rootstock-scales in the American representatives of this taxon are more fully hidden by roots than in the European type, Fernald made the former a distinct species, with an epithet referring to this character; the differences seem, however, insufficient for more than varietal segregation. A Swiss worker on this species, H. Christ, named and figured a number of "varieties" based on pinnule outline, and his epithet for the Narrow variety has 25 years' priority over Fernald's; it should be reduced to the status of form.

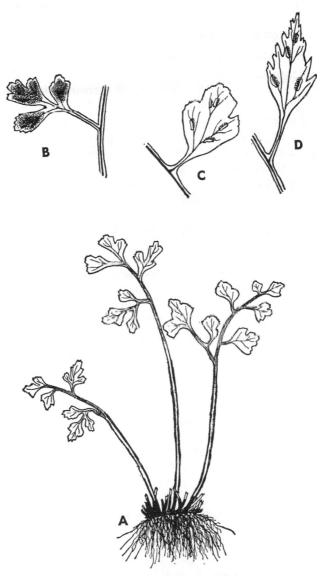

WALL-RUE SPLEENWORT

A. *Plant and*   B. *Pinna of type variety.*
Pinnules of: C. *Type and*   D. *Narrow variety, enlarged.*

Cliff Spleenwort—Bradley's Spleenwort

FEATURES: Stipe *ca.* ½ as long as blade, lustrous dark brown, this coloration extending to middle of rachis. Blade *ca.* 6 to 12 cm. long and 1.5 to 3 cm. broad. Pinnae oblong-triangular, serrate-toothed to jagged-lobed, the superior basal lobe forming an auricle. Sori medial, becoming blackish brown. The describer of this fern noted that its features suggest hybrid origin, and cytologic study indicates that it did originate as a hybrid between *A. montanum* and *A. platyneuron,* but that the chromosomes then doubled, so that it is now a tetraploid species.

RANGE: Rare, s. uplands up in our region to se. N.Y., s. Ohio, c. Ky., and w.-c. Mo.

HABITAT: Tight crevices in bare, often overhanging cliffs of sandstone, granite, and other lime-free rocks, what humus collects around its roots being always intensely acid. The statement that it grows on limestone, which gets copied from one fern book to another, is erroneous.

CULTURE: Unlikely to be successfully cultivated.

NOMENCLATURE:

Asplènium brádleyi D. C. Eaton, 1873 (GM, BB).

The epithet honors its first collector, W. H. Bradley. The preferred colloquial name refers to its habitat.

Sand Mountain Spleenwort—Graves' Spleenwort

Asplènium brádleyi × *pinnatifidum* =
Asplènium × *gràvesii* Maxon, 1918 (GM, BB).

This fern was discovered growing with the presumed parents by E. W. Graves, on Sand Mt. west of Trenton, Ga.; it combines their features in a striking way. They are both tetraploid, and cytologic study shows it to be, as expected, a hybrid of the same ploidy; its synthesis from a culture of mixed spores of the parents was attained by T. Darling, Jr., in 1957. In our region it is known only in se. Pa. and c. Ky.

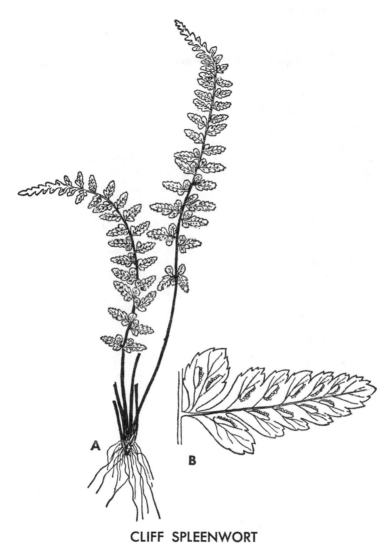

CLIFF SPLEENWORT
A. Plant. B. Pinna, enlarged.

Brown-stem Spleenwort—Ebony Spleenwort

FEATURES: Stipe short, like the rachis lustrous brown. Blades dimorphic, the sterile small, spreading, evergreen; fertile erect, *ca.* 18 to 35 cm. long and 2.5 to 5 cm. broad, with alternate superior-auricled pinnae, gradually reduced to mere wings at base, tardily deciduous. Pinnae in the type variety mostly under 3 cm. long, acutish, finely toothed, in var. *incisum ca.* 4 cm. long, acuminate, and irregularly coarse-toothed. (A southern variant, var. *bacculum-rubrum* [GM], with blades up to 60 cm. long and 12 cm. broad, grades into var. *incisum* in Va.) Blades in f. *hortonae* (named after its collector) all sterile, the pinnae deeply cut into frilly lobes. Sori numerous.

RANGE: Gulf states and common in our region up to a line from w. Me. to s. Wisc.; var. *incisum* mostly toward s.

HABITAT: Wooded slopes, humus-hummocks, and rock ledges, most luxuriant in subacid soil; often invading masonry.

CULTURE: Can be grown in well-drained humus, but short-lived if this is limed or fertilized.

NOMENCLATURE:

Asplènium platyneùron Oakes, 1878 (GM, BB).
(*Acrostichum platyneuros* L., 1753, *platyneuron*, 1763, basionym).
Asplenium ebeneum Aiton, 1789.

MAJOR VARIANTS:

A. platyneùron v. *incìsum* B. L. Robinson, 1908 (GM).
(*A. ebeneum* v. *incisum* Howe, 1869, basionym).
A. platyneuron f. *serratum* R. Hoffmann, 1922 (BB).
(*A. ebeneum* v. *serratum* Gray, 1873, basionym).
A. platyneùron f. *hórtonae* Clute, 1909 (GM, BB).
(*A. ebeneum* v. *hortonae* Davenport, 1901, basionym).

The colloquial translation of Aiton's epithet, used in some books, is inapt, in that ebony is black, whereas nothing about this fern is; a descriptive name accordingly seems preferable. Linnaeus' inappropriate epithet was based on a mixture of taxa. The first accepted variant is classed as the Incised variety, since its features show a geographic trend, the second as the Frilled form, because it is sporadic throughout.

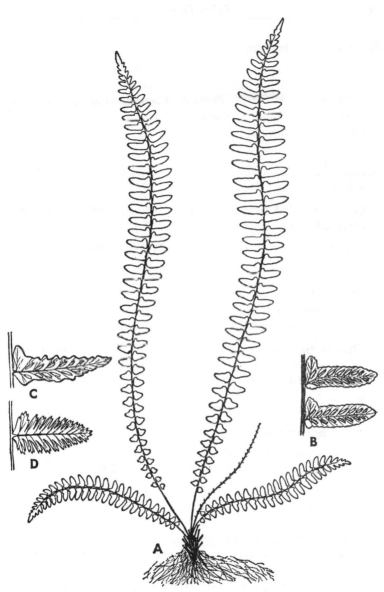

BROWN-STEM SPLEENWORT

A. *Plant, reduced.*   *Pinnae of:*   B. *Type variety.*
C. *Incised variety.*   D. *Frilled form.*

Black-stem Spleenwort

FEATURES: Fronds uniform, evergreen. Stipe *ca.* ¼ as long as blade, like rachis shining black. Blade *ca.* 13 to 25 cm. long and 1/10 as broad. Pinnae opposite, oblong with a low superior and sometimes also an inferior auricle, moderately reduced downward, entire or wavy margined. Sori few, medial.

RANGE: Tropical Amer. and Gulf states, up in our region to a line from c.-s. Pa. to e. Kans.

HABITAT: Shaded limestone ledges, the soil neutral or somewhat alkaline.

CULTURE: Worthy of trial in a shady, limestone rock garden.

NOMENCLATURE:

Asplènium resíliens Kunze, 1844 (GM, BB).
A. parvulum Martens & Galeotti, 1840, preoccupied.

This is the Spleenwort which might appropriately have been named for ebony, as both its stipe and rachis are of the same hue as that famous wood.

Virginia Spleenwort

Asplènium platyneùron × *trichómanes* =
Asplènium × *virgínicum* Maxon, 1939 (GM, BB).

When this taxon was first found, by William Palmer, in 1884, it was mistaken for the Black-stem Spleenwort, but its hybrid nature was subsequently recognized. As it combines the characters of the species treated on the preceding text page with those of that on the next, its parentage is manifest. The linear blade is *ca.* 18 mm. broad, with numerous well-spaced short pinnae, the lowest opposite and little reduced.

The find referred to was on rocks along the Potomac River in Alexandria-Arlington Co., Va. One other collection is known from the Delaware Water Gap, in N.J. or Pa., and one in N.C. Since the parents often grow close together, search may well lead to its discovery elsewhere.

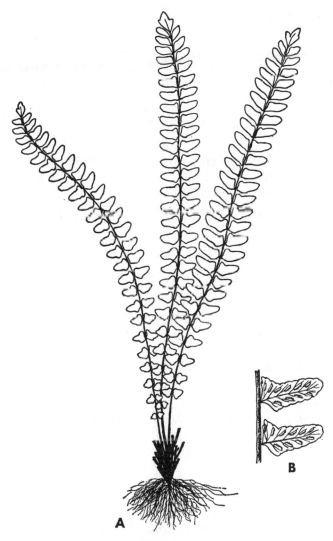

BLACK-STEM SPLEENWORT

A. *Plant, reduced.* B. *Pinnae.*

Maidenhair Spleenwort

FEATURES: Fronds uniform, evergreen, forming rosettes and tufts. Stipe *ca.* ⅓ as long as blade, like rachis dark brown. Blade *ca.* 8 to 15 cm. long and ⅒ as broad. Pinnae opposite, short, not auricled, crenate, or rarely lobed. Sori few.

RANGE: From N.S. to se. Minn., and down over our region, except in rock-free areas; also in s. uplands, w. N.A. (rare), and Eurasia.

HABITAT: Moist rock crevices, when on limestone often in the open, on noncalcareous rocks mostly in the shade. Soil neutral to moderately acid.

CULTURE: Can be grown in rock gardens, but rarely thrives.

NOMENCLATURE:

Asplènium *trichómanes* L., 1753 (GM, BB).
A. melanocaulon Muhlenberg, 1810.

Proposal of the second technical name was based on the view that the American representative of the species is distinct from the European, but this is not now accepted.

Shenandoah Spleenwort—Stotler's Spleenwort

Asplènium × *stótleri* Wherry, 1925 (GM, BB).
A. pinnatifidum × *bradleyi* (? BB).
A. pinnatifidum × *platyneuron* (GEF, GM), withdrawn herewith.
A. pinnatifidum × *trichómanes* Wherry, new interpretation.

This spleenwort, intermediate in its features between the two now suggested as its parents, was discovered by Dr. T. C. Stotler, an amateur naturalist of Harpers Ferry, W. Va. The stipe and lower rachis are lustrous dark brown. The oblong-triangular pinnae are cut into rounded lobes with nearly entire margins. It occurred on a single west-facing cliff of mica schist along the Shenandoah River south of Charles Town, Jefferson Co., W. Va.; the first-named parent grew nearby, the second 500 feet away. Over the years the rocks have dried out and all three have vanished, so the hybrid is now extinct. Its unreduced mother-cells sometimes yielded new plants, but no cultures are known to remain alive.

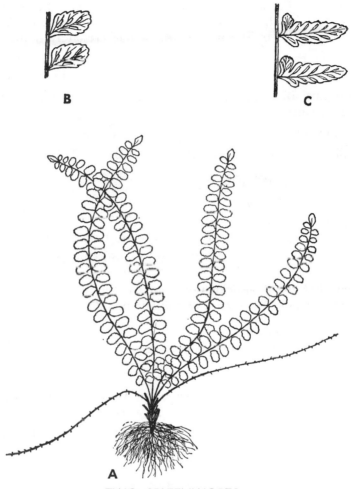

TWO SPLEENWORTS

Maidenhair: A. *Plant, reduced.* B. *Pinnae.*
Shenandoah: C. *Pinnae.*

Green Spleenwort

FEATURES: Fronds tufted, uniform, subevergreen. Stipe ca. ½ as long as blade, brown; rachis green. Blade *ca.* 6 to 12 cm. long and 8 to 15 mm. broad; pinnae crenately toothed.

RANGE: From subarct. e. Can. down to w. Me., n. Vt., and ne. tips of Mich. and Wisc.; also w. N.A. and n. Eurasia.

HABITAT: Bleak limestone ledges and talus, the soil neutral. Not cultivated.

NOMENCLATURE:

Asplènium víridè Hudson, 1762 (GM, BB).

ASPLENIUM HYBRIDS

Wherry's Spleenwort

Asplènium × *whérryi* D. M. Smith, 1961.
Asplènium brádleyi × *montànum* Wherry, 1935 (GEF).

Known in nw. N.J., se. Pa., and Ky. on siliceous rocks.

Sand Mountain Spleenwort

Asplènium brádleyi × *pinnatífidum*—see p. 156.

Pinnate Spleenwort

Asplènium montànum × *pinnatífidum*—see p. 152.

Kentucky Spleenwort

Asplènium pinnatífidum × *platyneùron* Wagner, 1954 (BB). = A. × *kentuckyénse* McCoy, 1936, as species.

Resembles a brown-rachis, symmetrically basally lobed *A. pinnatifidum;* rare, where the parents grow close together.

Shenandoah Spleenwort

Asplènium pinnatífidum × *trichómanes*—see p. 162.

Virginia Spleenwort

Asplènium platyneùron × *trichómanes*—see p. 160.

Miss Clermont's Spleenwort

Asplènium rùta-murària × *trichómanes* =
A. × *clermóntae* Syme, 1886.

Recorded from Vermont by Davenport in **1906.**

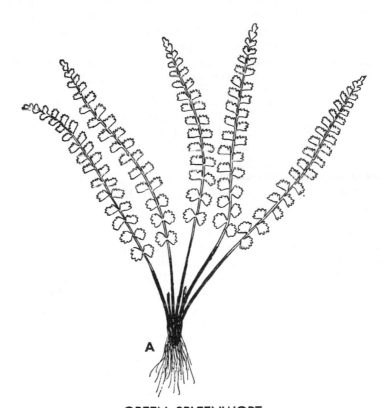

GREEN SPLEENWORT

A. *Plant, reduced.*   B. *Pinnae.*

Walking Spleenwort—Scott's Spleenwort

Asplènium ✕ *ebenoìdes* R. R. Scott, 1865, as species.
A. *platyneùron* ✕ *Camptosòrus rhizophýllus* Slosson, 1902.
Asplenosorus ebenoides Wherry, 1937 (GM, BB) invalid.

For 35 years subsequent to its naming, fern students argued over the possible hybrid origin of this taxon. The matter was then settled by Miss Margaret Slosson, who cut strips from prothallia of the presumptive parents in such a way that only antheridia or archegonia were present on any one, and planted these side by side in a moist chamber. In several cases, sperms of the one species actually fertilized the eggs of the other, and the sporophytes which arose showed all essential features of the natural plants.

In most of its known occurrences *A.* ✕ *ebenoides* produces, as usual with hybrids, only shrunken, lifeless spores; in one area, near Havana, Ala., however, the spores are viable and have blown around and started colonies over considerable territory. This phenomenon, which puzzled the earlier observers, can now be explained: At this locality chromosome-doubling has occurred, so the plants represent a tetraploid species.

The term *Asplenosorus* was proposed in 1937, but as no Latin diagnosis was supplied, it is invalid according to the *Code*. Under the view that *Camptosorus* is not a full-fledged genus it is unnecessary anyway. The hybrid combines the characters of its parents, with which it grows, but its fronds are cut in bizarre patterns, varying exceedingly even on the same individual plant. The brown color of the stipe usually extends well up the midrib; the blade may be shallowly or deeply cut into short obtuse or long acuminate lobes. The tip may be short or elongate, then often rooting.

Unexpected Spleenwort

Asplènium rùta-murària ✕ *Camptosòrus* E. L. Braun, 1939.
Asplenosorus ✕ *inexpectatus* E. L. Braun, 1940.
Asplènium ✕ *inexpectàtum* Morton, 1956.

Combines the characters of the parents; found once by Miss Braun in s. Ohio.

WALKING SPLEENWORT

A. Plant.

WALKING FERNS : *CAMPTOSÒRUS*

This genus was proposed by Link in 1833 to comprise an American and an Asian species; the name is from the Greek for flexuous, in reference to the wavy lines of sori. It is really only a subgenus of *Asplenium*. Its features are given below.

Walking Fern

FEATURES: Fronds spreading and arching. Stipe variable in length, brown only at very base. Blade simple, thinnish but evergreen, *ca.* 13 to 25 cm. long and 1.5 to 3 cm. broad near base, long-triangular, tapering to a slender "tail" which often roots at tip. Margin entire, sinuate or anomalously jaggedly cut. Basal auricles rounded or sometimes pointed, then occasionally tip-rooting, rarely obsolete (as in its Asian relative). Veins areolate. Sori short-linear, lying along vein-branches scattered in various positions over the blade. Chromosomes like those of *Asplenium*, with some species of which it hybridizes.

RANGE: From w. Me., s. Que., n. Mich., and se. Minn., down over our region to s. upland valleys.

HABITAT: Most frequent on shaded limestone ledges, occasional on other rocks, mossy clay banks, and rarely tree trunks, also invading crumbling masonry; soil circumneutral.

CULTURE: Desirable for a shady rock garden; not easy to establish, but if mulched by a limestone-favoring moss may in time proceed to "walk" over the rocks.

NOMENCLATURE:

Camptosòrus rhizophýllus Link, 1833 (GM, BB).
(*Asplenium rhizophylla* L., 1753; *rhizophyllum*, 1763, basionym).

The colloquial name refers to the way the plants seem to "walk around" by producing new ones at blade-tips. Linnaeus applied the equivalent epithet to a motley lot of ferns, but it is now restricted to the one he had from "Virginia and Canada." The genus *Camptosorus* is not really distinct from *Asplenium*, but is here retained in accordance with long usage.

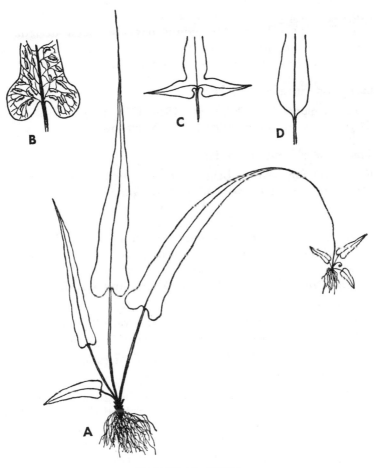

WALKING FERN

A. *Plant, reduced.*   *Blade-bases of:*   B. *Type form.*
C. *Long-auricled form.*   D. *Obsolete-auricled form.*

HARTS-TONGUE FERNS : *PHYLLÌTIS*

An ancient term for the European Harts-tongue Fern was proposed as a genus name by Hill in 1756, and validated by Ludwig a year later. The genus has also been designated *Scolopendrium,* but this is regarded as preferably a species epithet. Its features are those of the taxa described below.

European Harts-tongue Fern

Phyllìtis scolopéndrium Newman, 1844 (GM, BB).
(*Asplenium scolopendrium* L., 1753, basionym).

American Harts-tongue Fern

FEATURES: Stipe short, bearing scales which in the type variety are mixed broad and narrow, but in var. *americana* all narrow, with a long hair-tip. Blade evergreen, simple, *ca.* 18 to 35 cm. long and 2.5 to 5 cm. broad, the base auricled, the margins sinuate, and the tip obtusish, tending to become crested. Free tip of vein-forks in the type swollen and lying near margins, in our variety narrow and 1 mm. back.

RANGE: Rare and widely disjunct in N.B., Ont., nw. N.Y. and n. Mich.; also Tenn. The type variety is common in Eu., and is reported as an occasional escape in our region.

HABITAT: Cool shaded ledges and talus of limestone, the soil circumneutral.

CULTURE: The European variety can be grown in a shady rock garden. The American one rarely thrives there, however, because of the difficulty in keeping its roots ever cool and moist yet well-drained, and of protecting it from slugs. Conservationists have rescued clumps from quarries and set them out in seemingly favorable spots, without much success.

NOMENCLATURE:

Phyllìtis scolopéndrium v. *americàna* Fernald, 1935 (GM, BB).
Phyllitis fernaldiana Löve, 1954.

The suggestion that this should be classed as a separate species is based on the discovery that while the European variety is diploid, the American one is tetraploid; their morphologic differences seem, however, too slight.

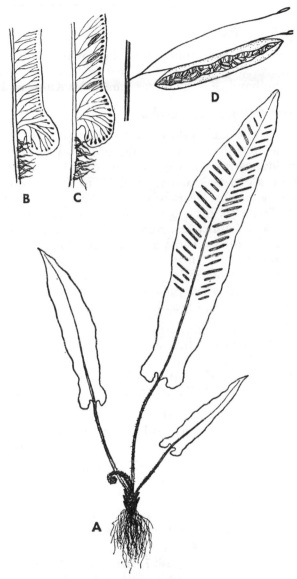

HARTS-TONGUE FERN

A. *Plant, reduced.*   *Blade-base of:*   B. *American and*
C. *European variety.*   D. *Sorus, enlarged.*

BRACKENS : *PTERÍDIUM*

This genus differs from *Pteris* in having under an indusioid reflexed marginal strip a true scarious indusium covering the band of sori; it was named by Kuhn in 1879.

(East-American) Bracken—Brake

FEATURES: Rootstock cord-like, widely creeping and branching, with sparse-hairy tip, sending up a row of huge coarse but deciduous fronds. Stipe woody, *ca.* 20 to 40 cm. long. Blade *ca.* 25 to 50 cm. long and 38 to 75 cm. broad, triangular, somewhat ternately 2- to 3-pinnate. As worked out by Tryon in 1941, 3 varieties are represented. In the Type variety *latiusculum* and the Hairy v. *pubescens* the terminal pinnule-segments are *ca.* 4 times as long as broad, the second differing in being often 2 to 3 times as tall and more pubescent beneath, and the indusia being ciliate. In the Tailed variety, v. *pseudocaudatum,* the segments are *ca.* 8 times as long as broad, and the tissue is glabrous.

RANGE: Var. *latiusculum,* from subarct. Can. well over our region; also southw. and scattered westw. Var. *pubescens,* only n. Mich. and s. Man.; widespread in the west. Var. *pseudocaudatum,* throughout the s. states, ranging n. in our region to L.I., N.Y., and in midlands to Kans.

HABITAT: Open or thinly wooded flats and slopes, in rather barren sandy or loamy soil, its reaction varying from strongly to moderately acid, or in bleak climates to neutral.

CULTURE: Too coarse and rapid-spreading for garden use.

NOMENCLATURE:

Pterídium aquilinum Kuhn, 1879, var. latiúsculum Underwood, (in Heller's Catalog), 1909 (GM, BB).
(*Pteris aquilina* L., 1753, basionym of species).
(*Pteris latiuscula* Desvaux, 1827, basionym of variety).
Pteridium latiusculum Hieronymus, 1914 (GEF).

MAJOR VARIANTS:

Pterídium aquilinum v. pubéscens Underwood, 1900 (GM, BB).
Pterídium aquilinum v. pseudocaudàtum Heller, 1900 (GM, BB).
(*Pteris aquilina* v. *pseudocaudata* Clute, 1900, basionym).
Pteridium latiusculum pseudocaudatum Maxon, 1919 (GEF).

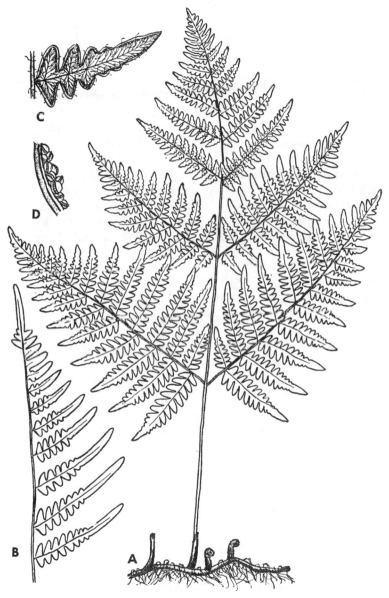

BRACKEN

A. *Plant, reduced.*   B. *Pinna-tip of Tailed variety.*
C. *Pinnule and*   D. *Enlarged soral strip of type variety.*

MAIDENHAIR FERNS : ADIÁNTUM

Early European naturalists were impressed by a fern which while growing in wet places seemed always to have dry leaves, and named it adiantum from the Greek for never wet. This was taken up as a genus name by Linnaeus in 1753. Only a few species were known to him, but over a hundred have since been discovered in mild-temperate and tropical regions.

Its typical members are characterized by a black stipe and rachis and by a unique arrangement of the spore-bearing organs: At intervals along segment-margins a scarious half-moon or crescent-shaped flap turns under and bears sori on its inner surface, thus constituting an inverse-indusium.

Southern Maidenhair Fern

FEATURES: Rootstock slender, creeping, sending up fronds throughout the growing season, bearing narrow brown scales. Stipe *ca.* ¾ as long as blade, which is ca. 15 to 30 cm. long and 10 to 20 cm. broad with a flexuous rachis, and 2- or 3-pinnate. Pinnules few, rhombic to fan-shaped, with lunate inverse-indusia. While the main fronds are soon wilted by frost, a few short ones may be subevergreen.

RANGE: Warm-temperate zones around the world. S. states, sporadically up to s. Va. and Ky.; also locally escaped from cultivation up to s. N.Y.

HABITAT: Moist limestone cliffs, walls of sinks, margins of springs, and cataracts of limy water, the roots wet but the fronds dry. Soil mildly alkaline.

CULTURE: Readily grown on porous limestone, tufa, etc., in a cool greenhouse in our region.

NOMENCLATURE:

Adiántum capillus-véneris L., 1753 (GM, BB).

AMERICAN VARIANT:

Adiantum capillus-veneris v. *protrusum* Fernald, 1950.

The epithet applied to this variety refers to its rootstock extending beyond the season's fronds.

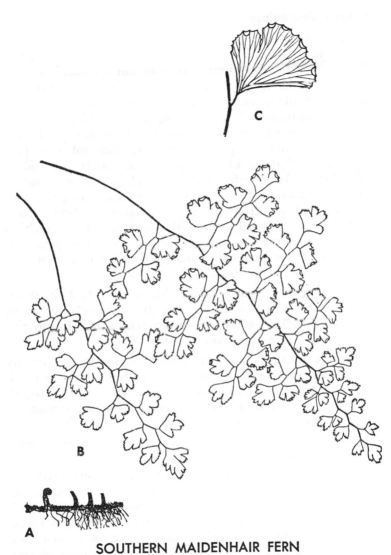

SOUTHERN MAIDENHAIR FERN

A. *Rootstock.*   B. *Fronds, reduced.*   C. *Pinnule, enlarged.*

Northern Maidenhair Fern

FEATURES: Rootstock stoutish, creeping, bearing light brown scales, sending up a row of fronds. Stipe erect, *ca.* 20 to 40 cm. long, forked into diverging curved rachises from the upper side of which *ca.* 5 to 7 pinnae arise, yielding a fan-shaped blade *ca.* 13 to 25 cm. high and 18 to 35 cm. broad. Pinnules obliquely triangular to oblong, with a major vein along lower margin from which multiple forked veins arise, and at upper margin cut into lobes in part tipped by lunate to oblong inverse-indusia. In **A.** *pedàtum* f. *laciniàtum* Weatherby 1937 (GM; *A. pedatum* v. *laciniatum* Hopkins, 1910, basionym) the pinnules lacy-cut. Var. *aleuticum* differs from the type in having a shorter rootstock, more crowded fronds, shorter less curved rachises and fewer pinnae; its tissue is bluish green in hue (although the type variety becomes similarly colored when it invades soils high in magnesium).

RANGE: Type var., from N.S. to Minn. and e. Neb. down over our region; also in s. uplands and rarely lowlands, and w. N.A. Var. *aleuticum,* from Nf. to n. Vt. and nw. Wisc.; and more abundantly in nw. N.A.

HABITAT: Type var., chiefly in humus-rich woods, occasionally on shaded rocky slopes, the soil being subacid to neutral. Var. *aleuticum,* in more exposed situations, in our region only on magnesian limestone and serpentine, though in the west on various kinds of rocks.

CULTURE: The highly decorative type variety thrives in cultivation, and should be in every woodland garden. Besides the lacy-cut f. *laciniatum* above noted, a few fern gardeners in our region have an unnamed one with the young growth red-tinted and the mature foliage bronzy. Rock gardeners here also grow a tiny variant, originally found in Oregon. The variety *aleuticum* should be a good subject for limestone rock gardens, at least in areas of cool climate.

NOMENCLATURE:

Adiántum pedàtum L., 1753 (GM, BB).

NORTHWESTERN VARIANT:

A. pedàtum [v.] β *aleùticum* Ruprecht, 1845 (GM, BB).

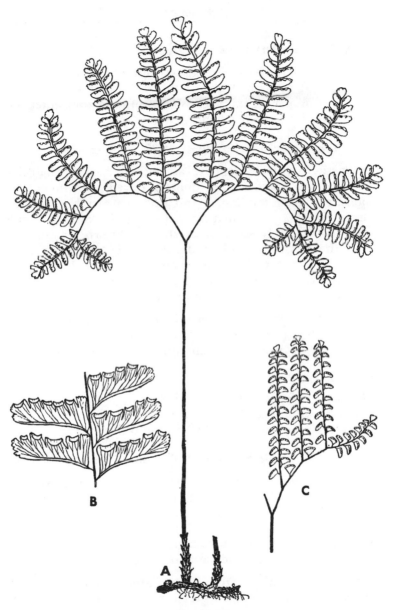

NORTHERN MAIDENHAIR FERN

Type variety: A. *Plant, reduced.* B. *Pinnules.*
Northwestern variety: C. *Blade-division, reduced.*

CLAW FERNS AND FALSE-CLOAK FERNS

These two ferns have several attributes in common: They have no real common names, and authorities differ widely as to their proper technical classification; and they enter our region only to a minor extent.

Claw Fern—*Onýchium* Kaulfuss, 1820: one species

FEATURES: Rootstock slender, ascending, bearing hair-like dark brown scales. Fronds densely tufted, firm but deciduous, the blade tending to roll up when dry but to open again after a rain, markedly dimorphic. Sterile fronds short-lived, rarely seen. Stipe shining brown, glabrous, 2 to 4 times as long as blade. Fertile blade triangular, 2- or 3-pinnate, *ca.* 3 to 6 cm. long and 2 to 4 cm. broad. Pinnules narrowly oblong, sharp-pointed, the sori marginal, well covered by a scarious indusioid margin.

RANGE AND HABITAT: Widespread in w. N.A.; in our region known only at 2 points in Que. on serpentine rock and 1 in Ont. on magnesian limestone. Not cultivated.

NOMENCLATURE:

Onýchium dénsum Brackenridge, 1854.
Cheilanthes siliquosa Maxon, 1918 (GM).
Pellaea densa Hooker, 1858 (BB); doubtfully valid.

False-cloak Fern—*Notholaèna* R. Brown, 1810: one species

FEATURES: Rootstock short, brown-scaly, sending up a tuft of tiny monomorphic fronds. Stipe dark brown, glabrous, slightly longer than the triangular 3-pinnate blade, which is *ca.* 2.5 to 5 cm. long and 1.5 to 3 cm. broad, white-powdery beneath. Sori forming a marginal band without any suggestion of an indusium (hence, "false-cloak").

RANGE AND HABITAT: Scattered over Mo., adj. Neb., and e. Kans.; also further sw., in crevices of limestone and other calcareous rocks. Not cultivated.

NOMENCLATURE:

Notholaèna dealbàta Kunze, 1848 (GM).
(*Cheilanthes dealbata* Pursh, 1814, basionym).
Pellaea dealbata Prantl, 1882 (BB).

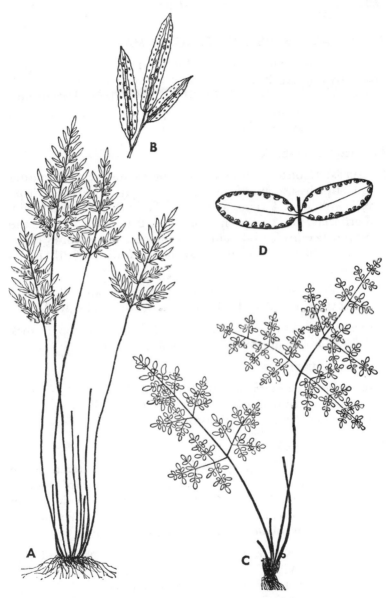

TWO MARGINAL-FRUITING FERNS

Claw Fern: A. *Plant, reduced.*   B. *Pinnules, enlarged.*
False-Cloak Fern: C. *Plant.*   D. *Pinnules, enlarged.*

ROCK-BRAKE FERNS : CRYPTOGRÁMMA

This genus name, signifying hidden rows of sori, was proposed by Robert Brown in 1823. It comprises a few small cold-climate rock ferns, with deciduous dimorphic fronds, the margins of the fertile pinnules not modified in texture, yet reflexing to form indusioid strips.

American Rock-brake

FEATURES: Rootstock stoutish, bearing slender scales, holding old stipe-bases, and sending up a tuft of fronds. Stipe yellowish, *ca.* 1½ times as long as the 2- to 3-pinnate blade. Sterile lax, *ca.* 3 to 6 cm. long and 2 to 4 cm. broad, the pinnulets elliptic and vein-tips enlarged. Fertile ones erect, *ca.* 5 to 10 cm. long and 3 to 6 cm. broad, the divisions linear.

RANGE: From arct. e. Can. down to n. Ont. and Man. and disjunct on Isle Royale, L. Superior, Mich.; also w. N.A.

HABITAT: Bleak and barren situations, often on open rock slides, the soil mostly subacid. Not cultivated.

NOMENCLATURE:

Cryptográmma acrostichoìdes R. Brown, 1823.
C. crispa v. *acrostichoides* Clarke, 1880 (GM, BB).
(*Osmunda crispa* L., 1753, basionym).

Slender Rock-brake

FEATURES: Rootstock thread-like, the fronds scattered. Stipe brown and scaly below, green and glabrous upward, slightly longer than blade. Sterile blades *ca.* 4 to 8 cm. long and 3 to 6 cm. broad, with obovate crenate pinnules or segments. Fertile blades ⅓ larger, with the segments entire.

RANGE: From Nf. to Ont. and down to n. N.J. and Pa., disjunct in W.Va., to nw. Mich. and ne. Minn. down to n. Ill. and e. Ia.; also w. mts. and Eurasia.

HABITAT: Cool moist shaded crevices of limestone and calcareous shale, the soil circumneutral. Not cultivated.

NOMENCLATURE:

Cryptográmma stélleri Prantl, 1882 (GM, BB).
(*Pteris stelleri* S. G. Gmelin, 1768, basionym).

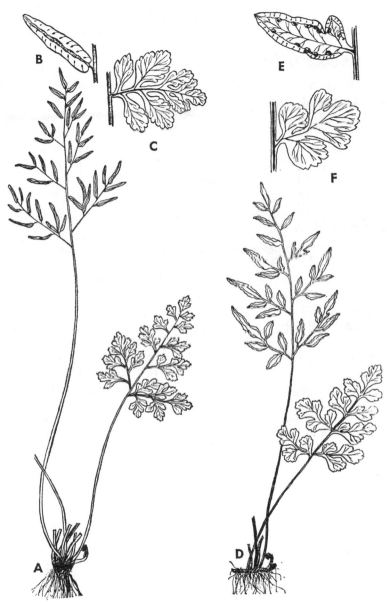

TWO ROCK-BRAKES

American: A. *Plant, reduced.*   B. *Fertile and*
C. *Sterile pinnules.*
Slender: D. *Plant, reduced.*   E. *Fertile and*
F. *Sterile pinnules.*

CLIFF-BRAKES : *PELLAÈA*

This genus name, derived from a Greek word for dusky, was proposed by Link in 1841. Its members are small to moderate-sized tufted rock ferns, with stipe and pinnae jointed at base, our species barely dimorphic, bluish-hued, coriaceous and subevergreen. The sori are borne in long sub-marginal bands at tips of vein-branches, covered by continuous scarious reflexed indusioid marginal strips.

Smooth Cliff-brake

FEATURES: Rootstock-scales copious though not matted, forming a conspicuous red-brown mass. Stipe *ca.* ⅔ as long as blade, blackish brown, bearing a few long narrow toothed scales. Rachis lustrous brown. Blade decidedly bluish green, glabrous, *ca.* 6 to 12 cm. long and 2.5 to 5 cm. broad, pinnate with the pinna-stalks curving upward out from the rachis, the pinnae all simple or the lower ternately divided. Sterile blades rather the smaller and more evergreen, their pinnae and pinnules tending to be elliptic. Fertile divisions oblong, the pale indusioid margins conspicuous.

RANGE: Frequent in the sw. part of our region, rarer and scattered n. and e., though extending to Vt., s. Ont., and Man.; locally in s. uplands, with varieties in w. mts.

HABITAT: Tight dry crevices in bleak vertical or overhanging cliffs, most frequently in limestone, but occasionally in calcareous shale and sandstone, also invading firm masonry. Soil circumneutral.

CULTURE: Difficult to cultivate, since when set among rocks, the herbage tends to dry up before new roots form.

NOMENCLATURE:

Pellaèa glabélla Mettenius, 1869 (GM).
Pellaea atropurpurea var. *bushii* Mackenzie, 1902 (BB).

This and the next-treated taxon differ in so many details that they are here maintained as distinct at species level, rather than classing the first as mere variety of the second.

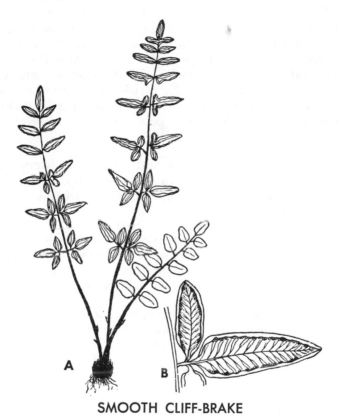

SMOOTH CLIFF-BRAKE

A. *Plant, reduced.*   B. *Pinnules, enlarged.*

Hairy Cliff-brake—Purple Cliff-brake

FEATURES: Rootstock-scales copious, matted, their mass being whitish in the middle and gray-buff marginally. Stipe *ca.* ⅔ as long as blade, brownish black, bearing both scales and stiff hairs, the rachis also rough-hairy. Blade not so bluish a green as the preceding, *ca.* 10 to 20 cm. long and 5 to 10 cm. broad, 1- to 3-pinnate, (the division more complex toward blade-base) with the pinna-stalks extending straight out from rachis. Sterile blades more ever-green and smaller than the fertile, and often less sub-divided, their pinnae and pinnules elliptic. Fertile divisions tending to be oblong, the pale indusioid margins conspicuous.

RANGE: Mex., Rocky Mt. states, and s. uplands, extending in our region from Kans. to Va., sparingly up to se. Minn. and n. Mich., and more frequently eastw. to Ind., s. Ont., and nw. Vt.

HABITAT: Cliffs, ledges, talus slopes, and rarely gravelly banks, often on limestone, but also on other rocks, including sandstone, shale, and granite, as well as invading masonry. Soil circumneutral to slightly acid.

CULTURE: As it grows in less bleak situations than the next-preceding species, this is more readily grown in the rock garden, and is fairly ornamental.

NOMENCLATURE:

Pellaèa atropurpùrea Link, 1841 (GM, BB).
(*Pteris atropurpurea* L., 1753, basionym).

This fern was discovered by John Clayton at a "Point Lookout" on the Rappahannock River in Virginia in the early 1700s. Its stipe and rachis are actually scarcely "purple."

According to GM, the above two taxa represent the genus *Pellaea* in our region. In BB, on the other hand, these two are regarded as pertaining to the same species, while the taxa herein named *Notholaena dealbata* and *Onychium densum* are made additional members of *Pellaea*.

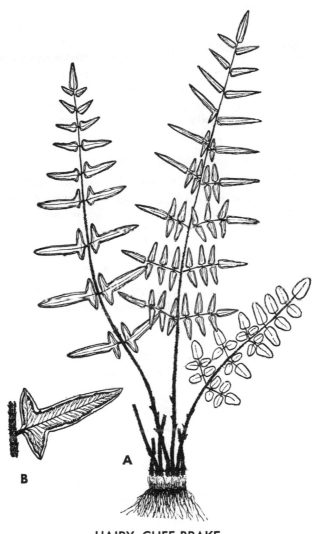

HAIRY CLIFF-BRAKE

A. *Plant, reduced.*   B. *Pinnule, enlarged.*

LIP FERNS : CHEILÁNTHES

The name of this group refers to a fancied lip-like aspect of the strips of reflexed indusioid tissue. The technical name, from the Greek for marginal flowers, was proposed by Swartz in 1806. The plants are moderate-sized monomorphic subevergreen rock ferns with 2- to 3-pinnate blades. The sori are borne near segment margins at enlarged vein-tips, covered by green reflexed indusioid flaps.

Smooth Lip Fern—Alabama Lip Fern

FEATURES: Rhizome slender, bearing narrow orange-brown scales. Stipe black, *ca.* ½ as long as blade, sparse-hairy. Blade nearly glabrous, *ca.* 8 to 15 cm. long and 2 to 4 cm. wide.

RANGE: Mex. and Ariz. northeastward, extending into our region in e. Kans., s. Mo. and sw. Va.

HABITAT: Crevices in cliffs of limestone and other calcareous rocks, the soil mildly alkaline. Not cultivated.

NOMENCLATURE:

Cheilánthes alabaménsis Kunze, 1847 (GM, BB).
(*Pteris alabamensis* Buckley, 1843, basionym).

Slender Lip Fern—Fée's Lip Fern

FEATURES: Rootstock short, bearing narrow orange-brown scales with dark medial stripe. Stipe purplish brown, about equal blade, hairy. Blade sparse-hairy above, densely so beneath, the hairs lustrous white, becoming brownish, *ca.* 3 to 6 cm. long and 1.5 to 3 cm. broad. Fronds curling up when dry, opening and reviving after rain.

RANGE: W. mts., entering our region in Kans. and Mo., extending n. to c. Wisc., and locally to nw. Ky.

HABITAT: Dry rock crevices, in our region most often limestone, the soil circumneutral. Not cultivated.

NOMENCLATURE:

Cheilánthes feèi Moore, 1857 (GM, BB).

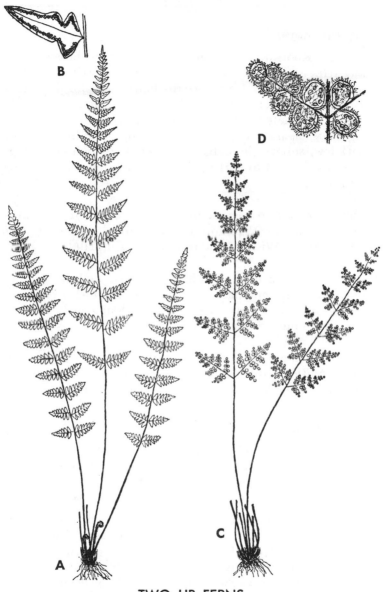

TWO LIP FERNS

Smooth: A. *Plant, reduced.* B. *Pinnule.*
Slender: C. *Plant.* D. *Pinnule, enlarged.*

Hairy Lip Fern

FEATURES: Rootstock thickish, bearing narrow brown medially dark scales. Fronds somewhat spaced. Stipe *ca.* ⅔ as long as blade, dark brown, coarse-hairy as is also the rachis. Blade dark green, *ca.* 8 to 15 cm. long and 3 to 6 cm. broad, 2-pinnate with the pinnules deeply cut into oblong segments, sparse-hairy above and copiously so beneath. Sori few, submarginal, barely covered by indusioid flaps. The fronds tend to curl up in dry weather but revive after a rain.

RANGE: The easternmost member of the genus: from e. Kans. to Va. up to se. N.Y. and sw. Ct., with a disjunct station on the Minn.-Wisc. boundary; also in s. uplands.

HABITAT: Open or thinly shaded rock ledges and talus slopes, northw. chiefly on shale and other rocks which break into slabs, but southw. also on limestone. Soil mostly subacid, less commonly circumneutral.

CULTURE: Being adaptable to a wide range of climate and soil conditions, this is the easiest member of the genus to grow in the rock garden, and is well worth trying.

NOMENCLATURE:

Cheilánthes lanòsa D. C. Eaton, 1859 (BB).
(*Nephrodium lanosum* Michaux, 1803, in part, basionym).
Cheilanthes vestita Swartz, 1806 (GM).
(*Adiantum vestitum* Sprengel, 1804, in part, basionym).

The nomenclature of this taxon is confused. Michaux, in proposing the epithet, gave some characters which fit this and some which apply better to the one treated next. As his type specimen represents only the present taxon, however, his epithet, in Eaton's combination, has long been accepted for this. Holding that the type is not authentic and that the part of the description applying to the second taxon should be given precedence, Fernald used in GM the later epithet of Swartz (although its description likewise covers two taxa). He then shifted Michaux's epithet to the following taxon, which is going to confuse workers who follow GM strictly.

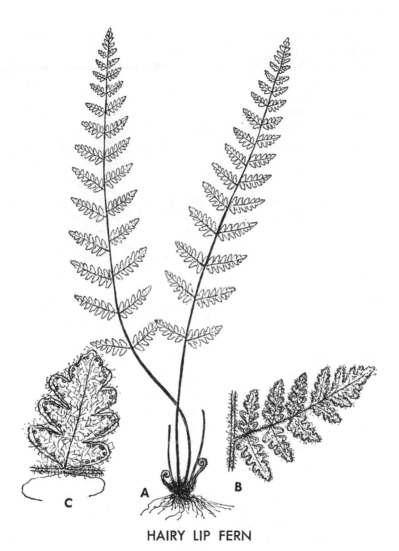

HAIRY LIP FERN

A. *Plant, reduced.*   B. *Pinna.*   C. *Pinnule, enlarged.*

Woolly Lip Fern

FEATURES: Rootstock thick, bearing long narrow medially dark brown scales, sending up tufted fronds; most unusually, these in bud are not coiled as in most ferns, but are merely bent. Stipe *ca.* ⅔ as long as blade, brown, bearing, as does the rachis, both hairs and scales. Blade bright green, sparsely hairy above and densely so beneath, the hairs white, becoming reddish, *ca.* 13 to 25 cm. long and 3 to 6 cm. broad, 3-pinnate with the pinnulets round (a good distinction from the preceding taxon). Sori well-covered by indusioid margins.

RANGE: From Mex. to Ariz. and s. uplands, extending into our region to s.-centr. Va. and ne. W. Va.

HABITAT: Open cliffs and ledges of various rocks—in our region granite, sandstone, limestone, and shale—the soil circumneutral to subacid.

CULTURE: A very attractive fern, well deserving of cultivation in a mild-climate rock garden.

NOMENCLATURE:

Cheilánthes tomentòsa Link, 1833 (BB).
Cheilanthes lanosa D. C. Eaton, 1859 (GM).
(*Nephrodium lanosum* Michaux, 1803, applicable to this taxon if at all only in part).

For many years the nomenclature of this taxon was supposedly settled, and Link's epithet universally used, but Fernald in 1946 threw it into confusion. He assumed that Michaux's epithet *lanosum* fitted only the present taxon, ignoring the fact that Michaux's description is equivocal and could apply about as well to the preceding one—as most fern students hold it does, the sheet in Michaux's herbarium actually representing only the latter. The resulting use of Eaton's combination for the present taxon in the 8th edition of *Gray's Manual* is most regrettable. Changes in long-established nomenclature should be made not on the basis of inferences or guesses but on sound evidence, which has not been adduced in this case. Return to long-established usage is favored in the present *Guide*.

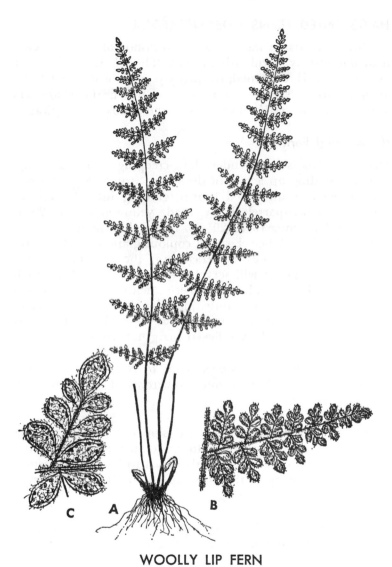

WOOLLY LIP FERN

A. *Plant, reduced.*   B. *Pinna.*   C. *Pinnule, enlarged.*

HAY-SCENTED FERNS : *DENNSTAÈDTIA*

This genus name was proposed in honor of an early German botanist by Bernhardi in 1801. Though ignored, as far as our region is concerned, for many years, it is now generally accepted for a single taxon here, of which the characters are given below. Other members of the genus are tropical.

Hay-scented Fern

FEATURES: Rootstock slender, long-creeping and branching, hairy, sending up a row of deciduous fronds. Stipe shorter than blade, shining red brown, grading into the yellow-brown rachis, sparsely hairy. Blade yellow-green, *ca.* 20 to 40 cm. long and 10 to 20 cm. broad, bipinnate with the pinnules sharp-lobed, bearing copious gland-tipped whitish hairs exhaling a hay-like fragrance; the presence of this peculiar indument will serve to distinguish this from various Lady Ferns and Marsh Ferns, with which beginners may confuse it. Sori minute, globular, borne in a cup-like indusium at vein-tips (an especially primitive character) and partly covered by reflexed marginal teeth.

RANGE: From Va. to e. Mo. and up to Nf., Que., Ont., O., and sw. Ind., with a disjunct occurrence in n. Mich.; also s. uplands.

HABITAT: Open or thinly wooded slopes, less often at bog margins, in barren strongly to moderately acid soil. Being unpalatable to grazing animals, tends to become a pasture weed. The ability of this seemingly delicate fern to thrive in open sun is surprising.

CULTURE: Though a beautiful fern, this spreads too rapidly for safe introduction into a small garden.

NOMENCLATURE:

Dennstaèdtia punctilòbula Moore, 1857 (GM, BB).
(*Nephrodium punctilobulum* Michaux, 1803, basionym).
Dicksonia punctilobula Gray, 1848, retained in successive editions of the *Manual* until 1908.

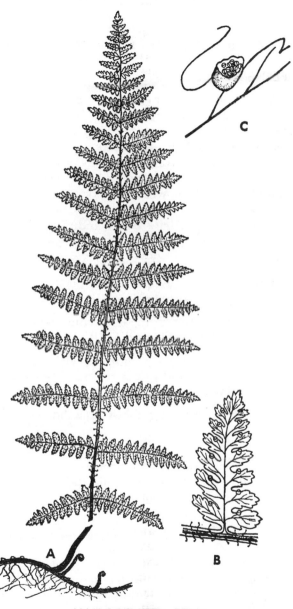

HAY-SCENTED FERN

A. *Plant, reduced.*   B. *Pinnule.*   C. *Sorus, enlarged.*

2. Filmy Fern Family : *Hymenophyllàceae*

FILMY FERNS : *TRICHÓMANES*

An ancient Greek term for some now unknown small hairy fern was made a genus name by Linnaeus in 1753. The members have a slender superficial creeping and branching rootstock covered by black hairs and roots, sending up (or down) a row of small lax often drooping fronds. Stipe short, winged. Blade entire to dissected, its tissue only one cell thick, accordingly translucent and showing a play of color. Sporangia borne in a soral cluster on a marginal bristle-like extension of a vein, surrounded at base by an indusioid sheath.

Appalachian Filmy Fern

FEATURES: Blade *ca.* 5 to 10 cm. long and 2 to 4 cm. broad, deeply pinnately dissected. Veins bearing scattered hairs.

RANGE: Rare and scattered in s. uplands, and up in our region to w. W. Va., s. O., and s. Ill.

HABITAT: Shaded permanently moist crevices and cavernous hollows in sandstone and gneiss rocks, often hanging from the roof. Soil intensely acid.

CULTURE: Can be grown in a moist greenhouse grotto.

NOMENCLATURE:

Trichómanes radicáns Swartz, 1806, unnamed variety.
Trichomanes boschianum Sturm, 1861 (GM, BB).
Vandenboschia radicans Copeland, 1938.

Since it seems to differ from the subtropical *T. radicans* only in its smaller size, this is here regarded as a variety.

Another genus of this family, *Hymenophýllum* J. E. Smith, 1793, differing from the above in having the indusioid sheath split, is represented in our region by a gametophyte: This consists of strips of green tissue with marginal buds. It is known from the mountains of Va. to Ky. and s. Ohio, in habitats like the Appalachian Filmy Fern. Its sporophyte stage has never been discovered, and deserves search by fern students.

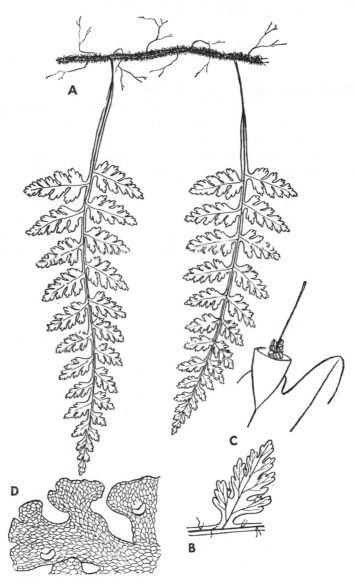

APPALACHIAN FILMY FERN

A. *Plant.*　B. *Segment.*　C. *Sorus, enlarged.*
D. *Gametophyte of unidentified Hymenophyllum.*

3. Climbing Fern Family : Schizaeàceae

CURLY-GRASS FERNS : SCHIZAÈA

This genus name, derived from the Greek for split, was proposed by J. E. Smith in 1793; although not the earliest, it has been so widely used that it is generally accepted. Its members are mostly small unfern-like plants. In our single species the rootstock is short, slender, erect, and hairy. The fronds are strongly dimorphic, the sterile being grass-like and the fertile consisting of a wiry stipe tipped by a small blade divided into narrow segments. The sporangia, borne in two rows on the latter, are ovoid with a group of annulus cells at the smaller end. All but this species grow in the tropics or the southern hemisphere.

(American) Curly-grass Fern

FEATURES: Sterile fronds numerous, resembling curly grass blades, *ca.* 3 to 6 cm. long. Fertile few, *ca.* 5 to 10 cm. high, the blade *ca.* 3 mm. long, with several segments.

RANGE: Restricted to s. N.J., N.S., and Nf. A report from Ont. has never been confirmed. While traditionally rare, actually abundant locally, but often overlooked because of its diminutive size.

HABITAT: In N.J., chiefly in litter at the base of "White Cedar" (*Chamaecyparis*) trees, sometimes on sandy flats under other trees, in damp hummocks of fine-leaved sorts of Sphagnum moss, only exceptionally spreading into the wet, coarse-leaved Sphagnums of bogs. In the two northeastern areas, on moist ledges and springy slopes, and in damp peaty barrens. Soil in all cases rich in humus but low in mineral nutrients, and intensely acid. The fact that the alleged Ontario occurrence was said to be deep in limy water on a lake shore adds to its incredibility.

CULTURE: Would be possible only in sterile peaty sand kept permanently moist by acid water.

NOMENCLATURE:

Schizaèa pusilla Pursh, 1814 (GM, BB).

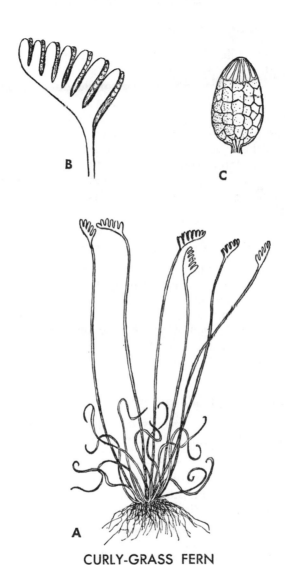

CURLY-GRASS FERN

A. *Plant.*   B. *Fertile blade, enlarged.*
C. *Sporangium, enlarged.*

CLIMBING FERNS : *LYGÒDIUM*

At least five different genus names were proposed for this group of plants in 1801; by general agreement *Lygodium*, derived by Swartz from the Greek for flexuous, is accepted. The genus is characterized by fronds with a short stipe and a long twining rachis. The pinnae are dimorphic, broad sterile ones being borne in the lower part, and relatively narrow or otherwise modified fertile ones toward the tip. The spores are produced in rather large curved sporangia with a terminal group of annulus cells, borne in double rows beneath segments. All but our species are subtropical or tropical.

(American) Climbing Fern—Hartford Fern

FEATURES: Rootstock black, wiry, widely creeping and branching, sending up a row of twining delicate but evergreen fronds. Stipe dark brown. Blade yellow green, *ca.* 50 to 100 cm. long. Pinnae alternate, the sterile ones consisting of a forking stalk, each division bearing a palmately lobed blade *ca.* 3 to 6 cm. across. Fertile ones repeatedly forked, with little leafy tissue.

RANGE: From e. Va. to c. Ky. and up to s. N.H., e. N.Y., and s. O.; also in s. uplands and rarely lowlands.

HABITAT: Moist thickets, springy slopes, and bog margins, the soil sandy, rich in humus but poor in nutrients, and intensely acid.

CULTURE: Rarely successful, in that few horticulturists will go to the trouble to maintain the necessary bed of acid soil, kept moist with non-limy water.

NOMENCLATURE:

Lygòdium palmàtum Swartz, 1806 (GM, BB).
(*Gisopteris palmata* Bernhardi, 1801, basionym).

The alternative name of this taxon refers to its having been the subject of the first conservation law to be applied to a fern, passed by the Connecticut legislature in 1869. While this law did lessen its tearing up for evanescent ornamentation, the subsequent expansion of agriculture destroyed most of its occurrences in that state.

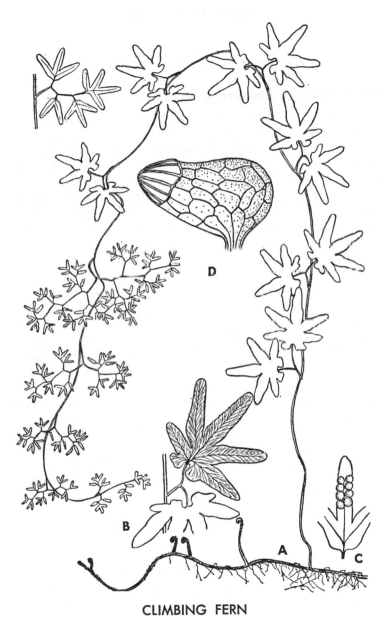

CLIMBING FERN

A. *Plant, reduced.*　　B. *Sterile division.*　　C. *Fertile division.*
D. *Sporangium, enlarged.*

4. Royal Fern Family : *Osmundàceae*

ROYAL FERNS : OSMÚNDA

This genus name, derived from Osmunder, a Saxon mythological character, was proposed by Linnaeus in 1753. Its members have a massive rootstock holding densely crowded old roots and stipe-bases, sending up a tuft of huge firm but deciduous fronds. The sporangia are relatively large, ovoid with obscure annulus, and borne openly in stalked complex clusters. The spores are unusual in being green and short-lived. The basal chromosome number is 22, low for a fern.

Cinnamon Fern

FEATURES: Stipe pinkish, *ca.* ½ as long as blade, floccose-hairy. Blades dimorphic, the sterile *ca.* 35 to 70 cm. long and 13 to 25 cm. broad, pinnate with the sessile pinnae cut into subfalcate obliquely acutish segments. Rachis pilose and bearing on under side a conspicuous tuft of brownish hairs at each pinna-base. Fertile fronds 2-pinnate, arising in spring, without leafy tissue, soon becoming cinnamon brown, early withering. Many variants of this taxon have received epithets. The only one possibly meriting varietal rank is v. **glandulosa** Waters, 1902; this has the blade covered with glistening gland-tipped hairs, and is said to occur in isolated colonies from the Gulf states up in our region from Va. to e. Pa. and R.I. Others are mere forms with anomalously cut pinnae or bearing both fertile and sterile tissue on a single frond. The most curious of the latter is f. *cornucòpiaefolia* Clute, 1908, in which the lobes are in part modified into funnel-like structures.

RANGE: From W. Indies and s. states, up nearly throughout our region, though rare toward w. and n. Can.

HABITAT: Swamps, bog-margins, wooded stream banks, and wet situations generally, where the soil is fairly acid.

CULTURE: Desirable in a moist shady garden if this is on a large enough scale for such a massive plant.

NOMENCLATURE:

Osmúnda cinnamòmea L., 1753 (GM, BB).

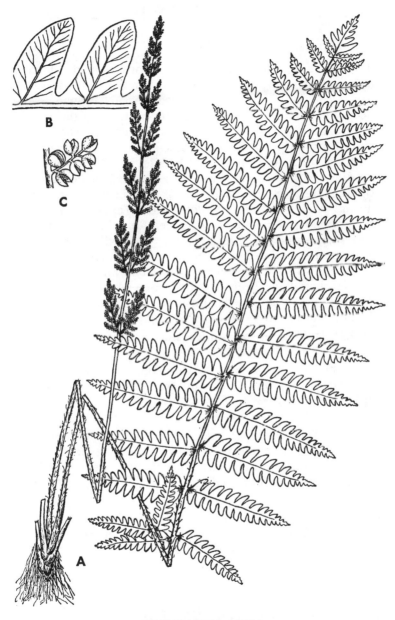

CINNAMON FERN

A. *Plant with fertile and sterile fronds, reduced.*
B. *Sterile segments.*   C. *Group of sporangia.*

Interrupted Fern—Clayton's Fern

FEATURES: Stipe yellowish, nearly ½ as long as blade, floccose-hairy when young but glabrous at maturity. Blade *ca.* 45 to 90 cm. long and 15 to 30 cm. broad. Pinnae sessile, deeply cut into segments which, in contrast to the preceding taxon, are relatively broad, bilaterally symmetrical, and obtusish-tipped. Rachis sparse-pubescent, the hairs not forming tufts at pinna-bases. Fertile fronds characterized by dimorphic pinnae: While those toward blade base and tip remain as in the sterile ones, the tissue in *ca.* 2 to 6 medial pinnae becomes obsolete, and is replaced by clusters of sporangia, at first blackish green, turning dark brown, and then withering. Fronds with the medial pinna-tissue only partly replaced by sporangia are occasional. This species seems to develop fewer variants than the preceding, but epithets have been assigned to one with the pinnae divided into long lobed pinnules, and another with the pinnae tending to be short, triangular, and irregularly cut in a frilly pattern.

RANGE: From subarct. Can. down over our region, though rare on the Coastal Plain and w. of Miss. R.; also in s. uplands, and represented by a hairy var. in e. Asia.

HABITAT: Wooded slopes and hummocks in swamps, only exceptionally mingling with the preceding taxon. Soil sub-acid to circumneutral, relatively rich in mineral nutrients. Fertile fronds are produced most freely in fairly open areas.

CULTURE: An especially good subject for the woodland garden, requiring neither so moist nor so acid conditions as the other two members of the genus.

NOMENCLATURE:

Osmúnda claytoniàna L., 1753 (GM, BB).

Discovered in Virginia by John Clayton in the early 1700s, this fern was named in his honor by Linnaeus. The most used colloquial name refers to the way the fertile pinnules interrupt the regular rows of sterile ones.

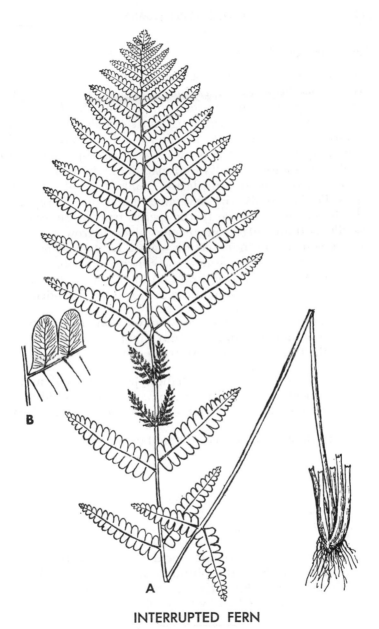

INTERRUPTED FERN

A. *Plant, reduced.*   B. *Sterile segments.*

(American) Royal Fern

FEATURES: Only remotely resembling our other members of the genus. Stipe *ca.* ¾ as long as blade, in some forms glaucous green, in others reddish, glabrous. Blade in average forms *ca.* 38 to 75 cm. long and 25 to 50 cm. broad, in dwarf variants in bleak situations only ½ this size, in especially favorable places twice as high, 2-pinnate with stalked divisions. Pinnules well-spaced, oblong with oblique base and obtuse to acutish tip, somewhat pubescent on axes. Fertile fronds with several terminal pinnae replaced by clusters of sporangia. In the species type, of Eurasia, the fertile portion bears conspicuous black narrow scales, in our taxon few or none. Form names have been assigned to variants with leafy tissue accompanying the sporangia, or with the latter appearing lower on the blade, and to others with the pinnules anomalously narrowed or rounded.

RANGE: Trop. Amer. and s. states, up over our region to Nf., n. Que. and Ont., and e. Minn., more frequent in lowlands than uplands, and rare w. of the Miss. R.

HABITAT: Bogs, swamps, and shallow pools, the soil usually strongly acid; occasionally on hummocks in non-acid areas, but then producing non-viable spores and not spreading.

CULTURE: Desirable for a large-scale bog- or water-garden.

NOMENCLATURE:

Osmunda regalis β Linnaeus, 1753.
Osmúnda regàlis v. spectábilis Gray, 1856 (GM, BB).
(*O. spectabilis* Willdenow, 1810, basionym).

Alternative colloquial names include: Locust Fern, in allusion to resemblance of the pinnules to leaflets of the Locust tree (*Robinia*); and Flowering Fern, in that the clusters of sporangia are supposed to look like flowers.

A hybrid between Osmúnda claytoniàna and O. regàlis, discovered in Conn. and first interpreted by H. G. Rugg, was named in his honor O. × rúggii by Tryon in 1940. It combines the features of the parents in a striking way.

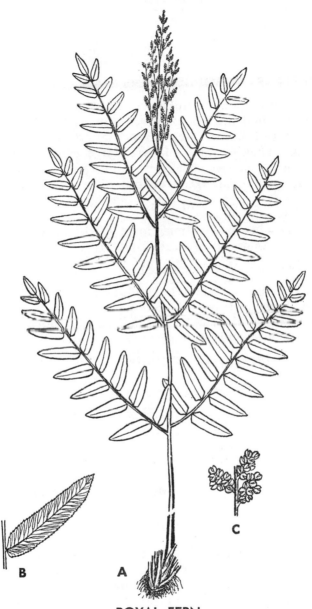

ROYAL FERN

A. *Plant, reduced.*   B. *Sterile pinnule.*   C. *Sporangia.*

5. Water Fern Family : *Salviniàceae*

POND FERNS—MOSQUITO FERNS : AZÓLLA

This genus name, of unknown derivation, was proposed by Lamarck in 1783. The plants are unfern-like free-floating groups of tiny bronzy green fronds attached to branching rootstocks. They produce relatively large female spores and minute male ones which aggregate into masses from which protrude small arrow-like structures termed glochidia.

Azólla mexicàna Presl, 1861 (BB).

Floating lobes ¾ to 1 mm. long; glochidia several-celled. From trop. Amer. up Miss. lowlands to Kans. and Wisc.

Azólla caroliniàna Willdenow, 1810 (GM, BB).

Floating lobes ca. ⅗ mm. long; glochidia one-celled. Chiefly in Gulf states and W.I.; in our region widely scattered in isolated spots in Mass., N.Y., and O.; probably chiefly escaped.

6. Water-clover Family : *Marsileàceae*

WATER-CLOVERS : MARSÍLEA

This genus was named in honor of an Italian naturalist, Marsigli, by Linnaeus in 1753. The plants have a wiry rootstock rooted in mud, sending up a row of fronds with a long stipe and floating blade; the latter is subequally divided into 4 pinnae, and so resembles a 4-leaf clover, though with veining like other ferns. Male and female spores are produced in blackish ellipsoidal structures termed sporocarps, borne on branching stalks at or near stipe-base.

Midland Water-clover—Marsílea mucronàta A. Braun, 1847 (GM, BB). Pinnae *ca.* 6 to 12 mm. long, pubescent, as are the solitary sporocarps. From s. states up in the prairies to sw. Minn., Kans., and s. Can., in muddy sloughs and depressions in grassland, often only seasonally filled with water.

The **European Water-clover,** M. quadrifòlia L., 1753 (GM, BB), with glabrous pinnae 13 to 25 mm. long, has escaped in widely scattered ponds and sluggish streams.

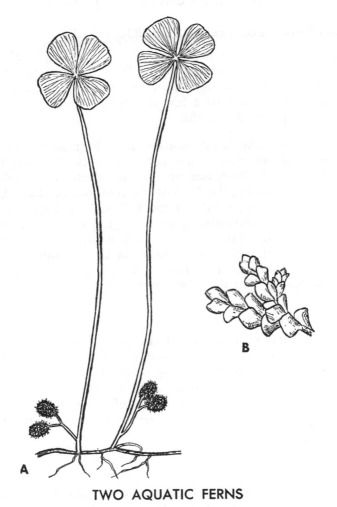

TWO AQUATIC FERNS

A. European Water-clover.   B. Pond Fern, *enlarged*.

7. Adders-tongue Family : *Ophioglossàceae*

ADDERS-TONGUE FERNS : *OPHIOGLÓSSUM*

Early herbalists named this group of ferns ophioglossum from a fancied resemblance of the fertile segment to a snake tongue, and that was taken up as a genus name by Linnaeus in 1753. There are only a few species, but they occur practically throughout the world.

The unfern-like plants consist of a short erect shallowly buried rootstock with a few cord-like roots spreading horizontally from its base, one or more of which may develop a new plant at its tip. The top of the rootstock produces buds, from which a stipe (also termed "common stalk") arises, sometimes only annually, again 2 or 3 times a year; the stipe forks several cm. up into an elliptic or ovate blade, and a fertile segment which bears near its tip a double row of globular to ellipsoidal sporangia, lacking an annulus, more or less immersed in the stem-tissue.

Limestone Adders-tongue

FEATURES: Plant *ca.* 10 to 20 cm. high, often 2 or 3 in a clump, or rootstock producing new ones several times a year. Stipe *ca.* 4 to 8 cm. long. Blade elliptic, *ca.* 4 to 8 cm. long and 1.5 to 3 cm. broad, apiculate, its veins in 2 series: larger, roughly hexagonal, groups of heavy ones enclosing smaller polygonal groups of fine ones. Fertile segment *ca.* 1½ times as long as blade.

RANGE: Mex. and s. states, and extending up in our region to n. Va., s. O., s. Ind., w. Ill., c. Mo., and e. Kans.

HABITAT: Mostly rooted in pockets of clay and locally forming large colonies, on thinly vegetated slopes over outcrops of limestone or calcareous shale; soil circumneutral or somewhat alkaline.

CULTURE: Possible in a mild-climate limestone rock garden, if this is not infested by slugs or rodents.

NOMENCLATURE:

Ophioglóssum engelmánni Prantl, 1883 (GM, BB).

LIMESTONE ADDERS-TONGUE

A. *Group of plants, reduced.*
B. *Bit of sterile blade, enlarged.*

Adders-tongue Fern

FEATURES: Plant up to *ca.* 30 cm. high and stipe to 15 cm. long. Blade rounded at tip; veins uniform, forming narrow areoles enclosing solitary free veinlets. In the Coast form, f. *arenarium,* yellowish in hue, narrowly elliptic with long-tapering ends, *ca.* 3 to 5 cm. long and 1 to 2 cm. broad, with only 5 to 7 basal veins; spores uniquely warty. In the Widespread variety, v. *pseudopodum,* blade dull pale green, elliptic or approximately so, short-tapering to apex and gradually to base, *ca.* 4 to 8 cm. long and 1.5 to 3 cm. broad, with 7 to 9 basal veins; spores reticulate. In the Southeastern variety, var. *pycnostichum,* blade lustrous dark green, ovate with abruptly tapering base, *ca.* 4 to 8 cm. long and 2 to 4 cm. broad, with 9 to 11 basal veins; sporangia tending to be compressed, and stem base having a persistent dark sheath, as in the European type. Fertile segment *ca.* 10 to 20 cm. long.

RANGE: Taxon *arenarium,* N.J. lowlands; t. *pseudopodum,* from Que. to se. Man. and down over our region, rare s. of lat. 40°; t. *pycnostichum,* from c. N.J. to s. Va. and w. Ky. to c. Mo.; also s. states.

HABITAT: The 3 taxa respectively in acid peaty sand, in mildly acid loam of meadows and open woods, and in circumneutral soil of limy meadows and humus-rich woods.

CULTURE: Too susceptible to fungi, slugs, etc., for culture.

NOMENCLATURE:

Ophioglóssum vulgàtum L., 1753 (BB).

AMERICAN VARIANTS:

O. vulgàtum f. *arenàrium* Clute, 1901.
(*O. arenarium* E. G. Britton, 1897, basionym).
O. vulgàtum v. *pseudópodum* Farwell, 1916 (GM).
(*O. vulgatum* f. *pseudopodum* Blake, 1913, basionym).
O. vulgàtum v. *pycnóstichum* Fernald, 1939 (GM).

Workers who prefer not to pay attention to minor details may merely recognize the species and ignore the American variants (BB); for the benefit of those who wish to study the plants more closely, three of the latter are here discussed.

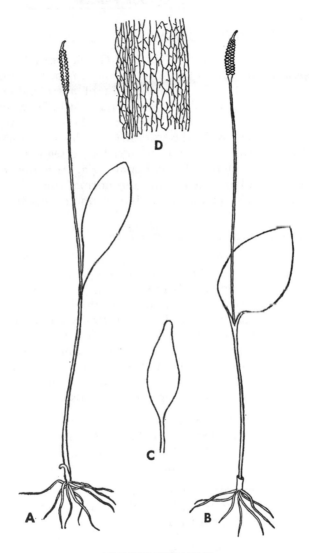

ADDERS-TONGUE

Plant of: A. *Widespread and*   B. *Southeastern variety,*
reduced.   C. *Blade of coast form, reduced.*
D. *Bit of sterile blade, enlarged.*

GRAPE FERNS (BOTRÝCHIUM)

This genus name, derived from a Greek word for cluster of grapes, in allusion to the grouped sporangia, was proposed by Swartz in 1801. The plants consist of a crown-like rootstock, sending out at base a few coarse cord-like roots, and on top bearing buds, which develop a shoot each year. At varying distances up, in the several taxa, the stipe forks into an inclined sterile blade and an erect fertile segment bearing toward its tip clustered globular sporangia. In many colonies much-dwarfed plants accompany the normal ones. The usual basal chromosome number is 45, but in one group 46.

Least Grape Fern—Small Grape Fern

FEATURES: Plant arising in early spring, withering by mid-summer, fleshy, pale bluish green. Height up to 20 cm., but much-reduced individuals frequent. Stipe in Type var. *ca.* 1½ to 3, in Mid 4 to 8 and in High 6 to 12 cm. long. Blade short-stalked, elliptic or in forms ovate, in Type var. *ca.* ½ to 1 cm. long and broad, in Mid 2 to 4 long and half as broad, in High 1 to 2 long and ½ cm. broad; divided into rounded, broad-based lobes and pinnae, in dwarfs entire. Fertile segment *ca.* twice as long as blade, the latter sometimes bearing sporangia also.

RANGE: From arct. e. Can. down over our region, widely scattered southw.; Type v. to Ct., se. Pa., and n. Ind., Mid, Me. to Pa. and n. O., High to c. Md. and s. Wisc. The type and other varieties and forms also in Eurasia.

HABITAT: Chiefly meadows and barrens northw., and in leaf litter of damp woods southw. Soil mostly subacid. Too delicate for successful cultivation.

NOMENCLATURE:

Botrýchium *símplex* E. Hitchock, 1823 (GM, BB).
B. *simplex* v. *simplex* (BB); typical [v.] (GM) = type var.

   MAJOR VARIANTS:

B. *símplex* v. *laxifòlium* Clausen, 1937 (GM) = Mid. v.
B. *simplex* f. *laxifolium* Fernald, 1949 (BB).
B. *símplex* v. *tenebròsum* Clausen, 1937 (GM, BB) = High v.
(*B. tenebrosum* A. A. Eaton, basionym).

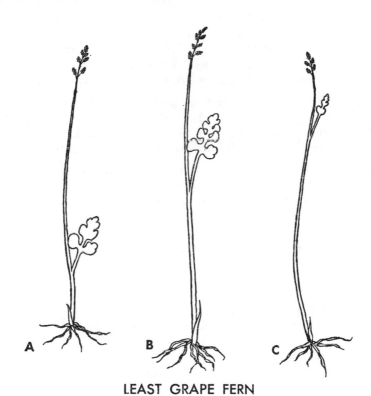

LEAST GRAPE FERN

Plants of: A. *Type variety.*   B. *Mid variety.*
C. *High variety.*

Moonwort

FEATURES: Plant arising in spring, the tissue in type variety pale bluish green, withering in summer. Stipe *ca.* 1.5 to 3 cm. long. Blade subsessile, oblong, *ca.* 2 to 4 cm. long and 1 to 2 cm. broad, with *ca.* 3 to 5 pairs of crowded fan or half-moon-shaped pinnae standing straight out from rachis. Blade-tip abruptly reduced to a few irregular segments. Taxon *onondagense* differs in having a brighter green color, and spaced, narrowly fan-shaped pinnae.

RANGE: Type, from subarct. e. Can. down in our region to Me., n. Vt., c. Ont., to *ca.* lat. 44° in Mich., n. Wisc., n. tip of Minn., and Man.; also in w. N.A. nad Eurasia. The var. *onondagense,* s. Vt. to nw. N.Y. and ne. Minn.

HABITAT: Type, in grassy meadows and limestone barrens, and var. *onondagense,* wooded slopes, also over limestone, the soil circumneutral. Not cultivated.

NOMENCLATURE:

Botrýchium lunària Swartz, 1801 (GM, BB).
(*Osmunda lunaria* L., 1753, basionym).

MAJOR VARIANT:

B. lunària v. *onondagénsè* House, 1923 (BB).
(*B. onondagense* Underwood, 1903, basionym).

Mingan Moonwort

FEATURES: Resembling the above species, but differing in: Tissue yellowish green. Stipe *ca.* 2 to 4 cm. long. Blade trough-shaped, with *ca.* 5 to 8 pairs of well-spaced obovate or narrowly fan-shaped pinnae which tend to slope up toward the rachis. Blade-tip regularly reduced to a group of small rounded pinnae. Cytologically tetraploid.

RANGE: From subarct. e. Can. down in our region to Vt., n. N.Y., Mich., and Wisc.; also nw. N.A.

HABITAT: Similar to preceding; likewise not cultivated.

NOMENCLATURE:

Botrýchium minganénsè Marie-Victorin, 1927.
B. lunaria v. *minganense* Dole, 1937 (BB).
B. lunaria f. *minganense* Clute, 1938 (GM).

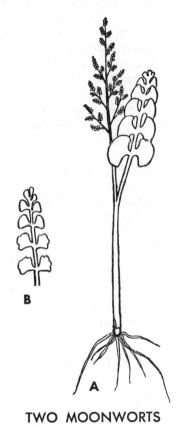

TWO MOONWORTS

A. *Plant* of Moonwort.   B. *Blade* of Mingan Moonwort.

Matricary Grape Fern—Daisy-leaf Grape Fern

FEATURES: Plant arising in spring, to a height of *ca.* 13 to 25 cm., the tissue pale bluish green, lasting to early summer. Stipe *ca.* 8 to 15 cm. long. Blade short-stalked, triangular-oblong, *ca.* 2½ to 5 cm. long and 2 to 4 cm. broad, cut into well-spaced bluntish toothed pinnae. Half-size plants often accompany normal ones. Several variants differing in blade features have been named, the more notable being: f. compositum Milde, 1858, with blade ternately divided; f. gracile Weatherby, 1935 (*B. neglectum* f. *g.* House, 1924, basionym), pinnae entire; and f. palmatum Milde, 1858, blade broadly triangular. Fertile segment *ca.* 4 to 8 cm. long.

RANGE: Common from Nf. to Minn., increasingly less so southw. but extending at both high and low alt. to Va. The Eurasian relative is more fleshy, but not nomenclatorially separated; a var. occurs in the Rocky Mts.

HABITAT: Woods and damp thickets, in subacid or rarely circumneutral humus-rich loam. May be found mingled with the other species of "Lesser Grape Ferns," but, being adapted to milder climatic conditions than these, often occurs alone. The search for these tiny plants, and the correct naming of them after collection, is recommended to every fern student as a rewarding undertaking.

CULTURE: Though seemingly more adaptable than its relatives, this fern is about as difficult to keep alive in a fern garden, as the usual pests overwhelm it sooner or later.

NOMENCLATURE:

Botrýchium matricariaefòlium A. Braun, 1845 (GM).
B. matricariifolium, altered spelling (BB).
B. neglectum Wood, 1847, lacking priority.
B. ramosum Ascherson, 1864, not valid under the Code.

The *Code of Nomenclature* requires that original spelling must be retained, except for typographic or orthographic errors; so Braun's spelling of the epithet is accepted here, even though some workers feel that the rules for forming Latin words in use in his day were not correct.

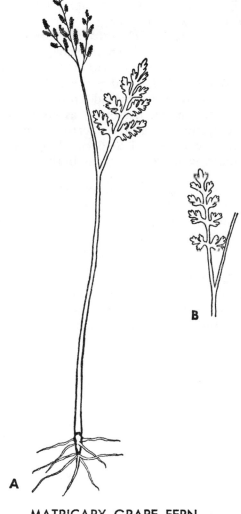

MATRICARY GRAPE FERN

A. Plant of triangular-blade form.   B. Blade of oblong form.

Triangle Grape Fern—Lanceolate Grape Fern

FEATURES: Plant appearing in spring, attaining a height in type v. of *ca.* 6 to 12, in v. *angust.* 13 to 25 cm., the tissue dark green, persisting well through summer. Stipe *ca.* 5 times as long as blade, which is nearly sessile, triangular, *ca.* 1.5 to 3 cm. long and broad, cut into a few pairs of rather sharp-pointed, toothed pinnae. Pinnae in the type v. decidedly fleshy and crowded, in v. *angustisegmentum,* as this epithet implies, narrower, as well as more widely spaced and thinnish textured. Fertile segment in type v. *ca.* 2 to 4, in v. *angust.* 3 to 6 cm. long. Half-size plants often accompany normal ones in both vars.

RANGE: Type var., from Greenl. and subarct. e. Can. down in our region to n. Me.; also in w. N.A. mts. and Eurasia. Var. *angustisegmentum,* endemic in our region, from w. Nf. to c. Minn., becoming increasingly rare southw., though reaching c. N.J. at low alt. and sw. Va. in the mts.

HABITAT: The Type var. grows in meadows and barrens where the soil remains cold through the season. Var. *angustisegmentum,* in humus-rich woods and hummocks in swamps, tolerating moderately high summer temperatures. Soil mostly subacid.

CULTURE: Rarely survives transplanting to a garden, being soon destroyed by fungi, slugs, mice, etc.

NOMENCLATURE:

Botrýchium lanceolàtum Ångström, 1854 (GM, BB).
(*Osmunda lanceolata* S. G. Gmelin, 1768, basionym).
B. lanceolatum v. *lanceolatum* (BB) = type var.

EAST-AMERICAN VARIANT:

B. l. v. *angustisegméntum* Pease & Moore, 1906 (GM, BB).
B. angustisegmentum Fernald, 1915.
B. l. ssp. *angustisegmentum* Clausen, 1937.

The two taxa here concerned are accepted as varietally distinct in the interest of uniformity, although subspecies status would be preferable.

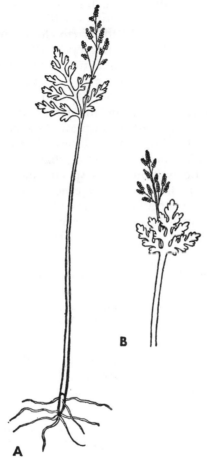

TRIANGLE GRAPE FERN

A. *Plant of East-American variety.*
B. *Upper part of widespread (type) variety.*

Rattlesnake Fern

FEATURES: Plant arising in spring, to a height of *ca.* 38 to 75 cm. (dwarfs frequent). Stipe *ca.* 18 to 35 cm. long. Blade triangular, sessile, *ca.* 13 to 25 cm. long and 1½ times as broad, ternately divided into repeatedly pinnate divisions, yellow green, withering in autumn. Sporangia in a dense compound panicle, maturing in late spring. In type var., blade membranous with well-spaced divisions, and sporangia scarcely 1 mm. in diameter, opening widely at maturity. In var. *europaeum,* plant ⅛ smaller, blade more coriaceous, with fewer more crowded divisions, and sporangia *ca.* 1.5 mm. in diameter, barely opening. Unlike most other Botrychiums, this species has a basal chromosome number of 46; it is moreover usually tetraploid. These differences could be regarded as justifying its assignment to a distinct genus, the earliest name for which is *Japanobotrychium,* Masamune, 1931.

RANGE: Type var., one of the commonest of ferns, from N.B. to Minn. and down throughout our region except in areas of barren or strongly acid soils; also in s. and occasionally in w. states. Var. *europaeum,* from subarct. e. Can. down to *ca.* lat. 44°, from Me. to Minn.; also w. N.A. and Eurasia.

HABITAT: Type var., humus-rich woods, the soil circumneutral to subacid. Var. *europaeum,* damp woods, chiefly coniferous, and brushy barrens, the soil mostly decidedly acid.

CULTURE: A highly ornamental plant, readily grown in a woodland garden, in fertile soil often becoming larger than in the wild.

NOMENCLATURE:

Botrýchium virginiànum Swartz, 1801 (GM, BB).
(*Osmunda virginiana* L., 1753, basionym).
Japanobotrychium virginianum Nishida, 1958.
Osmundopteris virginiana Small, 1938.

GEOGRAPHIC VARIANT:

B. virginiànum v. *europaèum* Ångström, 1854 (GM, BB).

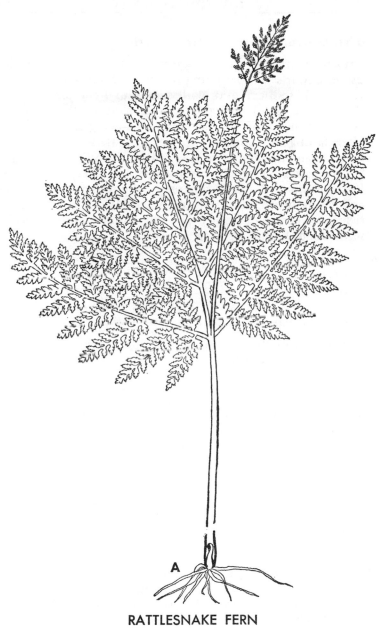

RATTLESNAKE FERN

A. *Plant, reduced.*

Leather Grape Fern—Broad Grape Fern

FEATURES: Plant appearing in early summer, bright green, its tissue thick-fleshy, becoming leathery. Stipe in the type var. *ca.* 1½ to 3 cm. and blade-stalk 2 to 4 cm. long, in the Widespread var. 3 to 6 and 4 to 8 cm. respectively. Blade evergreen, not bronzing in winter, yellowing in spring but often lasting into summer, subpentagonal; in type var. *ca.* 2.5 to 5 cm. long and 3 to 6 broad, in the Widespread var. 8 to 15 and 13 to 25 respectively, ternately 2-pinnate. Pinnules divided into segments, the terminal ones about as long as broad, subacute, their margins of thick yellow tissue, shallowly or rarely jaggedly blunt-toothed. Fertile segment *ca.* 3 times as long as blade.

RANGE: Type var., from subarct. Can. to c. Minn. and down to *ca.* lat. 44° from Me. to Wisc., with intergrading forms to ne. Pa. Widespread var., from Que. to Minn., down the mts. to n. Va., and w. to n. Ind., Ill., and Ia.; these and other variants also in w. N.A. and Eurasia.

HABITAT: Damp thickets, meadows, and barrens, in mostly subacid soil. Not cultivated.

NOMENCLATURE:

Botrýchium multifidum J. G. Gmelin, 1759 (GM, BB).
(*Osmunda multifida* S. G. Gmelin, 1768, basionym).
B. multifidum v. *multifidum* (BB) = type var.

WIDESPREAD VARIANT:

B. multifidum v. *intermèdium* Farwell, 1916 (GM, BB).
(*B. ternatum* v. *australe* subv. *intermedium* D. C. Eaton, 1879, basionym).

This species and its multiple variants have received dozens of names in their range over the northern hemisphere, but only the above seem worth listing here. It is deemed the most specialized member of the evergreen Grape Fern group, sometimes classed as the distinct genus *Sceptridium* Lyon, 1905. The taxa of this group are exceedingly variable, and seemingly grade into one another, so that specialists disagree markedly as to their proper classification. The juvenile stages of one often imitate adult stages of another.

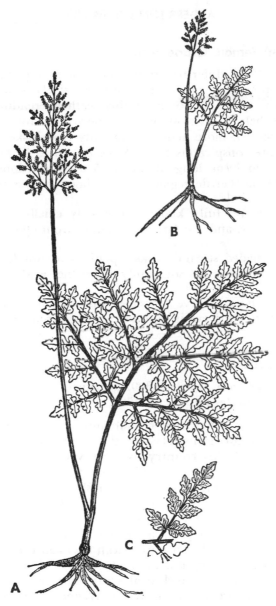

LEATHER GRAPE FERN

Plants of: A. Widespread and
B. Northern (type) variety, both reduced.   C. Pinnule.

(American) Ternate Grape Fern

FEATURES: Plant differing from average-sized representatives of the preceding taxon in: habit relatively slender, the tissue thinnish and not becoming leathery, tending to be concave below; divisions usually more numerous, shorter, better spaced, more acute, marginally less thickened, and with more conspicuous teeth. Stipe *ca.* 2.5 to 5 and blade-stalk 3.5 to 7 cm. long. Blade *ca.* 5 to 10 cm. long and 8 to 15 broad. Fertile segment *ca.* 3 times as long as blade.

RANGE: Not yet fully known, seemingly chiefly in the St. Lawrence vy. and the Gr. L. lowlands, from Que. to Wisc.

HABITAT: Shaded stream banks, openings in woods, also invading old fields, the soil sandy and rather acid.

CULTURE: The attractive aspect of this fern may encourage attempts to cultivate it, but success seems unlikely.

NOMENCLATURE:

Botrýchium ternàtum Swartz, 1800, unnamed **relative.**
(*Osmunda ternata* Thunberg, 1784, basionym).

Confused by superficial resemblances, early students of North American ferns classed the widespread evergreen Grape Ferns of this country as mere varieties or forms of this primarily Asiatic taxon. This view was upheld as late as 1879 by D. C. Eaton in his sumptuously illustrated two volume work, *Ferns of North America.* The derived colloquial name Ternate Grape Fern continued in use in "popular" fern books for many years after that, but specialists gradually came to realize that the American taxa concerned deserve species independence, and after about 1910 the epithet *ternatum* vanished from technical treatments. It was, accordingly, quite a surprise when W. H. Wagner, working at the University of Michigan, announced in 1959 the discovery in that state (and subsequently elsewhere) of a relative of the Asiatic taxon. This resembles so closely small-lobed forms of *B. multifidum* v. *intermedium,* treated on the preceding text page, that beginners may have difficulty in telling them apart, but they are deemed worthy of separation here.

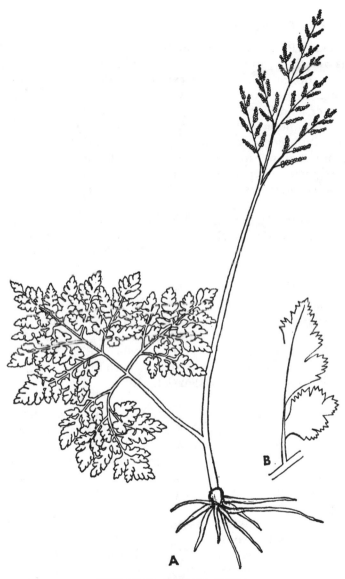

TERNATE GRAPE FERN

A. Plant, reduced.   B. Bit of margin, enlarged.

Blunt-lobe Grape Fern

FEATURES: Plant appearing in summer, seemingly rarer than its relatives, and not forming extensive colonies as they often do. Stipe *ca.* 2 to 4 cm. and blade-stalk 5 to 10 cm. long. Blade evergreen, remaining bright green through winter, tardily yellowing and withering, triangular, *ca.* 5 to 10 cm. long and 6 to 12 broad, ternately pinnate. Pinnae broadly oblong, divided into a few roundish close-set segments, toward tip notched at short intervals, the tip being a segment little longer than broad. Margins irregularly toothed. Fertile segment *ca.* 4 times as long as blade.

RANGE: From Que. to nw. Wisc., down in our region to lat. 39° at low alt. in N.J., Pa., and Md., and further s. in mts. of Va. and Ky.; also to sw. N.C. Not cultivated.

NOMENCLATURE:

Botrýchium oneidénsè House, 1921.
(*B. ternatum* v. *oneidense* Gilbert, 1901, basionym).
B. dissectum f. *oneidense* Clute, 1902 (GM).
B. obliquum v. *oneidense* Waters, 1903 (GEF).
B. multifidum v. *oneidense* Farwell, 1916 (BB).
B. dissectum v. *oneidense* Farwell, 1924.

When a succession of specialists fail to agree on the status of a taxon, or as to which, if any, species it should be subordinated, further study of its relationships are manifestly needed. Pending this, classification as a distinct species seems the simplest procedure. Identification of it should not be based on comparison of immature individuals of one taxon with mature plants of another; for juvenile plants of the broader lobed forms of t. *multifidum* as well as of t. *obliquum* (a later-treated taxon), may have lobes or segments much like those of adult t. *oneidense*. Identification of plants as closely related as these evergreen Grape Ferns can be safely made only on well-developed specimens, preferably with fertile segments.

A lowland form of this taxon, illustrated as Fig. 13 in Reed's *Ferns . . . of Md.* (1953) bears a striking resemblance to the more southern *Botrychium alabamense*.

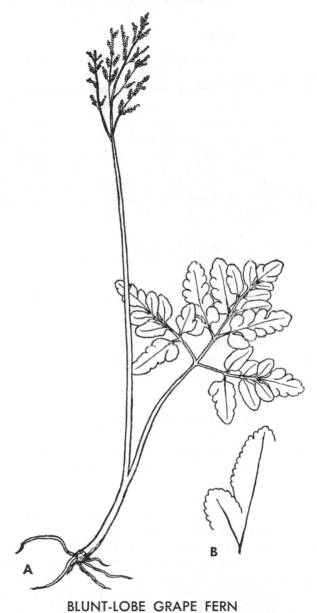

BLUNT-LOBE GRAPE FERN

A. Plant, reduced. *B. Bit of margin, enlarged.*

Sparse-lobe Grape Fern

FEATURES: Plant appearing in summer. Stipe *ca.* 3 to 5 cm. and blade-stalk 8 to 15 cm. long. Blade evergreen, in winter remaining bright green or at most becoming slightly bronzy at segment-tips, early the next spring yellowing and withering, triangular, *ca.* 5 to 10 cm. long and 6 to 12 broad, ternately pinnate. Pinnae in plants of our region mostly narrowly elliptic, sometimes with a few basal pinnules or lobes, but on the whole little divided, and in particular the margins above the middle uninterrupted by notches for long distances. Margins subserrately toothed. Fertile segment *ca.* 3 to 5 times as long as blade.

RANGE: S. states, and up in our region at low to moderate alt. to ne. Md., s. O. and Ind., and n. Mo.

HABITAT: Damp woods, swamp margins, and shaded stream banks, the soil mostly subacid.

CULTURE: Worth trying in a woodland garden, but only if slugs and rodents are under control.

NOMENCLATURE:

Botrýchium tenuifòlium Underwood, 1903.
B. obliquum v. *tenuifolium* Gilbert, 1903 (GEF).
B. ternatum obliquum f. *tenuifolium* Clute, 1905.
B. dissectum v. *tenuifolium* Farwell, 1924 (GM).

This southern taxon, ranging but a short distance up into our region, is often confused with depauperate phases of the far more widespread and correspondingly more familiar one treated on the next-following text page. Even in its most luxuriant state, however, it never approaches the commoner relative in extent of blade-division, and, moreover, shows much less tendency to become bronzed in winter, a feature which, as already pointed out, is of taxonomic significance in the evergreen Grape Ferns. Accordingly, even though it is far less readily distinguishable from t. *obliquum* than (over a vast area) t. *dissectum* is, its species independence is here maintained.

SPARSE-LOBE GRAPE FERN

A Plant, reduced.

Oblique Grape Fern—Coarse-lobe Grape Fern

FEATURES: Plant appearing in late summer. Stipe *ca.* 2 to 4 and blade stalk 5 to 10 cm. long. Blade evergreen, bronzing in winter and withering in spring, broad-triangular, *ca.* 4 to 8 cm. long and 6 to 12 broad (dwarfs occasional), often 3-pinnate below, but rapidly reduced to 1-pinnate upward. Tips of many divisions barely lobed triangular-oblong segments several times as long as wide. Margins bearing minute short teeth varying from symmetrical to subserrate. Fertile segment *ca.* 4 times as long as blade. Variability extreme.

RANGE: From N.S. to nw. Wisc. and down over our region, increasingly common southw.; also over s. states.

HABITAT: Damp woods, thickets, meadows, and barrens, the soil moderately acid.

CULTURE: Can be grown in a woodland garden, though usually destroyed by pests before long.

NOMENCLATURE:

Botrýchium oblíquum Muhlenberg, 1810 (GEF).
B. dissectum v. *obliquum* Clute, 1902 (BB).
B. dissectum f. *obliquum* Fernald, 1921 (GM).

Once more a vexing problem of classification arises. When a fern student visits, in the southern part of our region, one of the frequent areas where this and the next-following taxon grow together, he will find it difficult to understand why anyone would class them as mere varieties, let alone forms, of one another; for they are there more readily distinguishable than any other pair of taxa in the evergreen Grape Fern group. As a rule there will be no intermediates at all, or at most a rare individual of the taxon termed *B. dissectum* f. *confusum* on the following text page. If, however, he now travels northward to the Great Lakes lowlands, he will find intermediates to increase in frequency until they outnumber the extremes. It is this situation which leads most current workers to refuse to maintain them as distinct at species level. Until further study discloses the significance of these relationships, it is deemed simpler to maintain them as independent.

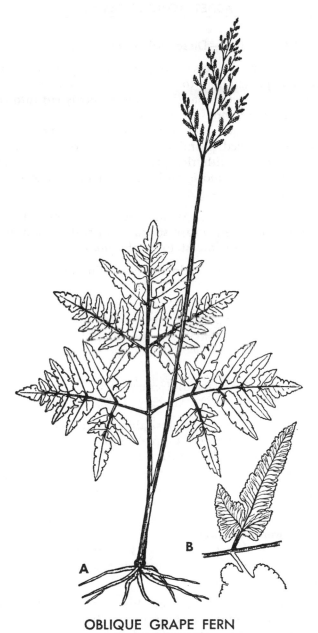

OBLIQUE GRAPE FERN

A. *Plant, reduced.* B. *Pinnule.*

Lace-leaf Grape Fern—Dissected Grape Fern

FEATURES: Like the preceding taxon in major respects, though stipe tending to be 1½ times as long; differing conspicuously in the margins being jaggedly cut into coarse teeth which are not at all serrate, but have entire sub-parallel sides and a truncate tip. The form-epithet *confusum* was applied to individuals so shallowly cut as to be readily confused with the preceding taxon; otherwise the present one is far more uniform than that, at least southward.

RANGE: From N.S. to se. Minn. and down over our region, becoming increasingly rare southw.; in s. states scattered in uplands only (in contrast to t. *obliquum*).

HABITAT AND CULTURE: As in the preceding taxon.

NOMENCLATURE:

Botrýchium disséctum Sprengel, 1804 (GM, BB).
B. dissectum v. *dissectum* (BB); typical [f.] (GM).

MAJOR VARIANT:

B. disséctum f. *confùsum* Bartholomew, 1951.
(*B. obliquum* f. *confusum* Wherry, 1942, basionym).

When anyone deems it desirable to reduce a southern member of the evergreen Grape Fern group to less than species status, the *Code* requires it to be placed under this, since it was the earliest to receive an epithet in such status. As noted under the preceding taxon, intergradation between it and the present one is so frequent in the Great Lake lowlands that reduction in status is there considered unavoidable. Southwardly, however, the two are so unlike in aspect that the beginner has no difficulty in distinguishing them, and as they also differ in range, they are here tentatively maintained as species.

While some workers consider this "skeletonized" state of the blade to represent an aberrant or "freak" development, study of the vascular strands and veins suggests that the present taxon is primitive, and the others have arisen by the gradual development of webbing between the ancestral narrow segments.

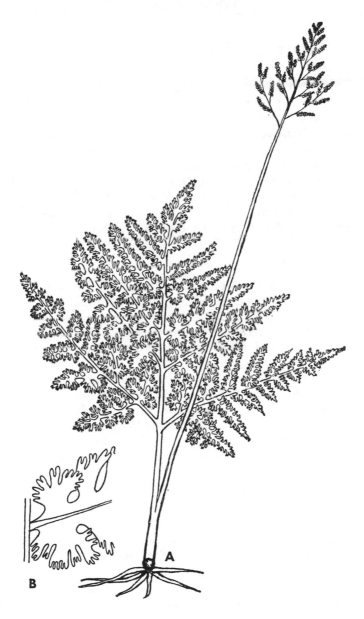

LACE-LEAF GRAPE FERN

A. Plant, reduced.   B. Bit of margin, enlarged.

Horsetail Family : *Equisetàceae*

HORSETAILS AND SCOURING-RUSHES : *EQUISÈTUM*

This ancient term, a Latinization of the colloquial one, was made a genus name by Linnaeus in 1753. The plants have an extensive underground system of jointed rootstocks bearing roots at nodes. The aerial stems are traversed by hollow tubes, termed canals, and bear ridges often roughened by silica deposits; their nodes are ringed by crown-like sheaths with teeth representing leaves but lacking green tissue. The green globular ribbon-appendaged spores are borne in ovoid sporangia in terminal cones.

Field Horsetail

FEATURES: Stems dimorphic. Fertile arising in early spring, succulent and soon withering, buff or pink with coarse flaring sheaths bearing blackish brown teeth, *ca.* 15 to 30 cm. high. Sterile stems appearing as the fertile fade, green, in typical forms erect and *ca.* 25 to 50 cm. high, but varying through many intermediates to prostrate, and from solitary to densely clumped. Nodes with flaring sheaths, the teeth brown-tipped, bearing whorls of stem-like but slender branches, horizontal to nearly erect, simple or with branchlets, 3- or 4-angled. While epithets have been coined for many variants, since these mostly occur in association with typical plants—indeed often arising from the same rootstocks—they are here not named. A northern variant with consistently 3-angled branches may be termed v. *boreàle* Ruprecht, 1846; (*E. boreale* Bongard, 1832, basionym).

RANGE: From arct. e. Can. down over our region, rare in lowlands and s. states; also w. N.A. and Eurasia.

HABITAT: Swamps, stream banks, meadows, and damp woods, often invading barren disturbed ground, notably railroad ballast and road fills, then developing forms. Soil subacid.

CULTURE: Too weedy for garden use.

NOMENCLATURE:

Equisètum arvénsè L., 1753.

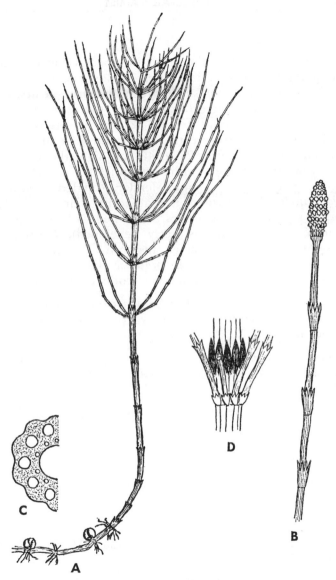

FIELD HORSETAIL

A. *Plant with sterile shoot and*   B. *Fertile shoot, both reduced.*
C. *Half section, enlarged.*   D. *Node, enlarged.*

Meadow Horsetail

FEATURES: Resembling the preceding species, but differing in respects here emphasized: Less dimorphic. Fertile shoots arising in early spring, pale green and firm, at first simple but soon developing green branches, the cone then withering, leaving a blunt stem-tip, otherwise like the sterile. The latter appearing early, lasting through summer, pale green, slender, mostly 20 to 40 cm. high, the sheath-teeth narrow, brown with white margin, the branches which emerge at their base simple, slender, 3-angled. First branch-internode shorter than the adjacent stem-sheath (in *E. arvense* longer). Stem-ridges roughened with silica granules (in *E. arvense* these scarcely developed). Central canal about half stem diameter in both, but those beneath grooves rather small in *E. pratense* (larger in *E. arvense;* text and diagrams in reference works contradictory).

RANGE: From subarct. e. Can. down over c. and w. N.E. to n. N.J., and Ont. to Man. down to se. Mich. and ne. Ia.; also in nw. N.A. and Eurasia.

HABITAT: Wooded alluvial flats, damp thickets, and limy meadows, the soil mostly circumneutral and rich in nutrients.

CULTURE: Might be grown in a cool woodland garden, but of no particular merit.

NOMENCLATURE:

Equisètum praténsè Ehrhart, 1784 (GM, BB).

Giant Horsetail

Equisètum telmateìa Ehrhart, 1783, v. *braùnii* Milde, 1865 (GM; not included in BB).

This American representative of a Eurasian species, assigned the above varietal epithet, resembles *E. arvense* but is much coarser and up to 5 times as large. It occurs chiefly toward the Pacific coast, but was found once in the Keweenaw peninsula of n. Mich.; the area, as a result of lumbering operations and subsequent thicket growth, is now an impenetrable wilderness. Not illustrated.

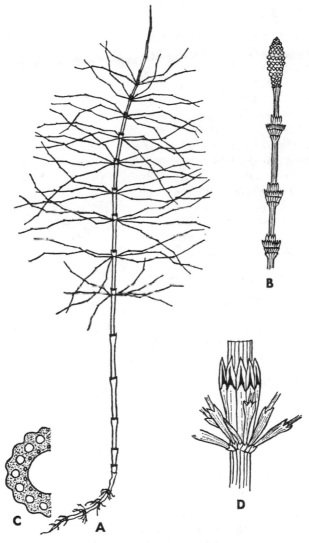

MEADOW HORSETAIL

A. *Plant with sterile shoot and*   B. *Fertile shoot, both reduced.*
C. *Half section, enlarged.*   D. *Node, enlarged.*

Woodland Horsetail

FEATURES: Stems subdimorphic, both sorts arising together in spring. Fertile stems promptly sending out branches, the cone later withering, leaving a flat stem-tip. Sterile bright green, *ca.* 20 to 60 cm. high, the loose sheaths with broad brown teeth united in groups of 2 or 3, the branches which emerge at their base slender, rebranched, the branchlets drooping attractively. Stem-ridges roughened by pointed silica granules; central canal over half the stem diameter. Branch-ridges roughened by silica in the type var., smooth in the others. Branchlets sparse in var. *pauciramosum,* copious in var. *multiramosum.*

RANGE: From subarct. e. Can. down over our region to low alt. in Md., the mts. of s. W. Va., s. Mich., and se. Ia.; also nw. N.A. and Eurasia. The type var. is rare eastw., though known to n. N.Y. and s. Que. Var. *pauciramosum* is commoner from Lab. and Nf. to N.E. while var. *multiramosum* seems the only one s. of lat. 41°.

HABITAT: Swamps, moist open woods, less commonly marshy meadows, occasionally invading sterile disturbed areas; soil mostly subacid.

CULTURE: Desirable but difficult to transplant.

NOMENCLATURE:

Equisètum sylváticum L., 1753 (GM, BB).

GEOGRAPHIC VARIANTS:

E. sylváticum v. *pauciramòsum* Milde, 1865 (GM, BB).
E. sylváticum v. *multiramòsum* Wherry, 1937.
(*E. s.* v. *pauciramosum* f. *multiramosum* Fernald, 1918, basionym, GM).

The view that the second-named variant deserves variety status is reaffirmed on the interpretation that this category pertains to taxa with definite geographic range—which the one in question has—whereas that of forma, previously assigned, applies to mere aberrant individuals within normal populations, certainly not the case here.

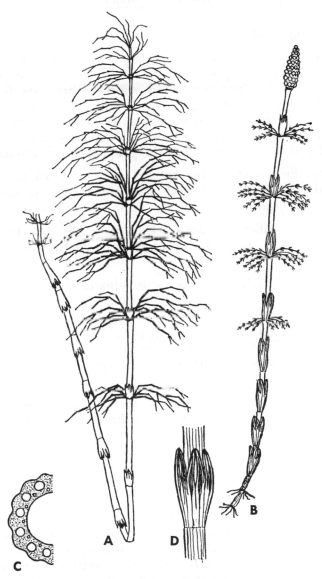

WOODLAND HORSETAIL

A. *Plant with sterile shoot and*   B. *Fertile shoot, both reduced.*
    C. *Half section, enlarged.*   D. *Node, enlarged.*

Water Horsetail

FEATURES: Stems uniform (as they are in all subsequent members of the genus), deciduous, *ca.* 50 to 100 cm. high, simple to bearing conspicuous whorls of branches. Ridges numerous, low, bearing scattered silica flakes but scarcely rough. Sheaths tight, with numerous narrow brown teeth. Central canal occupying most of stem, others barely developed. Cone *ca.* 1 to 2 cm. long, appearing in summer.

RANGE: From Greenl. and subarct. e. Can. down over our region to low alt. in n. Del., easternmost W. Va., and out to c. Ia.; also plains states, nw. N.A., and Eurasia.

HABITAT: Shallow to deep water of ponds and sluggish streams, river marshes and sometimes swamps. Soil circumneutral.

CULTURE: Suitable for a large-scale aquatic garden.

NOMENCLATURE:

Equisètum fluviátilè L., 1753 (GM, BB).
E. limosum L., 1753 = *E. fl.* f. *linnaeànum* Broun, 1938 (GM).
(*E. l.* f. *linnaeanum* Döll, 1857, basionym).

Linnaeus thought that the branched and unbranched forms of this taxon were distinct species, but the second is now considered a mere form of the first, as indicated in the naming.

Shore Horsetail

Equisètum × *litoràlè* Kühlewein, 1845 (as species; GM; ? BB).
= *E. arvénsè* × *fluviátilè* (GM).

While this taxon has been classed as a species, and again regarded as a mere variant of one or more other horsetails, the current view that it is a hybrid between those stated is based on its combining their features in a striking way, and in the spores, which it rarely produces in any case, being reportedly always abortive. The epithet refers to its usual stream-bank habitat, it commonly growing between the drier zone supporting the first-named parent and the wetter favored by the second. There are reports of it from Nf. to Pa.

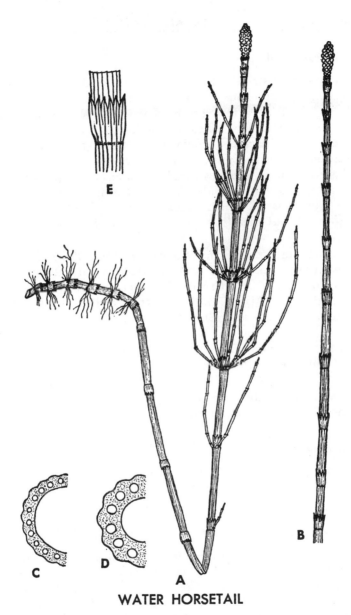

WATER HORSETAIL

A. Plant with branches, reduced. **B. Unbranched stem,** *reduced. Half sections of:* **C. Water and** **D. Shore** *Horsetail, enlarged.* **E. Node, enlarged.**

Marsh Horsetail

FEATURES: Stems *ca.* 25 to 50 cm. high, deciduous, simple to bearing conspicuous whorls of short or sometimes long branches. Ridges few, *ca.* 8, sharp, barely roughened by flat silica granules. Sheaths moderately flaring upward, their teeth blackish brown with broad to narrow pale scarious margins. Central canal only ⅛ the stem diameter, those under the grooves nearly as large. Cone produced in summer. Varying considerably in stem and branch details, on the basis of which several form epithets have been proposed, but these are here deemed unimportant.

RANGE: From Greenl. and subarct. e. Can. down into our region, becoming rare and scattered s. of lat. 45°, but known in s. Vt., c. Ct., e. N.Y. (reports in N.J. and Pa. doubtful), sw. Mich., and disjunct in c. Ill.; also n. Plains states, nw. N.A. and Eurasia.

HABITAT: Marshes, open swamps, stream banks, and ditches, the soil mostly circumneutral.

CULTURE: Might be grown in a cool-climate water garden, but of no particular merit.

NOMENCLATURE:

Equisètum palústrè L., 1753 (GM, BB).

AMERICAN VARIANT:

E. palustre var. *americanum* Marie-Victorin, 1927.

This variety was separated from the Eurasian type of the species on the basis of detailed observations made by Frère Marie-Victorin in his study of the *Equiseta* of Quebec. He considered the North American taxon to be distinguished by the sheath-teeth having decidedly broader pale margins than the typical Eurasian one. The validity of this has been questioned by subsequent workers, and the American variety is not accepted as distinct in GM or BB. The matter is too complicated for full treatment here, so the variant is merely listed.

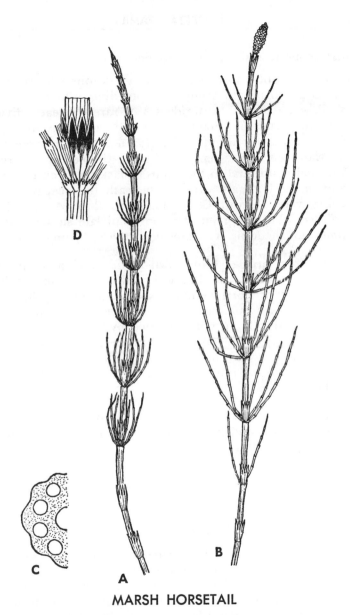

MARSH HORSETAIL

A. *Short-branched sterile stem.*
B. *Long-branched fertile stem.*   C. *Half section, enlarged.*
D. *Node, enlarged.*

Least Scouring-rush—Dwarf Scouring-rush

FEATURES: Plant a tuft of dark green flexuous wiry stems *ca.* 10 to 20 cm. high, evergreen, spreading into colonies by shallow rootstocks. Stem-ridges 3 or rarely 4, each divided into two parts by broad shallow grooves, so as to appear 6 (or 8), bearing minute silica granules. Sheaths loose, with 3 triangular white-margined teeth, tipped by a bristle. Internally, unusual in the genus in lacking a central canal, and in the 3 canals which lie beneath the deeper grooves being very narrow. Cone small, *ca.* 2 to 4 mm. long, pointed, blackish green, developing in late summer, sometimes not shedding its spores until the following spring.

RANGE: From arct. e. Can. down in our region to nw. Ct., sw. N.Y., s. Mich., ne. Ill., and c. Minn.; also in nw. N.A. and n. Eu. Reports of this taxon occurring farther s. in our region are dubious: An often repeated statement that it extends into Pa. is not supported by herbarium material. There is one specimen alleged to have been collected at only moderate altitude in N.C., but this is too much of a disjunction of an otherwirse arctic and cool-climate species to be credible.

HABITAT: Litter of coniferous or less often deciduous woods, springy slopes, and hummocks in swamps, the soil subacid or rarely circumneutral.

CULTURE: Invasive and without horticultural merit.

NOMENCLATURE:

Equisètum scirpoìdes Michaux, 1803 (GM, BB).

The Equisetums thus far treated are considered to represent an advanced subdivision of the genus, in that they have a deciduous habit and normal branching; they are the ones which merit the colloquial name Horsetails. In contrast, the present taxon and those which follow belong to a subdivision deemed more primitive, being chiefly evergreen and simple-stemmed, the branches, if any, developing only irregularly; they constitute the Scouring-rushes. The Least Scouring-rush is taken up first, since it is specialized in its reduced size and obsolete central canal.

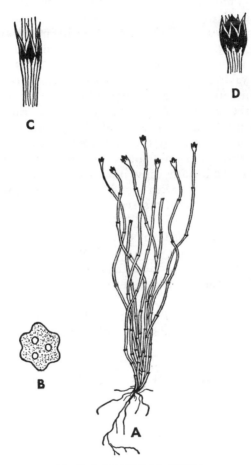

LEAST SCOURING-RUSH

A. *Plant.*   B. *Stem-section, enlarged.*   C. *Node, enlarged.*
D. *Tip of fertile stem, enlarged.*

Variegated Scouring-rush

FEATURES: Stem slender, *ca.* 20 to 40 cm. high, evergreen. Ridges *ca.* 5 to 10, deeply grooved, bearing a row of small silica granules on each part. Sheaths moderately flaring, often banded dark and light green with blackish summit, the teeth at first bristle-tipped, but the bristles tending to break away. Central canal *ca.* ½ stem diameter. Cone produced in late summer, sharp-pointed, partly enclosed by uppermost sheath. T. *jesupi* is said to differ from the type in averaging larger in all its parts, and in having tighter sheaths with more persistent bristles. T. *nelsoni,* in the stems being only subevergreen, in having the ridges barely grooved, with only one row of granules, and like the preceding var. with persistent bristles. Further study is needed to decide the status of the three taxa.

RANGE: Type, arct. e. Can. down to w. Ct., and nw. N.Y., along Gr. L. to se. Ia. and e. Neb.; also w. N.A. and Eurasia. The two variant taxa, often not clearly distinguishable, from Mass. to Minn.

HABITAT: Damp sandy flats, stream banks, hard-water spring runs, and limy marshes, the soil circumneutral or mildly alkaline.

CULTURE: Might be grown in a cold-climate water garden.

NOMENCLATURE:

Equisètum variegàtum Schleicher, 1807 (GM, BB).

MAJOR VARIANTS (PROBABLY HYBRIDS):

E. variegàtum v. *jésupi* A. A. Eaton, 1901 (GM, BB).
E. jesupi A. A. Eaton, 1904.
E. variegàtum v. *nélsoni* A. A. Eaton, 1904 (GM, BB).
E. nelsoni Schaffner, 1926.

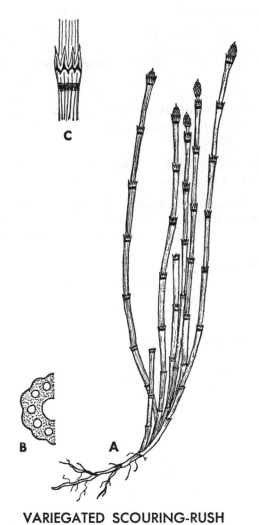

VARIEGATED SCOURING-RUSH

A. Plant, reduced.   B. Half section, enlarged.
C. Node, enlarged.

Smooth Scouring-rush

FEATURES: Stem herbaceous in texture and deciduous, *ca.* 40 to 80 cm. high, simple (or, as in subsequent members, producing irregular branches where injured). Ridges low, with few flat silica granules, smooth to the touch. Sheaths flaring, greenish gray with basal black band, the narrow blackish teeth soon falling. Central canal ¾ stem diameter. Cone produced in summer, ellipsoidal with conspicuously rounded tip.

RANGE: From ne. O. at intervals across Mich. to nw. Minn. and Kans.; widespread further w., from Can. to Mex.

HABITAT: Moist or seasonally dry prairie land, and clayey depressions; invading roadsides and other disturbed areas. Soil circumneutral to subacid. Of no cultural interest.

NOMENCLATURE:

Equisètum laevigàtum A. Braun, 1844 (BB).
E. kansanum Schaffner, 1912 (GM).

Intermediate Scouring-rush

FEATURES: Stem firm and evergreen (at least in mild climates), *ca.* 50 to 100 cm. high. Ridges bearing a row of low strips of silica, thereby somewhat rough. Sheaths and teeth as in the preceding taxon. Central canal ⅘ stem diameter. Cone produced in summer, subcylindric with a conspicuous firm sharp tip. The spores are reportedly abortive, and the way in which this combines the features of the preceding and following taxa indicates hybrid origin.

RANGE: Widely scattered from Vt. to Va., and Mo., where presumably introduced, but native from w. N.Y. to c. Minn.; scattered in s. uplands and abundant in w. U.S.

HABITAT: Moist sandy land, often invading disturbed soil, this usually circumneutral. Of no cultural interest.

NOMENCLATURE:

Equisètum × *ferríssii* Clute (as species), 1904.
E. hyemale v. *affine* × *laevigatum* Hauke, 1960.
E. hyemale [v.] *intermedium* A. A. Eaton ("*hiemale*") (GM).

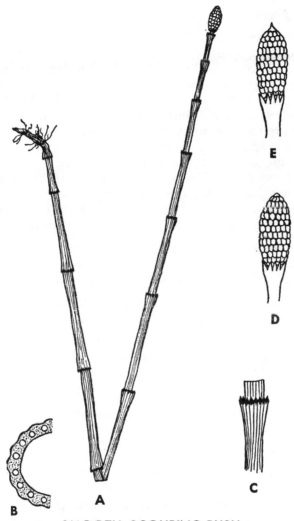

SMOOTH SCOURING-RUSH

A. Plant, reduced.   B. Half section, enlarged.
C. Node, enlarged.   D. Cone.
E. Cone of hybrid with following taxon.

Scouring-rush

FEATURES: Stem firm and evergreen. Ridges in the European type bearing a double row of silica granules, in the American variants a single row of silica strips, producing a markedly rough surface. Sheaths cylindric, lying close against the stem, gray green with a blackish band at top and often at base. Central canal ⅔ the stem diameter. Cone produced in summer, sharp-tipped.

E. h. v. *affine:* Stem *ca.* 40 to 80 cm. high and 5 to 10 mm. thick, the sheath-teeth mostly falling early.

E. h. v. *elatum:* Stem up to *ca.* 300 cm. high and to 20 mm. thick, the sheath-teeth falling only tardily. In both variants injury to rootstock-tips may lead to the solitary stems being replaced by a cluster of smaller ones.

RANGE: The American variants occur throughout our region, but the detailed distribution of the two has never been worked out; also far s. and w. The type is Eurasian.

HABITAT: Sandy shores, springy slopes, limy barrens, often invading disturbed soil, fills, railroad ballast, etc.; soil mostly circumneutral.

CULTURE: While rather striking, too weedy to cultivate.

NOMENCLATURE:

Equisetum hyemale L., 1753 (GM); *hiemale* (BB).

AMERICAN VARIANTS:

Equisètum hyemàlè v. *affinè* A. A. Eaton, 1903 (GM).
(*E. robustum* v. *affine* Engelmann, 1844, basionym).
E. hiemale v. *pseudohiemale* Morton, 1952 (BB).
(*Hippochaete prealta* v. *pseudohyemalis* Farwell, 1917, basionym).
Equisètum hyemàlè v. *elàtum; hiemale* v. *elatum* Morton, 1951.
(*E. laevigatum* γ *elatum* Engelmann, 1844, basionym).
E. prealtum Rafinesque, 1817 (misprint for *praealtum*) (GEF).
E. robustum A. Braun, 1844.

Correcting Linnaeus' epithets is disfavored here, for after all, he spoke and wrote, so surely could spell, Latin; moreover, our nomenclature starts with his work of 1753.

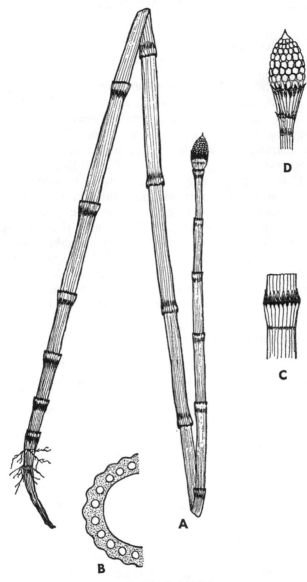

SCOURING-RUSH

A. *Plant, reduced.* B. *Half section, enlarged.*
C. *Node, enlarged.* D. *Cone.*

Quillwort Family : *Isoëtàceae*

QUILLWORTS : *ISÒËTES*

This genus was named by Linnaeus in 1753 from an ancient word meaning equal points. Its members are rather small aquatic plants with a more or less lobed, globular stem—technically a corm—buried in mud, with firm anchoring roots, and sending up a rosette of quill-like leaves, many of which have a sporangium in a swollen base. Some of these contain a large number of minute monolete spores, known as microspores, which are male; the others contain a moderate number of larger trilete ones, the megaspores, which are female. The species are distinguishable in part by the size, shape, and vascular system of the leaves, but most readily by the sculpture of the megaspores. As the certain identification of many of its members is a matter for specialists, the taxa are only briefly treated here, mostly as in GM.

Spiny-spored Quillwort

FEATURES: Leaves deep green, lax, varying exceedingly in number and length. Sporangium globose to ellipsoid, *ca.* 3.5 to 7 mm. long. Megaspores averaging ½ mm. in diameter, conspicuously covered by numerous spines.

RANGE: From Greenl. and subarct. e. Can. to c. Minn., and down to n. N.J., c. Pa., n. O., s. Mich., and sc. Wisc.; represented by vars. in nw. N.A. and Eurasia.

HABITAT: Lakes, ponds, and sluggish streams, usually rather deeply immersed, the water fairly cold through summer, mostly slightly acid.

CULTURE: This, like most other species, can be grown in an aquarium, although the tissues, especially the sporangia, are a favorite food of various kinds of fish.

NOMENCLATURE:

Isòëtes muricàta Durieu, 1864 (GM).
I. braunii Durieu, 1864 (GEF), preoccupied so not valid.
I. echinospora Durieu, 1864, vars. *braunii, muricata* and *robusta* Engelmann, 1867 (BB).

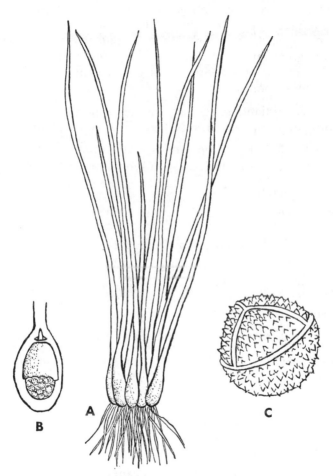

SPINY-SPORED QUILLWORT

A. *Plant.*   B. *Sporangium in leaf-base, enlarged.*
C. *Megaspore, enlarged*

Midland Quillwort—Black-based Quillwort

FEATURES: Leaves fairly numerous, firm, up to 3 mm. thick, bright green, at base shiny blackish brown or in a form merely grayish, negativing the second colloquial name. Sporangium up to 3 cm. long. Megaspores averaging ⅓ mm. in diameter, covered with crowded and somewhat confluent low projections.

RANGE: S. midland states, up in our region to n. Ill., sw. Minn., and adj. S.D. A s. N.J. taxon may be identical.

HABITAT: Shallow, often temporary, pools and ditches, meadows, and stream banks, in circumneutral mud.

NOMENCLATURE:

Isòëtes melanópoda Gay and Durieu, 1864 (GM, BB).

Limestone Quillwort—Butler's Quillwort

FEATURES: Leaves few, lax, triangular in section and 1 mm. thick, pale-based. Sporangium to 7 mm. long. Megaspores averaging ½ mm. in diameter, covered with numerous low mostly distinct wart-like projections.

RANGE: From s. midland uplands to e. Mo. and se. Kans.

HABITAT: Temporary pools and muddy depressions on limestone barrens and calcareous meadows.

NOMENCLATURE:

Isòëtes bútleri Engelmann, 1878 (GM, BB).

Virginia Quillwort

FEATURES: Leaves few, lax, quadrangular in section and 1 mm. thick, shining brown at base. Sporangium short. Megaspores barely ½ mm. in diameter, with irregular spaced low dots, some united into short ridges.

RANGE: Valleys of n.-c. Va.; with also a s. variety.

HABITAT: Temporary pools in clayey and sandy barrens, the soil slightly acid.

NOMENCLATURE:

Isòëtes virgínica Pfeiffer, 1937 (GM, BB).

A

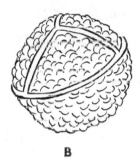

B

C

THREE QUILLWORTS

Megaspores of: A. Midland.   B. Limestone.
C. Virginia, *all enlarged.*

Shore Quillwort

FEATURES: Leaves few to numerous, firm, *ca.* 2 mm. thick. Sporangium to 7 mm. long. Megaspores averaging ½ mm. in diameter, with discrete crest-like ridges from the top of which extend well-spaced jagged teeth.

RANGE AND HABITAT: Represented by several varieties, from ne. Va. to R.I. and up to sw. Que., in shallow water along stream, or less commonly pond, shores.

NOMENCLATURE:

Isòëtes ripària Engelmann, 1846 (GM, BB).

In BB this taxon is divided into several varieties, but these are omitted here.

Sugary-spored Quillwort

FEATURES: Leaves rather few, lax, *ca.* 2 mm. thick, olive green. Sporangium subglobular, *ca.* 4 mm. across. Megaspores up to ½ mm. in diameter, with irregular crowded ridges bearing granulated-sugar-like dots. A var. *amesii* A. A. Eaton, 1903 (GM) = *I. riparia* v. *a.* Proctor, 1949 (BB) differs in having the stem 3 or 4 (instead of 2) lobed and the leaves more slender and numerous.

RANGE AND HABITAT: Type var., se. Va. to Del., and v. *amesii,* se. N.Y. to s. N.E., on tidal river shores.

NOMENCLATURE:

Isòëtes saccharàta Engelmann, 1867 (GM).
I. riparia v. *palmeri* Proctor, 1949 (BB).
(*I. saccharata* v. *palmeri* A. A. Eaton, 1901, basionym).

Eaton's Quillwort

FEATURES: Leaves numerous, coarse, and firm. Sporangium to 1 cm. long. Megaspores averaging ½ mm. in diameter, with numerous interwoven ridges like alligator skin.

RANGE AND HABITAT: From n. N.J. to s. N.H., deeply immersed in ponds, or sometimes on river shores.

NOMENCLATURE:

Isòëtes eàtoni Dodge, 1896 (GM, BB).

A

B

C

THREE QUILLWORTS

Megaspores of: A. Shore. B. Sugary-spored.
C. Eaton's, *all enlarged.*

Big-spored Quillwort

FEATURES: Leaves numerous, firm, round in section, abruptly pointed. Sporangium to 5 mm. long. Megaspores up to 1 mm. in diameter, the ridges all interlacing.

RANGE AND HABITAT: From Nf. and subarct. e. Can. to ne. Minn., down to n. N.J. (and disjunct in n. Va.), s. Mich., and c. Wisc.; cold lakes, ponds, and streams, mostly deep.

NOMENCLATURE:

Isòëtes macróspora Durieu, 1864 (GM, BB).

Tuckerman's Quillwort

FEATURES: Leaves numerous, lax, round in section, taper-pointed. Sporangium to 5 mm. long. Megaspores averaging ½ mm. in diameter, the ridges on the commissural faces subparallel, on the outer face netted.

RANGE AND HABITAT: From Nf. and subarct. e. Can. to s. Ont. and down to Ct. and e. N.Y.; shores of tidal streams and less often shallowly immersed in ponds.

NOMENCLATURE:

Isòëtes tuckermáni A. Braun, 1867 (GM, BB).

Pitted Quillwort

FEATURES: Similar to *I. tuckermani,* but the thick ridges forming a regular honeycomb-like network on all faces.

RANGE AND HABITAT: Known only in se. N.H. waters.

NOMENCLATURE:

Isòëtes foveolàta A. A. Eaton, 1896 (GM, BB).

Appalachian Quillwort—Engelmann's Quillwort

FEATURES: Leaves numerous, lax. Sporangium *ca.* 1 cm. long. Megaspores averaging ½ mm. in diameter, with thin ridges forming a honeycomb-like network on all faces.

RANGE AND HABITAT: From se. N.H. to e. Mo. and down over our region, and into s. uplands; in varied habitats, ponds, streams, river shores and even muddy ditches.

NOMENCLATURE:

Isòëtes engelmánni A. Braun, 1846 (GM, BB).

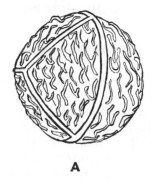

A

B

C

D

FOUR QUILLWORTS

Megaspores of: A. Big-spored. B. Tuckerman's. C. Pitted.
D. Appalachian, *all enlarged.*

Spike-moss Family : *Selaginellàceae*

SPIKE-MOSSES : *SELAGINÉLLA*

The distinctness of this genus was not recognized by Linnaeus, but was pointed out by Palisot de Beauvois in 1805; the name is diminutive of selago, an ancient term for plants of similar aspect. Its members resemble mosses but differ in having a vascular system—their stems and leaves are traversed by long tubular cells. The stems are often supported on "rhizophores," thread-like structures which branch and root at base. Finally, they produce spores of two sexes in separate globular sporangia borne at the base of specialized leaves, the sporophyls, in spike-like cones, to which the vernacular name refers. The basal chromosome number in this genus is 9, the lowest of any of our Pteridophytes.

Northern Spike-moss

FEATURES: Plant a mat-forming perennial, *ca.* 5 to 10 cm. high and broad. Leaves all alike, in multiple spiral rows, *ca.* 2 to 4 mm. long and 1 mm. broad, with sharp tip and sparsely ciliate margins. Sterile branches prostrate, sub-evergreen; fertile ones ascending, deciduous, their leaves grading upward into slightly longer sporophyls, more ciliate and in *ca.* 10 rows. Cone nearly cylindric, but with 4 rounded angles, *ca.* 2 to 4 cm. long. Megaspores—the larger, female ones—yellowish white, with low rounded tubercles on the 3 flat surfaces.

RANGE: From subarct. e. Can. to ne. Man. and down to the St. Lawrence vy. in Que. and along Gr. L. shores n. of lat. 44° to Minn.; also nw. N.A. and Eurasia.

HABITAT: Cold stream and lake shores, springy banks and mossy talus slopes, the soil circumneutral or mildly alkaline, warming up but little even in midsummer.

CULTURE: Of no horticultural interest.

NOMENCLATURE:

Selaginélla selaginoìdes Link, 1841 (GM, BB).
(*Lycopodium selaginoides* L., 1753, basionym).

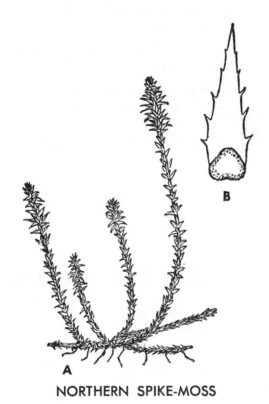

A

B

NORTHERN SPIKE-MOSS

A. *Plant.*   B. *Sporophyl with sporangium, enlarged.*

Rock Spike-moss

FEATURES: Plants small evergreen tufts, *ca.* 3 to 5 cm. high. Leaves narrow, densely crowded in multiple spiral rows, up to 2 mm. long and ½ mm. wide, ciliate, with a firm white terminal bristle. Cones square-prismatic, *ca.* 1 to 2 cm. long, the sporophyls ovate. Megaspores yellowish white, somewhat reticulate.

RANGE: From Que. to Man. and down over our region, rare on Coastal Plain and far westw.; also in s. uplands.

HABITAT: Full sun or rarely part shade, on dry siliceous rocks, coarse gravel, or rarely indurated sand (reports on limestone erroneous), the soil mostly subacid.

CULTURE: Can be grown in a lime-free rock garden.

NOMENCLATURE:

Selaginélla rupéstris Spring, 1838 (GM, BB).
(*Lycopodium rupestre* L., 1753, basionym).

Meadow Spike-moss

FEATURES: Plants forming extensive though short-lived yellow-green mats. Leaves scale-like, in 4 rows, the lateral the larger. Cones *ca.* ½ to 1 cm. long, cylindric and barely angled, the sporophyls like lateral leaves, in 4 rows. Megaspores white, reticulated.

RANGE: S. states and up over our region, rare northw. but reaching s. Me., sw. Que., n. Mich., and w. Ill.

HABITAT: Grassy meadows, muddy stream banks, and damp disturbed areas, the soil circumneutral to subacid.

CULTURE: Of no horticultural merit.

NOMENCLATURE:

Selaginélla àpus Spring, 1840; *apoda* Fernald, 1915 (GM, BB).
(*Lycopodium apodum* L., 1753, basionym).

The Linnaean epithet, signifying without feet, refers to a fancied resemblance to a swallow which roosts with its feet hidden. In the Latin of 1840 this became *apus*.

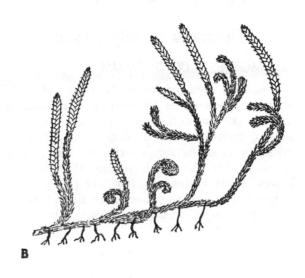

B

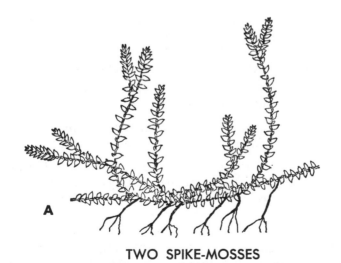

A

TWO SPIKE-MOSSES

Plants of: A. Meadow.   B. Rock.

Clubmoss Family : Lycopodiàceae

CLUBMOSSES : LYCOPÓDIUM

The term used for these plants in the Middle Ages, taken up as a genus name by Linnaeus in 1753, is derived from the Greek for wolf's foot, presumably in that they, like wolves, thrive in barren places. The plants consist of root-stocks or creeping stems with few coarse roots, sending up stems or branches with multiple rows of small scale-like leaves. Their spores, all alike, are produced in rounded sporangia borne near the base of modified leaves—the sporophyls —usually grouped in cylindric cones, rarely in zones on stems.

Crowfoot Clubmoss—Running-pine

FEATURES: Stem long-creeping in thin litter, its evergreen branches *ca.* 15 to 30 cm. high, rebranched in a fan-like pattern to which the epithet refers. Branchlets formed into flat strips *ca.* 1.5 to 2.5 mm. broad by the fused bases of 4 rows of close-set leaves: the top row narrow, appressed, the 2 side broad, spreading, and the bottom with only a tiny tail-like tip free. Annual constrictions in these lacking or obscure. Peduncle *ca.* 5 to 10 cm. long, often forking twice and bearing 4 cones *ca.* 2.5 to 5 cm. long.

RANGE: Common from s. Nf. to se. Minn., down over our region to Va. and e. Mo.; also in s. uplands.

HABITAT: Dry or rarely moist open woods, thickets, and grassy slopes, in mostly subacid humus-rich soil.

CULTURE: Desirable as a ground cover, but not readily transplanted, requiring treatment like cuttings: the air around the trimmed tops kept moist until new roots grow.

NOMENCLATURE:

Lycopòdium flabellifórmè Blanchard, 1911 (GEF).
(*L. complanatum* v. *flabelliforme* Fernald, 1901, basionym, GM, BB).

The question as to whether this taxon should be classed as a species or variety is discussed under the relative treated on the following text page.

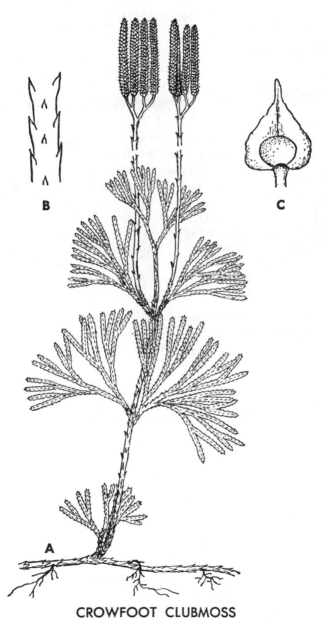

CROWFOOT CLUBMOSS

A. *Plant, reduced.*   B. *Under side of branchlet.*
C. *Sporophyl, enlarged*

Flat-branch Clubmoss

FEATURES: Stem a nongreen rootstock buried in the soil. Evergreen shoots *ca.* 13 to 25 cm. high, rebranched in an irregular, not fan-like, pattern. Branchlets formed into flat strips *ca.* 1.5 to 2 mm. broad by the fused bases of 4 rows of close-set leaves: the top row narrow, appressed, the 2 side broad, spreading, and the bottom with a small triangular free tip. Annual constrictions in these markedly developed and conspicuous. Peduncle *ca.* 3 to 6 cm. long, bearing 1, 2, or rarely more cones *ca.* 1.5 to 2.5 cm. long. From the type variety as above described, var. *canadense* differs in the stem being green and running only through litter (as in *L. flabelliforme*) and the branching somewhat more regular; var. *elongatum,* in the peduncles and cones *ca.* ⅕ longer. Both of these accompany the type and should be classed as forms.

RANGE: From arct. e. Can. down in our region to n. N.E., locally to w. Mass. and ne. Pa., to *ca.* lat. 43° in Mich. and Wisc., and to Man., c. Minn., and ne. Ia.; also in w. N.A. and Eurasia, with varietal representatives in mts. from Mex. to n. S.A.

HABITAT: Dry rocky or sandy barrens, open woods, and bog-margins, in decidedly acid soil which remains cool in summer. Not cultivated.

NOMENCLATURE:

Lycopòdium complanàtum L., 1753 (GM, BB).

MAJOR VARIANTS:

L. complanatum v. *canadense* Marie-Victorin, 1925.
L. complanatum f. *canadense* Porsild, 1935.
L. complanatum v. *elongatum* Marie-Victorin, 1925.

Whether this taxon should be classed as specifically or only varietally distinct from the one treated on the preceding text page is a matter of opinion. The first interpretation is accepted here in view of the rather impressive sum total of their contrasts, which involve stem-depth, branchlet arrangement and constrictions, cone number and size, and range. The second view, which is rather widely favored, is supported merely by the existence of occasional intermediates.

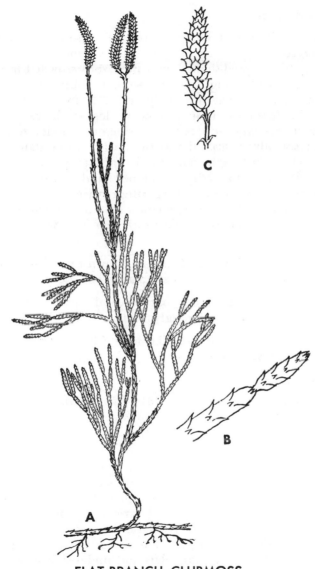

FLAT-BRANCH CLUBMOSS

A. *Plant, reduced.* B. *Under side of branchlet.* C. *Cone.*

Ground-cedar

FEATURES: Rootstock creeping well below soil surface. Shoots evergreen, *ca.* 15 to 30 cm. high, in the open glaucous green and funnel-shaped with numerous crowded branches, in the shade bright green with the branches sprawly. Branchlets formed into strips *ca.* 1.25 to 1.5 mm. broad by the fused bases of 4 rows of close-set leaves: the top row narrow and appressed, the side ones moderately broad and spreading, and the bottom with a subulate tip approaching in length that of adjacent lateral leaves. Annual constrictions markedly developed and conspicuous. Peduncle *ca.* 4.5 to 9 cm. long, often twice forked and bearing 4 short-stalked slender cones *ca.* 1.5 to 3 cm. long; the origin of Pursh's epithet, which signifies 3-spiked, unexplained.

RANGE: From Nf. to n. Minn. and down over our region to se. Va. and s. Ky.; also in s. uplands and Eurasia.

HABITAT: Sandy or rocky barrens and open woods, often coniferous, the soil strongly acid.

CULTURE: Ornamental but like most Clubmosses difficult to transplant successfully.

NOMENCLATURE:

Lycopòdium tristàchyum Pursh, 1814 (GM, BB).
L. chamaecyparissus A. Braun, 1843.

———

While typical forms of this taxon are distinctive enough, seeming intergrades with both *L. complanatum* and *L. flabelliforme* are not infrequent; as these mostly occur where the respective species grow together, their hybrid origin is suspected. Two that have received varietal epithets are:

L. tristachyum v. *habereri* Marie-Victorin, 1925 (*L. habereri* House, 1913, basionym). This is *ca.* twice as tall as the type var., with flatter branchlets and under-side leaves much smaller than the others.

L. t. v. *laurentianum* Marie-Victorin, 1925. Differing from the type in having the rhizome surficial, and the branchlets flatter. Both are designated *L. flabélliformè* × *L. tristàchyum* Marie-Victorin, 1925; their independent name would be *L.* × *hábereri* House, as species, 1913.

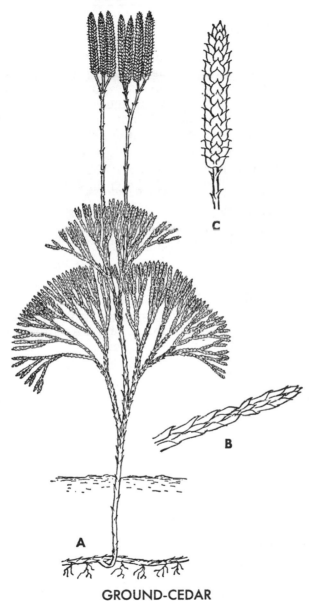

GROUND-CEDAR

A. *Plant, reduced.* B. *Under side of branchlet.* C. *Cone.*

Alpine Clubmoss

FEATURES: Rootstock shallowly creeping. Evergreen erect branches *ca.* 5 to 10 cm. high, repeatedly forked. Leaves in 4 rows, the upper and lateral *ca.* 5 mm. long, half-fused to stem, the upper narrower and more appressed, the lower only half as long, concave but not fused, the branch-outline thus flattish. Cones *ca.* to 2 cm. long.

RANGE: From arct. e. Can., down in our region locally to mid. Que. and n. Mich.; also nw. N.A. and Eurasia.

HABITAT: Cold slopes and acid meadows. Not cultivated.

NOMENCLATURE:

Lycopòdium alpìnum L., 1753 (GM, BB).

Savin-leaf Clubmoss

FEATURES: Like preceding, but *ca.* 13 to 25 cm. high. Leaves in 4 rows, about half-fused to stem, those of the top and bottom rows alike, narrow, appressed, of the lateral rows broader, with incurved tip, the branch-outline thus flat. Cone peduncled, *ca.* 2 to 4 cm. long.

RANGE: Nf. to n. Mich., down to n. N.E. and scattered, c. Mass., s. N.Y., ne. Pa., and w. Md.

HABITAT: Open woods, thickets, and bleak meadows, in cool strongly acid soil. Not cultivated.

NOMENCLATURE:

Lycopòdium sabinaefòlium Willdenow, 1810, GM; *sabinifolium,* (BB).

Sitka Clubmoss

FEATURES: Another similar plant, *ca.* 5 to 10 cm. high. Leaves narrow, in 5 like rows, fused to stem less than half their length, the branch-outline thus cylindric. Cones sessile, *ca.* 1 to 2 cm. long.

RANGE: Nf. to n. Vt. and ne. N.Y.; also nw. N.A.

HABITAT: Open rocky barrens in acid soil. Not cultivated.

NOMENCLATURE:

Lycopòdium sitchénsè Ruprecht, 1845 (BB).
L. *sabinaefolium* v. *sitchense* Fernald, 1923 (GM).

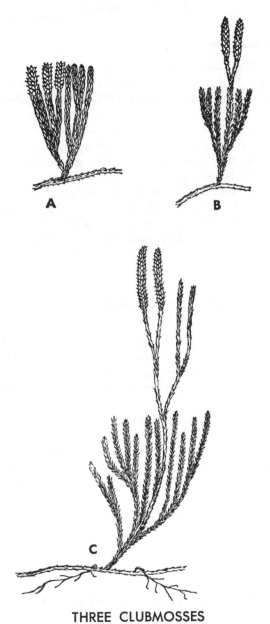

THREE CLUBMOSSES

Plants of: A. Alpine.   B. Sitka.   C. Savin-leaf.

Ground-pine—Tree Clubmoss

FEATURES: Rootstock creeping deep in soil. Evergreen erect stems *ca*. 13 to 25 cm. high, repeatedly branched upward, thus tree-like. Leaves lustrous dark green, on the branches in *ca*. 6 rows, all narrow and with free tip 3 to 5 mm. long. Cones sessile at branch-tips, *ca*. 3 to 5 cm. long. In the type variety the top leaves are appressed and the bottom much shortened too, rendering the branch-outline when viewed end-on flattish; this accordingly merits the colloquial name Flat-branch Ground-pine. In var. *dendroideum* the leaves in all rows are equal in length and spread, so its corresponding name is Round-branch Ground-pine. The latter variety also differs in tending to have slightly narrower leaves and more numerous, longer cones; habitat contrasts are noted below.

RANGE: Nf. to Man., down over our region to se. Va., s. Ky., w. Minn., and e. Ia.; also nw. N.A. and ne. Asia.

HABITAT: Type variety: chiefly in moist or seemingly dry humus-rich woods, less commonly grassy thickets, rocky barrens and bog-margins, its soil mostly subacid and fairly well supplied with nutrients. Var. *dendroideum*: bogs, mossy barrens, wooded rocky slopes, sandy flats, and moist woods in sterile areas, its soil mostly intensely acid and low in nutrients. (The correlation of branch-outline with soil features is interesting to observe; when close attention is paid to such details, the intergradation between the two varieties often alleged to occur will be found to be rare).

CULTURE: The lustrous dark green herbage makes these plants desirable for a woodland garden, but they will not thrive in enriched soil.

NOMENCLATURE:

Lycopòdium obscùrum L., 1753 (GM, BB) = type var.

MAJOR VARIANT:

L. obscùrum v. dendroìdeum D. C. Eaton, 1890 (GM, BB). (*L. dendroideum* Michaux, 1803, basionym).

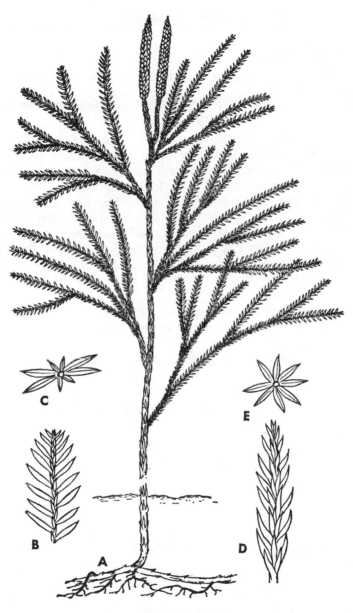

GROUND-PINE

A. *Plant, reduced.   Branchlet-tips of Flat-branch (type)*
variety: B. *Under side.*   C. *End view.*
D. *and* E., *same of Round-branch variety, all enlarged.*

Running Clubmoss

FEATURES: Stem creeping on surface, evergreen, sending up forking branches *ca.* 13 to 25 cm. high. Leaves yellowish green, in *ca.* 10 spiraled rows, linear-subulate, *ca.* 3.5 to 7 mm. long, with a bristle up to 3 mm. long at tip, all alike so that the branch-outline is cylindric. Tip of one or more branchlets sending up a slender leafy peduncle *ca.* 8 to 15 cm. long, simple or forked, bearing one or more slender cones *ca.* 4 to 8 cm. long. Several variants have been assigned epithets in the status of variety; all but one of them—taxon *monostachyon*—appear sporadically in the midst of normal populations and so would better be classed as forms. They are here listed alphabetically, but with the one exception not "accepted"; the mere freaks which have received form epithets are not included.

RANGE: From subarct. e. Can. to sw. Va. and e. Ky., c. Minn. and e. Ia.; also s. uplands, nw. N.A., and Eurasia.

HABITAT: Open woods, grassy thickets, rocky barrens, and bog-margins, in mostly subacid soil.

CULTURE: Would be desirable in an acid soil garden, but not easy to transplant, the plants tending to dry out and die before new roots form.

NOMENCLATURE:

Lycopòdium clavàtum L., 1753 (GM, BB).

v. *integerrimum* Spring, 1842. Leaves lacking a bristle.
v. *laurentianum* Marie-Victorin, 1925. Cones paired, at tip of peduncle-forks.
v. *megastachyon* Fernald & Bissell, 1910. Cone solitary.
One-cone variety, v. *monostachyon* Greville & Hooker, 1831. Peduncle under 2.5 cm. and solitary cone under 4 cm. long. From arct. e. Can. down to mts. of N.H., (also nw. N.A.).
v. *subremotum* Marie-Victorin, 1925. Peduncle multiply forked, with up to 6 cones.
v. *tristachyum* Hooker, 1840. Cones 3, at peduncle-tip.

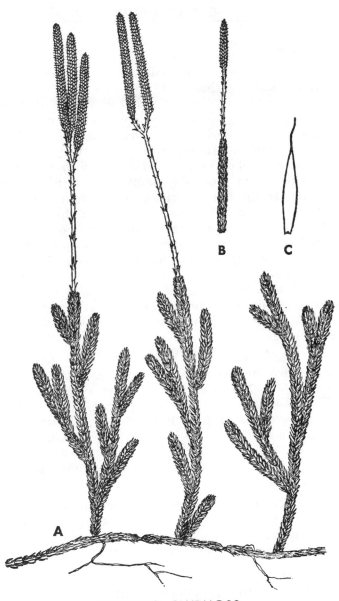

RUNNING CLUBMOSS

A. *Plant, reduced.*   B. *Stem-tip of One-cone variety.*
C. *Leaf, enlarged.*

Stiff Club-moss

FEATURES: Stem creeping on soil surface, sending up simple or few-forked branches *ca.* 13 to 25 cm. high, tipped with buds which winter over and renew growth another season, resulting in annual constrictions which suggested the epithet. Leaves dark green, evergreen, firm and sharp-pointed, uniform. In the type variety they spread horizontally and reflex in age, and are *ca.* 6 to 10 mm. long, and widest at or above the middle, with manifestly serrate margins. In the Entire variety, var. *acrifolium,* they differ in being widest below the middle with the margins obscurely serrate (or practically entire). The other two varieties have ascending or appressed leaves only 3 to 6 mm. long. In var. *alpestre* the leaves are about 1 mm. wide, flat, and somewhat serrate, in the Least variety, var. *pungens,* ½ mm. wide, concave, and essentially entire. (Intergradations are so frequent that these taxa might better be classed as forms.) Cones in all variants sessile, *ca.* 2 to 4 cm. long.

RANGE: From arct. e. Can. down to w. N.E., northernmost N.J., down the mts. to sw. Va., and se. Mich. to c. Minn.; also in nw. N.A. and Eurasia. The type var. and var. *acrifolium* have essentially the same range (although the latter seems absent from Europe). Var. *alpestre* is chiefly arctic, known in our region only down to n. N.H. Var. *pungens* in full development extends down to about lat. 43°, but in intermediate forms also along the Appalachians to W. Va.

HABITAT: Coniferous and less often deciduous woods, rocky barrens, and bog-margins, in sterile, strongly acid soil. The reduced varieties are found mostly on mossy ledges and bleak mountain slopes. Not cultivated.

NOMENCLATURE:

Lycopòdium annótinum L., 1753 (GM, BB).

MAJOR VARIANTS:

L. annótinum v. *acrifòlium* Fernald, 1915 (GM, BB).
L. annótinum v. *alpéstrè* Hartman, 1833 (GM).
L. annótinum v. *púngens* Desvaux, 1827 (GM, BB).
L. annotinum f. *pungens* Porsild, 1912.

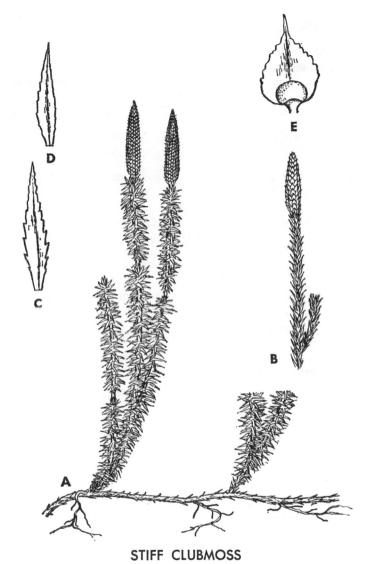

STIFF CLUBMOSS

A. *Plant, reduced.*   B. *Shoot-tip of Least variety.*
Leaves of: C. *Type variety and*   D. *Entire variety, enlarged.*
E. *Sporophyl, enlarged.*

Slender Clubmoss—Carolina Clubmoss

FEATURES: Stem short, prostrate, deciduous except for a small evergreen bud. Lateral leaves broadish, falcate, upcurved; 4 upper rows narrower, erect. Fertile branches few, *ca.* 6 to 12 cm. high, their leaves tiny and scattered. Cone slender, yellowish, *ca.* 2 to 4 cm. long (larger in the south).

RANGE: S. lowlands and toward the Atlantic coast, Va. to L.I. Related taxa occur nearly throughout the world.

HABITAT: Wet sandy flats and sphagnous meadows, the soil intensely acid. Not cultivated.

NOMENCLATURE:

Lycopòdium caroliniànum L., 1753.

Southern Clubmoss—Chapman's Clubmoss

FEATURES: Stem elongate, prostrate, deciduous except for evergreen buds. Leaves in many rows, uniform except that those under stem bend upward, coarse-ciliate. Fertile branches multiple, *ca.* 13 to 25 cm. high, well-covered by ascending leaves. Cone *ca.* 3 to 6 cm. long, slender, the sporophyls appressed, few-toothed below.

RANGE: S. states, and up over our region in coastal lowlands to Nf.

HABITAT: Sphagnum bogs, meadows, and wet sand barrens, in intensely acid soil. Not cultivated.

NOMENCLATURE:

Lycopòdium appréssum Lloyd & Underwood, 1900 *"adpressum."* (*L. inundatum* v. *appressum* Chapman, 1878, basionym). *L. inundatum* [v.] β *bigelovii* Tuckerman, 1843 (GM, BB). *L. chapmani* Underwood, 1901.

Whether this taxon should be classed as a species or a mere variety is a matter of opinion. The former interpretation is adopted here, since it is reasonably distinct in morphology from its relative *L. inundatum* (type); intergradation between them seems less frequent than implied in the literature, and in particular they are ecologically contrasted, being warm- and cold-climate plants, respectively.

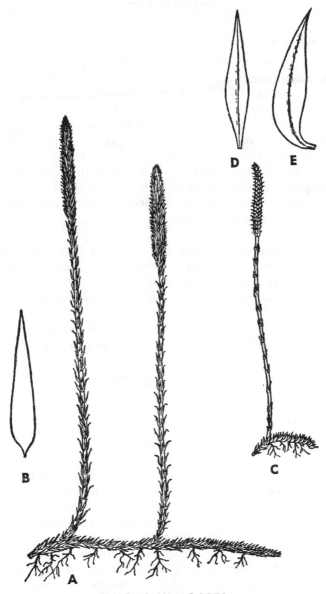

TWO CLUBMOSSES

Southern: A. *Plant.*   B. *Leaf, enlarged.*
Slender: C. *Plant.*   D. *Top leaf and*   E. *Side leaf of stem.*

Bog Clubmoss

FEATURES: Stem short or moderately elongate, but rarely extending more than a few cm. beyond the youngest fertile branch, deciduous but with an evergreen bud at tip, rooting throughout. Leaves in *ca.* 8 rows, the under ones twisted upward, entire or nearly so. Fertile branches very few, mostly only 1 or 2, their height in average colonies *ca.* 3.5 to 7 cm. (both dwarf and giant forms also occurring), their leaves spreading. Cone *ca.* 2 to 4 cm. long, the sporophyls green, abruptly widened toward base, with a single pair of teeth. When flooded, the stems and branches develop in bizarre patterns.

RANGE: Wholly unlike that of our other bog Clubmosses: from subarct. e. Can. and down in our region to a line from n. N.J. to ne. Ill., rare and scattered further s., though extending down the mts. to sw. Va.; also Eurasia.

HABITAT: Sphagnum bogs, shores of ponds and spring runs, and sterile clayey meadows, the soil intensely acid.

CULTURE: Possible in a cold bog garden.

NOMENCLATURE:

Lycopòdium inundàtum L., 1753 (GM, BB).

Traditionally this is a highly variable taxon, but it is so only to workers who are impressed by occasional seeming intergradation toward it exhibited by taxa of normally decidedly distinctive characters and ranges. Correspondingly, all other bog-dwelling Clubmosses of our region (except *L. carolinianum,* which is so manifestly unrelated) have at one time or another been classed as "varieties" of it, and some are still so maintained in reference works. The unravelling of the real relationships in this "difficult" group is a problem greatly needing attack by combined morphological, physiological, and cytological studies.

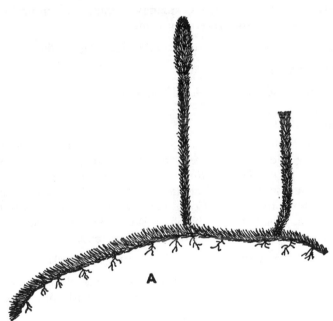

BOG CLUBMOSS

A. Plant.   B. Sporophyl, enlarged

Foxtail Clubmoss

FEATURES: Stem elongate, rooting at few points, between which it arches, deciduous except for evergreen buds. Leaves in many rows, the lower twisting upward, *ca.* 6 mm. long, with conspicuous marginal teeth. Fertile branches up to 20 cm. high, of stout aspect owing to the numerous spreading leaves *ca.* 1 cm. long. Cone *ca.* 3 to 5 cm. long and 1.5 cm. thick, the sporophyls narrow-'.ased, widely spreading, copiously ciliate.

RANGE: Gulf states and up in our region on Atlantic lowlands to Ct.; also tropical S.A.

HABITAT: Sphagnum bogs, springy slopes, and moist sandy pineland, the soil intensely acid.

CULTURE: Worth trying in a really acid bog garden.

NOMENCLATURE:

Lycopòdium alopecuroìdes L., 1753 (GM, BB).

Meadow Clubmoss

FEATURES: Stem elongate, rooting throughout and scarcely arching, deciduous except for a terminal evergreen bud. Leaves in *ca.* 8 rows, the lower twisted upward, *ca.* 7 mm. long, sparsely ciliate. Fertile branches *ca.* 10 to 20 cm. high, not stout in aspect. Cone *ca.* 3 to 6 cm. long and 6 to 12 mm. thick, the sporophyls somewhat widened at base and entire or few-toothed, spreading or ascending.

RANGE: Rare, Gulf states, and Atlantic lowlands to Mass.

HABITAT: Clayey or sandy meadows or less often sphagnum bogs, in moist strongly to moderately acid soil. Not cultivated.

NOMENCLATURE:

Lycopòdium inundàtum L., 1753, v. *elongàtum* Chapman, 1878 (BB).
L. alopecuroides v. *elongatum* Chapman, 1897.
L. inundatum v. *robustum* R. J. Eaton, 1931 (GM).

This little-known taxon grades into all of the other bog Clubmosses (except *L. carolinianum*). Whether it should indeed be classed as a variety or a species needs further study.

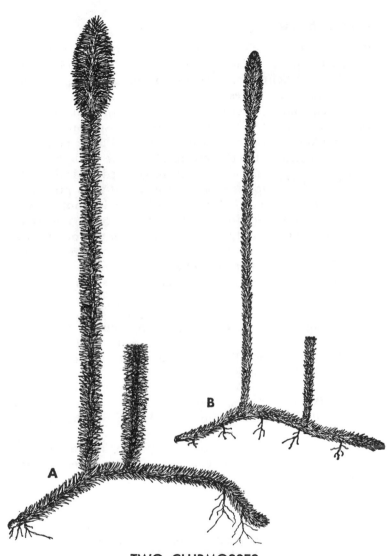

TWO CLUBMOSSES

Foxtail: A. *Plant, reduced.*
Meadow: B. *Plant, reduced.*

Shining Clubmoss

FEATURES: Stem-base creeping and rooting, holding persistent
withered leaves; upcurving stem forking several times,
reaching a height of *ca.* 13 to 25 cm., bearing crowded
shiny dark green leaves which remain evergreen for more
than one season. Leaves in *ca.* 6 rows, grouped in successive
zones of longer sterile ones and shorter sporophyls, producing a knobby aspect. Sterile leaves *ca.* 6 to 12 mm. long,
broadened and distinctly serrate above the middle, sporophyls *ca.* 4 to 8 mm. long, little broadened and obscurely
serrate to entire upward. Some upper leaf-axils producing
small two-lobed buds, which fall off and in contact with
moist humus sprout into new plants; though sometimes
mistaken for gametophytes, these have no sex organs and
constitute only vegetative reproductive-structures. Woodland *Lycopodium* gametophytes are subterranean, and,
contrary to the statements in some books, as large as peas
or even small grapes.

RANGE: From subarct. e. Can. down over our region, as far
w. as ne. Minn., c. Ia., and s. Ky.; also in s. uplands and
ne. Asia, though not Europe. Intermediates with the two
following taxa become frequent westw.

HABITAT: Wooded slopes, flats, stream banks, and swamp-
margins, the soil rich in humus and usually subacid.

CULTURE: Desirable for a woodland garden, the shiny evergreen foliage clothing the curiously knobby stems yielding
a striking effect.

NOMENCLATURE:

Lycopòdium lucídulum Michaux, 1803 (GM, BB).
Urostachys lucidulus Herter, 1909.

This and the two following taxa represent the most primitive division of the genus, in that their sporophyls are borne
in zones on leafy stems instead of in differentiated cones.
Some workers indeed regard them as constituting a distinct
genus, *Urostachys* Herter, 1909 (from Greek for tail spike,
first applied to a subgenus by Pritzel, 1900).

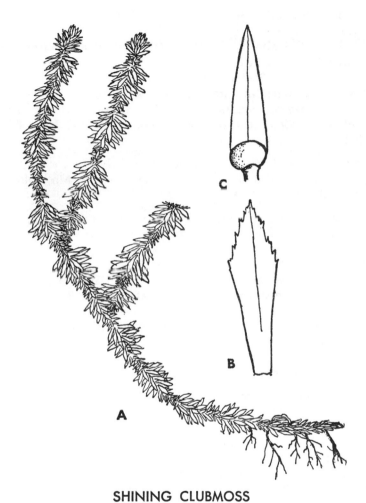

SHINING CLUBMOSS

A. *Plant, reduced.*   B. *Leaf and*   C. *Sporophyl, enlarged.*

Rock Clubmoss

FEATURES: Stem-base short-creeping and rooting, holding persistent withered leaves; upcurving stem forking at base and sparsely above, yielding tufts or, when on cliffs, festoons. Stem-length *ca.* 8 to 15 cm.; leaves bright green, not notably shiny. Sterile leaves *ca.* 5 to 9 and sporophyls 4 to 7 mm. long, the stem outline knobby. All leaves flat and somewhat narrowed at base, tending to taper from below middle, entire or only obscurely serrate. Buds with 2 longish lobes.

RANGE: Incompletely known, but seemingly from s. Ont. to ne. Minn., down to ne. Pa., c. Ky., and e. Mo.; also s. uplands and w. N.A.

HABITAT: Crevices in cliffs, rock ledges, and talus slopes, the soil subacid to neutral. Not cultivated.

NOMENCLATURE:

Lycopòdium poróphilum Lloyd & Underwood, 1900 (GM).
Urostachys lucidulus v. *porophyllus* Herter, 1909 (misprint).
L. lucidulum v. *occidentale* L. R. Wilson, 1932.
(*L. lucidulum* f. *occidentale* Clute, 1903, basionym).
L. × *buttersii* = *L. lucidulum* × *L. selago* v. *patens* Abbe, 1953.
L. selago v. *patens* Desvaux, 1827 (BB); = next species.

The problems as to the interpretation and the nomenclature of this taxon are highly complex, and further studies of them are needed. For many years it was supposed to be what had been named in Europe *L. selago* v. *patens,* but the only feature it has in common with that is the spreading ("patent") leaves. The Rock Clubmoss was named in species status in 1900, (the often misunderstood epithet coming from Greek for cavity-loving) and is so treated here, although the extent to which it seems to intergrade with the preceding taxon could well be regarded as justification for classifying it as a mere variety. Since it shows some approach to the following taxon as well, it might represent a hybrid between them; however, the chromosomes of all three are minute, numerous, and anomalous in behavior, so cannot be used to reach any conclusion. These spikeless Clubmosses may indeed all be descended from hybrids.

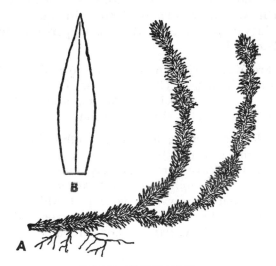

ROCK CLUBMOSS
A. *Plant, reduced.* B. *Leaf, enlarged.*

Mountain Clubmoss—Fir Clubmoss

FEATURES: Stem forking from base, in the type var. and var. *appressum* forming dense tufts, covered by dark green leaves which remain evergreen for more than one season. Height varying from *ca.* 5 to 10 cm. in the Appressed variety, var. *appressum,* to 15 to 30 cm. in the Spreading variety, var. *patens;* leaf-length uniform, so that the shoot outline is smoothly cylindric. Leaves swollen and concave at base, tapering upward, entire or obscurely toothed; length in var. *appressum ca.* 3 to 6, in the type var. 4 to 8 and in var. *patens* 5 to 10 mm. Upper axils producing small 2-lobed buds.

RANGE: From arct. e. Can. down at low alt. to Me. and increasingly higher to Ct., e. Pa., sw. Va. (and in highest s. mts.), w. to n. Mich., e. Minn., and c. Wisc.; also Eurasia, with vars. in the s. hemisphere.

HABITAT: Rocky barrens, ledges, and talus slopes, and bog margins, the soil mostly intensely acid. In the bleaker situations the leaves are relatively short and appressed, constituting var. *appressum.* In less severe environments the intermediate type var. is developed, while in relatively mild climates the stems tend to elongate and leaves to spread, resulting in v. *patens.* Not cultivated.

NOMENCLATURE:

Lycopòdium selàgo L., 1753 (GM, BB).
Urostachys selago Herter, 1909.

MAJOR VARIANTS:

L. selàgo v. *appréssum* Desvaux, 1827 (GM).
L. selàgo v. *pàtens* Desvaux, 1827 (GM).
(*Plananthus = Lycopodium patens* Palisot de Beauvois, 1805, basionym).

As pointed out by Bower in his *Origin of a Land Flora* (1908), the lack of differentiation between leaves and sporophyls marks this as the most primitive living vascular plant; his frontispiece represents the variant with spreading leaves. The epithet *patens* was based on Plate 56, Fig. 1 E in Dillenius' *Historia Muscorum* of 1741, which shows uniform leaves and so is erroneously applied to taxon *porophilum.*

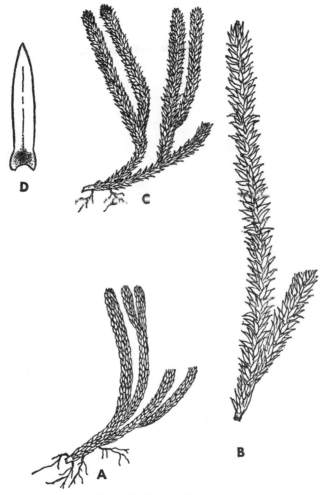

MOUNTAIN CLUBMOSS

Plants of varieties: A. *Appressed-leaf.* B. *Spreading-leaf.*
C. *Type.* D. *Leaf, enlarged.*

INDEXES

AUTHORS OF FERN NAMES

(The numerals following classifications indicate taxa named)

Abbe, Ernst C., 1905–   ; American taxonomist (1)
Adanson, Michel, 1727–1806; French taxonomist (1)
Aiton, William, 1731–1793; British taxonomist (1)
Alston, Arthur H. G., 1902–1958; British pteridologist (1)
Ångström, Johan, 1813–1879; Swedish taxonomist (2)
Ascherson, Paul F. A., 1834–1913; German taxonomist (1)

Bartholomew, Elizabeth A., 1912–   ; American taxonomist (1)
Benedict, Ralph C., 1883–   ; American pteridologist (4)
Bernhardi, Johann J., 1774–1850; German taxonomist (7)
Bissell, Charles H., 1857–1925; American taxonomist (1)
Blake, Sidney F., 1892–1959; American taxonomist (1)
Blanchard, William H., 1850–1922; American taxonomist (1)
Blasdell, Robert F., 1929–   ; American taxonomist (1)
Bolton, James, 17..–1799; British taxonomist (1)
Bongard, A. G. Heinrich, 1786–1839; Russian taxonomist (1)
Bory de St. Vincent, J. . . . , 1778–1846; French naturalist (3)
Brackenridge, William D., 1810–1893; American taxonomist (1)
Braun, Alexander C. H., 1805–1877; German taxonomist (10)
Braun, E. Lucy, 1889–   ; American taxonomist (2)
Britton, E. G. (Mrs. N. L.), 1858–1934; American taxonomist (1)
Broun, Maurice, 1906–   ; American naturalist (4)
Brown, Robert, 1773–1858; British taxonomist (6)
Buckley, Samuel B., 1809–1884; American taxonomist (1)
Butters, Frederick K., 1878–1945; American taxonomist (8)

Chapman, Alvan W., 1809–1899; American taxonomist (3)
Ching, Ren-Chang, 1899–   ; Chinese pteridologist (1)
Christ, K. Hermann H., 1833–1933; Swiss pteridologist (1)
Christensen, Carl F. A., 1872–1942; Danish pteridologist (5)

293

Clarke, Charles B., 1832–1906; British taxonomist (1)
Clarkson, Edward H., 1866–1934; American naturalist (1)
Clausen, Robert T., 1911–   ; American taxonomist (3)
Clute, Willard N., 1869–1950; American pteridologist (16)
Copeland, Edwin B., 1873–   ; American pteridologist (2)
Crane, F. W. (Mrs. C. W.), 1906–   ; American pteridologist (1)

Davenport, George E., 1833–1907; American pteridologist (7)
Desvaux, A. Niçaise, 1784–1856; French taxonomist (5)
Dodge, Raynal, 1844–1918; American pteridologist (1)
Dole, Eleazer J., 1888–   ; American taxonomist (1)
Döll, Johann C., 1808–1885; German taxonomist (1)
Dowell, Philip, 1864–1936; American pteridologist (6)
Druce, George C., 1850–1932; British taxonomist (1)
Durieu de Maisonneuve, M. C., 1797–1878; French pteridologist (5)

Eaton, Alvah A., 1865–1908; American pteridologist (9)
Eaton, Amos, 1776–1842; American taxonomist (2)
Eaton, Daniel C., 1834–1895; American pteridologist (10)
Eaton, Richard J., 1890–   ; American taxonomist (1)
Ehrhart, Friedrich, 1742–1795; German taxonomist (1)
Engelmann, George, 1809–1884; American taxonomist (8)

Farwell, Oliver A., 1867–1944; American taxonomist (11)
Fée, Antoine L. A., 1789–1874; French pteridologist (6)
Fernald, Merritt L., 1873–1950; American taxonomist (24)
Fiori, Adriano, 1865–   ; Italian taxonomist (1)
Fischer, Friedrich E. L., 1782–1854; Russian taxonomist (1)
Fournier, Eugène P. N., 1834–1884; French taxonomist (1)

Galeotti, Henri G., 1814–1858; Belgian taxonomist (1)
Gay, Jacques E., 1786–1864; Swiss taxonomist (1)
Gilbert, Benjamin D., 1835–1907; American pteridologist (9)
Gmelin, Johann G., 1709–1755; German taxonomist (1)
Gmelin, Samuel G., 1745–1774; Russian taxonomist (3)
Gray, Asa, 1810–1888; American taxonomist (11)
Gray, Frederick W., 1878–1960; American naturalist (2)
Gray, Samuel F., 1766–1828; British taxonomist (1)
Greville, Robert K., 1794–1866; British taxonomist (2)
Hahne, . . . ,   –   ; German taxonomist (1)

Hartman, Carl J., 1790–1849; Swedish taxonomist (1)
Hauke, Richard L., 1930–   ; American botanist (1)
Heller, A. Arthur, 1867–1944; American taxonomist (1)
Herter, Wilhelm G., 1884–1958; German-S. Amer. taxonomist (4)
Hieronymus, Georg H. E. W., 1846–1921; German taxonomist (1)
Hill, John, 1716–1775; British taxonomist (1)
Hitchcock, Edward, 1793–1864; American naturalist (1)
Hoffmann, Georg F., 1761–1826; German taxonomist (3)
Hoffmann, Ralph, 1870–1932; American taxonomist (1)
Hooker, (Sir) William J., 1785–1865; British taxonomist (5)
Hopkins, Lewis S., 1872–   ; American naturalist (1)
Hoppe, David H., 1760–1846; German taxonomist (1)
House, Homer D., 1878–1949; American taxonomist (3)
Howe, Elliot C., 1828–1899; American taxonomist (1)
Hudson, William, 1730–1793; British taxonomist (1)

Jacquin, Nikolaus J. von, 1727–1817; Austrian taxonomist (1)

Kaulfuss, Georg F., 1786–1830; German pteridologist (1)
Komarov, Nikolai F., 1901–1942; Russian taxonomist (2)
Kühlewein, Paul E., 1798–1870; German taxonomist (1)
Kuhn, Maximilian F. A., 1842–1894; German taxonomist (1)
Kunze, Gustav, 1793–1851; German pteridologist (4)

Lamarck, J. B. . . . de, 1744–1829; French naturalist (2)
Lawson, George, 1827–1895; Canadian naturalist (4)
Link, Johann H. F., 1767–1851; German taxonomist (6)
Linnaeus, Carl, 1707–1778; Swedish taxonomist (68)
Lloyd, Francis E., 1868–1947; Canadian taxonomist (2)
Löve, Askell, 1916–   ; Canadian taxonomist (1)
Ludwig, Christian G., 1709–1773; German taxonomist (1)

McCoy, Thomas N., 1908–   ; American pteridologist (1)
Mackenzie, Kenneth K., 1877–1934; American taxonomist (1)
Marie-Victorin, Frère, 1885–1944; Canadian taxonomist (9)
Martens, Martin, 1797–1863; Belgian taxonomist (1)
Masamune, Genkei, 1899–   ; Japanese botanist (1)
Maxon, William R., 1877–1948; American pteridologist (7)
Mertens, Franz C., 1764–1831; German taxonomist (1)
Mettenius, Georg H., 1823–1866; German taxonomist (2)

Michaux, André, 1746–1802; French-American taxonomist
   (15)
Milde, Carl A. J., 1824–1871; German pteridologist (2)
Moore, Albert H., 1883–   ; American taxonomist (1)
Moore, Thomas, 1821–1887; British pteridologist (3)
Morton, Conrad V., 1905–   ; American pteridologist (9)
Muhlenberg, G. Henry E., 1753–1815; American taxonomist
   (4)
Müller, Otto F., 1730–1784; Danish taxonomist (1)

Nakai, Takenoshi, 1882–1952; Japanese taxonomist (1)
Newman, Edward, 1801–1876; British pteridologist (4)
Nieuwland, Julius A. A., 1878–1936; American taxonomist (3)
Nishida, Tôji, 1874–1927; Japanese taxonomist (1)
Nuttall, Thomas, 1786–1859; American taxonomist (1)

Oakes, William, 1799–1848; American taxonomist (1)

Palisot de Beauvois, Ambroise . . ., 1752–1820; French pteri-
   dologist (2)
Palmer, William, 1856–1921; American naturalist (1)
Pease, Arthur S., 1881–   ; American naturalist (1)
Pfeiffer, Norma E., 1889–   ; American botanist (1)
Porsild, Alf E., 1901–   ; Canadian taxonomist (3)
Poyser, William A., 1882–1928; American naturalist (1)
Prantl, Karl A. E., 1849–1893; German taxonomist (3)
Presl, Karel B., 1794–1852; Austrian pteridologist (8)
Proctor, George R., 1920–   ; American pteridologist (2)
Pursh, Frederick T., 1774–1820; American taxonomist (3)

Rafinesque, Constantine S., 1783–1840; Naturalist (2)
Raymond, L. F. Marcel, 1915–   ; Canadian taxonomist (1)
Reed, Clyde F., 1918–   ; American naturalist (1)
Robinson, Benjamin L., 1864–1935; American taxonomist (3)
Robinson, John, 1846–1925; American naturalist (1)
Roth, Albrecht W., 1757–1834; German pteridologist (4)
Rugg, Harold G., 1883–1957; American pteridologist (1)
Ruprecht, Franz J., 1814–1870; Russian taxonomist (6)
Rylands, Thomas G., 1818–1900; British taxonomist (1)

Schaffner, John H., 1866–1939; American taxonomist (2)

Schkuhr, Christian, 1741–1811; German taxonomist (1)
Schleicher, Johann C., 1768–1834; Swiss taxonomist (1)
Schmidel, Casimir C., 1718–1792; German taxonomist (1)
Schott, Heinrich W., 1794–1865; Austrian pteridologist (5)
Scott, Robert R., 1827–1877; American naturalist (1)
Shaver, Jesse M., 1888–   ; American pteridologist (1)
Sim, Robert, 1828–1882; British botanist (1)
Slosson, Margaret, 1874–   ; American pteridologist (6)
Small, John K., 1869–1938; American taxonomist (6)
Smith, Dale M., 1928–   ; American taxonomist (1)
Smith, (Sir) James E., 1759–1828; British taxonomist (4)
Spenner, Fridolin C. L., 1798–1841; German taxonomist (1)
Sprengel, Curt P. J., 1766–1833; German taxonomist (5)
Spring, Anton F., 1814–1872; Belgian taxonomist (3)
Sturm, Johann W., 1808–1865; German taxonomist (1)
Swartz, Olof P., 1760–1818; Swedish pteridologist (16)
Syme, —,   –   ; British botanist (2)
Taylor, Thomas M. C., 1904–   ; Canadian taxonomist (3)
Thunberg, Carl P., 1743–1828; Swedish taxonomist (1)
Tidestrom, Ivar, 1864–1956; American taxonomist (2)
Todaro, Agostino, 1818–1892; Italian naturalist (1)
Torrey, John, 1796–1873; American taxonomist (1)
Trudell, Harry W., 1884–   ; American naturalist (1)
Tryon, Rolla M., 1916–   ; American pteridologist (7)
Tuckerman, Edward, 1817–1886; American naturalist (1)

Underwood, Lucien M., 1853–1907; American pteridologist
     (10)

Wagner, Warren H., Jr., 1920–   ; American pteridologist
     (1)
Waters, Campbell E., 1872–1955; American pteridologist (2)
Watt, David A. P., 1830–1917; Canadian pteridologist (3)
Weatherby, Charles A., 1875–1949; American pteridologist
     (7)
Wherry, Edgar T., 1885–   ; American naturalist (26)
Willdenow, Karl L., 1765–1812; German taxonomist (7)
Wilson, Leonard R., 1906–   ; American botanist (1)
Winslow, Evelyn James, 1870–   ; American botanist (1)
Wood, Alphonso, 1810–1881; American taxonomist (1)
Woynar, Heinrich, 1865–1917; Austrian taxonomist (1)

The biographical data for less well-known authors were obtained from the card file of botanists begun by the late John H. Barnhart, and maintained by his successor, Harold W. Rickett, in the library of the New York Botanical Garden. Should any reader of this *Guide* have information as to dates of birth or death of individuals for whom this information seems to be lacking, or detect any errors in the above list, it will be appreciated if they call attention to them.

SIGNIFICANCE OF EPITHETS
OF SPECIES AND LESSER TAXA

abbeae: in honor of Mrs. Ernst C. Abbe, 96

acrifolium: sharp-leaved, 276

acrostichoides: resembling an *Acrostichum,* 100, 138, 180

aculeatum: prickly, 102

acuminatum: tapering to a point, 60

adpressum: turned toward a support, 278

affine: related to, 250

alabamense (-is) : of Alabama, 186, 226

aleuticum: of the Aleutian Islands, 176

alopecuroides: resembling an *Alopecurus* (Foxtail Grass) , 282

alpestre (-is) : of high mountains, 134, 276

alpina (-um) : of the Alps, 88, 270

americana (um) : of America, 118, 134, 170, 242

anadenium: lacking glands, 118

angustifolia (-um) : narrow-leaved, 136, 146

angustisegmentum: narrow-segmented, 218

angustum: narrow, 142

annotinum: yearly, 276

apoda (-um) : without a foot, 262

appalachiana: of the Appalachians, 94

appressum: pressed against a support, 278, 290

apus: without a foot, 262

aquilina (-um) : like an eagle, 172

arenarium: of sand, 210

areolata (-um) : having areoles, 146

arvense: of fields, 234

asplenioides: resembling an *Asplenium,* 144

atropalustris: of a dark swamp, 124

atropurpurea: dark purple, 182, 184

australe: southern, 222

austriaca: of Austria, 118 (120, 122)

bacculum-rubrum: of Baton Rouge, 158

bellii: in honor of John Bell, 88

benedictii: in honor of R. C. Benedict, 130
bigelovii: in honor of Jacob Bigelow, 278
bipinnatifidum: twice pinnately cut, 60, 116
boottii: in honor of William Boott, 128
boreale: northern, 234
boschianum: in honor of R. B. van den Bosch, 198
bradleyi: in honor of F. H. Bradley, 156
braunii: in honor of Alexander Braun, 98, 236, 252
bulbifera: bearing bulbs, 82
bushii: in honor of B. F. Bush, 182
butleri: in honor of G. D. Butler, 254
buttersii: in honor of F. K. Butters, 286

cambricoides: resembling taxon *cambricum,* 80
campyloptera (-um) : bent-winged, 118
canadense (-is) : of Canada, 266
capillus-veneris: like Venus' hair, 174
caroliniana (-um) : of Carolina, 206, 278
cathcartiana: in honor of Ellen Cathcart, 92
celsa: held high, 110
chapmani: in honor of A. W. Chapman, 278
cinnamomea: like cinnamon, 200
clavatum: club-shaped, 274
claytoniana: in honor of John Clayton, 202
clermontae: in honor of Miss Clermont, 164
clintoniana (-um) : in honor of G. W. Clinton, 108
complanatum: flattened, 266
compositum: compound, 216
confusa (-um) : confusing, 96, 230, 232
connectile (-is) : joined together, 68
cornucopiaefolia: with cornucopia-like leaves, 200
crispa (-um) : curled, 100, 180
cristata (-um) : crested, 106
cryptolepis: with hidden scales, 154
cyclosorum: with round sori, 140

dealbata: whitened, 178
deltoideum: triangular, 60
dendroideum: tree-like, 272
densa (-um) : compact, 188
diaphanum: translucent, 84
dickieana: in honor of a Mr. Dickie, 86

dilatata (-um) : expanded, 118
disjuncta (-um) : disconnected, 64
dissectum: dissected, 226, 228, 230, 232
dowellii: in honor of Philip Dowell, 128
dryopteris: an oak fern, 64

eatonii: in honor of A. A. Eaton, 256
ebeneum: like ebony, 158
ebenoides: resembling taxon *ebeneum*, 166
echinospora: prickly-spored, 252
elatius, elatum: tall, 142, 250
elegans: elegant, 116
ellipticum: elliptical, 144
elongatum: elongate, 266, 282
engelmanni: in honor of George Engelmann, 208, 258
europaeum: of Europe, 220

féei: in honor of A. L. A. Fée, 186
fernaldiana: in honor of M. L. Fernald, 170
ferrissii: in honor of J. H. Ferriss, 248
filix-femina: a female fern, 140, 144
filix-mas: a male fern, 114
flabelliforme: fan-shaped, 264
fluviatile: of streams, 240
foveolata: pitted, 258
fragile (-is) : brittle, 84
fragrans: fragrant, 104
fructuosa (-um) : fruitful, 130

gaspense: of the Gaspé region, Que., 134
germanica: of Germany, 78
glabella: smoothish, 90, 182
glandulosa: glandular, 200
goldiana (-um) : in honor of John Goldie, 112
gracile (-is) : slender, 90, 216
gravesii: in honor of C. B. Graves, 100; E. W., 156

habereri: in honor of J. V. Haberer, 268
haleana: in honor of Josiah Hale, 74
hexagonoptera: with hexagonal wings, 66
hiemale: variant spelling of hyemale, 250
hortonae: in honor of Frances B. Horton, 158

hyemale (Linnaeus' spelling) : of winter, 248, 250
hyperborea: far northern, 84

ilvense (-is) : of Elba, 90
inexpectatus (-um) : unexpected, 166
incisum: sharply cut, 100, 158
integerrimum: entire, 274
intermedia (-um) : 122, 222, 248
inundatum: covered by water, 278, 280

jesupi: in honor of H. G. Jesup, 246

kansanum: of Kansas, 248
kentuckyense: of Kentucky, 164

laciniatum: slashed, 176
laevigatum: smoothed, 248
lanceolatocristata (-um) : like t. *cristata* but lanceolate, 120
lanceolatum: lanceolate, 218
lanosa (-um) : woolly, 188, 190
latiuscula (-um) : broadish, 172
laurentiana (-um) : of the St. Lawrence region, 84, 268, 274
laxifolium: weak-leaved, 212
leedsii: in honor of A. N. Leeds, 130
limosum: of mud, 240
linnaeana (-um) : in honor of Linnaeus, 64, 240
litorale: of shores, 240
lonchitis: (ancient name for) a narrow-leaved plant, 102
lucidulum: somewhat shiny, 284, 286
lunaria: moon-like, 214

mackayi: in honor of A. H. Mackay, 84
macrospora: large-spored, 258
marginale (-is) : marginal, 116
matricariaefolium: with leaf like a *Matricaria*, 216
maxonii: in honor of W. R. Maxon, 96
megastachyon: giant-spiked, 274
melanocaulon: black-stemmed, 162
melanopoda: black-footed, 254
mexicana: of Mexico, 206
michauxianum (-ii) : in honor of André Michaux, 58, 142
minganense: of the Mingan islands, 214

mohrioides: resembling a *Mohria*, 102
montana (-um) : of mountains, 80, 152, 164
mucronata: abruptly pointed, 206
multifidum: much-divided, 100, 222, 226
multiramosum: much-branched, 238
muricata: with sharp projections, 252

neglectum: overlooked, 216
nelsoni: in honor of N. L. T. Nelson, 246
nodulosa: lumpy, 78
noveboracense (-is) : of New York, 70

obliquum: oblique, 226, 228, 230, 232
obscurum: hidden, 272
obtusa (-um) : blunt, 96
obtusilobata: blunt-lobed, 76
occidentale: western, 286
ohionis: of Ohio, 154
oneidense: of Oneida Co., New York, 226
onondagense: of Onondaga Co., New York, 214
oregana: of Oregon, 92

palmatum: palm-shaped, 196
palmeri: in honor of T. C. Palmer, 256
palustre (-is) : of marshes, 74, 242
parvulum: smallish, 160
patens: spreading, 286, 288
pauciramosum: few-branched, 238
pedatum: decreasing outward, like the toes, 176
pensylvanicum (old spelling) : of Pennsylvania, 78
phegopteris: a beech fern, 68
pinnatifidum: pinnately cut, 150, 152, 156
pittsfordensis: of Pittsford, Massachusetts, 132
platyneuron (-os) : broad-veined, 158 (164)
polypodioides: resembling a *Polypodium*, 58, 68
porophilum: cavity-loving, 286
poyseri: in honor of W. A. Poyser, 130
pratense: of meadows, 236
prealta (-um) (misprint for prae-) : very tall, 250
protrusa (-um) : protruding, 86, 174
pseudocaudata (-um) : imitating taxon *caudatum*, 172
pseudohiemale (-hyemale) : imitating taxon *hiemale*, 250

pseudopodum: with a false foot, 210
pubescens: hairy, 74, 172
punctilobula (-um) : with small pointed lobes, 192
pungens: sharp-pointed, 276
purshii: in honor of F. T. Pursh, 98
pusilla: very small, 92, 194
pycnocarpon (-us) : with crowded fruits, 136
pycnostichum: with crowded rows, 210

quadrifolia: four-leaved, 206

radicans: with roots, 198
ramosum: branched, 218
regalis: royal, 204
remotiuscula: remotish, 104
resiliens: springy, 160
rhizophylla (-um, -us) : with rooting leaves, 168
riparia: of beaches, 256
robertiana: resembling St. Robert's geranium, 62
robusta (-um) : stout, 250, 252, 282
rubellum: reddish, 142
ruggii: in honor of H. G. Rugg, 204
rupestre (-is) : of rocks, 262
ruta-muraria: rue of the walls, 154

sabinaefolium (sabinifolium) : with Savin-like leaves, 270
saccharata: sugary, 256
scirpoides: resembling a *Scirpus,* 244
scolopendrium: (ancient name for) a parallel-marked plant, 170
scopulina (-um) : of rocky places, 94, 102
selaginoides: resembling taxon *Selago,* 260
selago: (ancient name for) a small fir-like plant, 286, 288
sensibilis: sensitive, 76
separabilis: spaced, 124
serratum: saw-toothed, 158
siliquosa: like a cylindric seed-pod, 178
simplex: simple, 212
simulans, simulata (-um) : imitating, 72, 84
sitchense: of Sitka, Alaska, 140, 270
slossonae: in honor of Margaret Slosson, 128
spectabilis: showy, 204

spinulosa (-um) : with small spines, (118) , 120, (122)
stelleri: in honor of G. W. Steller, 180
stotleri: in honor of T. C. Stotler, 162
struthiopteris: an ostrich-like fern, 78
subremotum: moderately remote, 274
subtenuifolium: rather slender-leaved, 154
subtripinnatum: not quite tripinnate, 144
sylvaticum: of woodlands, 238

telmateia: of puddles, 236
tenebrosum: of shady places, 212
tennesseensis: of Tennessee, 82
tenuifolium: slender-leaved, 228
ternata (-um) : divided into 3 parts, 222, 224, 226, 228
thelypterioides: resembling a *Thelypteris*, 138
thelypteris: a female fern, 74
tomentosa: densely woolly, 190
trichomanes: a tangled mass of hair, (160) , 162, (164)
tripinnatifida: three times pinnately cut, 116
triploidea: with 3-fold chromosome complement, 132
tristachyum: three-spiked, 268, 274
trudelli: in honor of H. W. Trudell, 152
tuckermani: in honor of Edward Tuckerman, 258

uliginosa (-um) : of swamps, 128

variegatum: variegated, 246
vestita (-um) : clothed, 188
virginiana (-um) : of Virginia, 60, 220
virginica (-um) : of Virginia, 48, 160
viride: green, 164
vulgare, vulgatum: common, 60, 210

wherryi: in honor of the author of this *Guide,* 130, 164

INDEX TO TECHNICAL NAMES

(Accepted names are in bold-face, rejected ones in light-face)

INDEX TO COLLOQUIAL NAMES

A CATALOG OF SELECTED
DOVER BOOKS
IN ALL FIELDS OF INTEREST

A CATALOG OF SELECTED DOVER
BOOKS IN ALL FIELDS OF INTEREST

CONCERNING THE SPIRITUAL IN ART, Wassily Kandinsky. Pioneering work by father of abstract art. Thoughts on color theory, nature of art. Analysis of earlier masters. 12 illustrations. 80pp. of text. 5⅜ x 8½. 23411-8 Pa. $4.95

ANIMALS: 1,419 Copyright-Free Illustrations of Mammals, Birds, Fish, Insects, etc., Jim Harter (ed.). Clear wood engravings present, in extremely lifelike poses, over 1,000 species of animals. One of the most extensive pictorial sourcebooks of its kind. Captions. Index. 284pp. 9 x 12. 23766-4 Pa. $14.95

CELTIC ART: The Methods of Construction, George Bain. Simple geometric techniques for making Celtic interlacements, spirals, Kells-type initials, animals, humans, etc. Over 500 illustrations. 160pp. 9 x 12. (Available in U.S. only.) 22923-8 Pa. $9.95

AN ATLAS OF ANATOMY FOR ARTISTS, Fritz Schider. Most thorough reference work on art anatomy in the world. Hundreds of illustrations, including selections from works by Vesalius, Leonardo, Goya, Ingres, Michelangelo, others. 593 illustrations. 192pp. 7⅛ x 10¼. 20241-0 Pa. $9.95

CELTIC HAND STROKE-BY-STROKE (Irish Half-Uncial from "The Book of Kells"): An Arthur Baker Calligraphy Manual, Arthur Baker. Complete guide to creating each letter of the alphabet in distinctive Celtic manner. Covers hand position, strokes, pens, inks, paper, more. Illustrated. 48pp. 8¼ x 11. 24336-2 Pa. $3.95

EASY ORIGAMI, John Montroll. Charming collection of 32 projects (hat, cup, pelican, piano, swan, many more) specially designed for the novice origami hobbyist. Clearly illustrated easy-to-follow instructions insure that even beginning papercrafters will achieve successful results. 48pp. 8¼ x 11. 27298-2 Pa. $3.50

THE COMPLETE BOOK OF BIRDHOUSE CONSTRUCTION FOR WOODWORKERS, Scott D. Campbell. Detailed instructions, illustrations, tables. Also data on bird habitat and instinct patterns. Bibliography. 3 tables. 63 illustrations in 15 figures. 48pp. 5¼ x 8½. 24407-5 Pa. $2.50

BLOOMINGDALE'S ILLUSTRATED 1886 CATALOG: Fashions, Dry Goods and Housewares, Bloomingdale Brothers. Famed merchants' extremely rare catalog depicting about 1,700 products: clothing, housewares, firearms, dry goods, jewelry, more. Invaluable for dating, identifying vintage items. Also, copyright-free graphics for artists, designers. Co-published with Henry Ford Museum & Greenfield Village. 160pp. 8¼ x 11. 25780-0 Pa. $10.95

HISTORIC COSTUME IN PICTURES, Braun & Schneider. Over 1,450 costumed figures in clearly detailed engravings—from dawn of civilization to end of 19th century. Captions. Many folk costumes. 256pp. 8⅜ x 11¾. 23150-X Pa. $12.95

STICKLEY CRAFTSMAN FURNITURE CATALOGS, Gustav Stickley and L. & J. G. Stickley. Beautiful, functional furniture in two authentic catalogs from 1910. 594 illustrations, including 277 photos, show settles, rockers, armchairs, reclining chairs, bookcases, desks, tables. 183pp. 6½ x 9¼. 23838-5 Pa. $11.95

AMERICAN LOCOMOTIVES IN HISTORIC PHOTOGRAPHS: 1858 to 1949, Ron Ziel (ed.). A rare collection of 126 meticulously detailed official photographs, called "builder portraits," of American locomotives that majestically chronicle the rise of steam locomotive power in America. Introduction. Detailed captions. xi+ 129pp. 9 x 12. 27393-8 Pa. $13.95

AMERICA'S LIGHTHOUSES: An Illustrated History, Francis Ross Holland, Jr. Delightfully written, profusely illustrated fact-filled survey of over 200 American lighthouses since 1716. History, anecdotes, technological advances, more. 240pp. 8 x 10¾. 25576-X Pa. $12.95

TOWARDS A NEW ARCHITECTURE, Le Corbusier. Pioneering manifesto by founder of "International School." Technical and aesthetic theories, views of industry, economics, relation of form to function, "mass-production split" and much more. Profusely illustrated. 320pp. 6⅛ x 9¼. (Available in U.S. only.) 25023-7 Pa. $9.95

HOW THE OTHER HALF LIVES, Jacob Riis. Famous journalistic record, exposing poverty and degradation of New York slums around 1900, by major social reformer. 100 striking and influential photographs. 233pp. 10 x 7⅞. 22012-5 Pa. $11.95

FRUIT KEY AND TWIG KEY TO TREES AND SHRUBS, William M. Harlow. One of the handiest and most widely used identification aids. Fruit key covers 120 deciduous and evergreen species; twig key 160 deciduous species. Easily used. Over 300 photographs. 126pp. 5⅜ x 8½. 20511-8 Pa. $3.95

COMMON BIRD SONGS, Dr. Donald J. Borror. Songs of 60 most common U.S. birds: robins, sparrows, cardinals, bluejays, finches, more–arranged in order of increasing complexity. Up to 9 variations of songs of each species. Cassette and manual 99911-4 $8.95

ORCHIDS AS HOUSE PLANTS, Rebecca Tyson Northen. Grow cattleyas and many other kinds of orchids–in a window, in a case, or under artificial light. 63 illustrations. 148pp. 5⅜ x 8½. 23261-1 Pa. $5.95

MONSTER MAZES, Dave Phillips. Masterful mazes at four levels of difficulty. Avoid deadly perils and evil creatures to find magical treasures. Solutions for all 32 exciting illustrated puzzles. 48pp. 8¼ x 11. 26005-4 Pa. $2.95

MOZART'S DON GIOVANNI (DOVER OPERA LIBRETTO SERIES), Wolfgang Amadeus Mozart. Introduced and translated by Ellen H. Bleiler. Standard Italian libretto, with complete English translation. Convenient and thoroughly portable–an ideal companion for reading along with a recording or the performance itself. Introduction. List of characters. Plot summary. 121pp. 5¼ x 8½. 24944-1 Pa. $3.95

TECHNICAL MANUAL AND DICTIONARY OF CLASSICAL BALLET, Gail Grant. Defines, explains, comments on steps, movements, poses and concepts. 15-page pictorial section. Basic book for student, viewer. 127pp. 5⅜ x 8½. 21843-0 Pa. $4.95

THE CLARINET AND CLARINET PLAYING, David Pino. Lively, comprehensive work features suggestions about technique, musicianship, and musical interpretation, as well as guidelines for teaching, making your own reeds, and preparing for public performance. Includes an intriguing look at clarinet history. "A godsend," *The Clarinet,* Journal of the International Clarinet Society. Appendixes. 7 illus. 320pp. 5⅜ x 8½. 40270-3 Pa. $9.95

HOLLYWOOD GLAMOR PORTRAITS, John Kobal (ed.). 145 photos from 1926-49. Harlow, Gable, Bogart, Bacall; 94 stars in all. Full background on photographers, technical aspects. 160pp. 8⅜ x 11¼. 23352-9 Pa. $12.95

THE ANNOTATED CASEY AT THE BAT: A Collection of Ballads about the Mighty Casey/Third, Revised Edition, Martin Gardner (ed.). Amusing sequels and parodies of one of America's best-loved poems: Casey's Revenge, Why Casey Whiffed, Casey's Sister at the Bat, others. 256pp. 5⅜ x 8½. 28598-7 Pa. $8.95

THE RAVEN AND OTHER FAVORITE POEMS, Edgar Allan Poe. Over 40 of the author's most memorable poems: "The Bells," "Ulalume," "Israfel," "To Helen," "The Conqueror Worm," "Eldorado," "Annabel Lee," many more. Alphabetic lists of titles and first lines. 64pp. 5³⁄₁₆ x 8¼. 26685-0 Pa. $1.00

PERSONAL MEMOIRS OF U. S. GRANT, Ulysses Simpson Grant. Intelligent, deeply moving firsthand account of Civil War campaigns, considered by many the finest military memoirs ever written. Includes letters, historic photographs, maps and more. 528pp. 6⅛ x 9¼. 28587-1 Pa. $12.95

ANCIENT EGYPTIAN MATERIALS AND INDUSTRIES, A. Lucas and J. Harris. Fascinating, comprehensive, thoroughly documented text describes this ancient civilization's vast resources and the processes that incorporated them in daily life, including the use of animal products, building materials, cosmetics, perfumes and incense, fibers, glazed ware, glass and its manufacture, materials used in the mummification process, and much more. 544pp. 6⅛ x 9¼. (Available in U.S. only.) 40446-3 Pa. $16.95

RUSSIAN STORIES/PYCCKNE PACCKA3bl: A Dual-Language Book, edited by Gleb Struve. Twelve tales by such masters as Chekhov, Tolstoy, Dostoevsky, Pushkin, others. Excellent word-for-word English translations on facing pages, plus teaching and study aids, Russian/English vocabulary, biographical/critical introductions, more. 416pp. 5⅜ x 8½. 26244-8 Pa. $9.95

PHILADELPHIA THEN AND NOW: 60 Sites Photographed in the Past and Present, Kenneth Finkel and Susan Oyama. Rare photographs of City Hall, Logan Square, Independence Hall, Betsy Ross House, other landmarks juxtaposed with contemporary views. Captures changing face of historic city. Introduction. Captions. 128pp. 8¼ x 11. 25790-8 Pa. $9.95

AIA ARCHITECTURAL GUIDE TO NASSAU AND SUFFOLK COUNTIES, LONG ISLAND, The American Institute of Architects, Long Island Chapter, and the Society for the Preservation of Long Island Antiquities. Comprehensive, well-researched and generously illustrated volume brings to life over three centuries of Long Island's great architectural heritage. More than 240 photographs with authoritative, extensively detailed captions. 176pp. 8¼ x 11. 26946-9 Pa. $14.95

NORTH AMERICAN INDIAN LIFE: Customs and Traditions of 23 Tribes, Elsie Clews Parsons (ed.). 27 fictionalized essays by noted anthropologists examine religion, customs, government, additional facets of life among the Winnebago, Crow, Zuni, Eskimo, other tribes. 480pp. 6⅛ x 9¼. 27377-6 Pa. $10.95

FRANK LLOYD WRIGHT'S DANA HOUSE, Donald Hoffmann. Pictorial essay of residential masterpiece with over 160 interior and exterior photos, plans, elevations, sketches and studies. 128pp. 9¼ x 10¾. 29120-0 Pa. $12.95

THE MALE AND FEMALE FIGURE IN MOTION: 60 Classic Photographic Sequences, Eadweard Muybridge. 60 true-action photographs of men and women walking, running, climbing, bending, turning, etc., reproduced from rare 19th-century masterpiece. vi + 121pp. 9 x 12. 24745-7 Pa. $12.95

1001 QUESTIONS ANSWERED ABOUT THE SEASHORE, N. J. Berrill and Jacquelyn Berrill. Queries answered about dolphins, sea snails, sponges, starfish, fishes, shore birds, many others. Covers appearance, breeding, growth, feeding, much more. 305pp. 5¼ x 8¼. 23366-9 Pa. $9.95

ATTRACTING BIRDS TO YOUR YARD, William J. Weber. Easy-to-follow guide offers advice on how to attract the greatest diversity of birds: birdhouses, feeders, water and waterers, much more. 96pp. 5³⁄₁₆ x 8¼. 28927-3 Pa. $2.50

MEDICINAL AND OTHER USES OF NORTH AMERICAN PLANTS: A Historical Survey with Special Reference to the Eastern Indian Tribes, Charlotte Erichsen-Brown. Chronological historical citations document 500 years of usage of plants, trees, shrubs native to eastern Canada, northeastern U.S. Also complete identifying information. 343 illustrations. 544pp. 6½ x 9¼. 25951-X Pa. $12.95

STORYBOOK MAZES, Dave Phillips. 23 stories and mazes on two-page spreads: Wizard of Oz, Treasure Island, Robin Hood, etc. Solutions. 64pp. 8¼ x 11. 23628-5 Pa. $2.95

AMERICAN NEGRO SONGS: 230 Folk Songs and Spirituals, Religious and Secular, John W. Work. This authoritative study traces the African influences of songs sung and played by black Americans at work, in church, and as entertainment. The author discusses the lyric significance of such songs as "Swing Low, Sweet Chariot," "John Henry," and others and offers the words and music for 230 songs. Bibliography. Index of Song Titles. 272pp. 6½ x 9¼. 40271-1 Pa. $9.95

MOVIE-STAR PORTRAITS OF THE FORTIES, John Kobal (ed.). 163 glamor, studio photos of 106 stars of the 1940s: Rita Hayworth, Ava Gardner, Marlon Brando, Clark Gable, many more. 176pp. 8⅜ x 11¼. 23546-7 Pa. $14.95

BENCHLEY LOST AND FOUND, Robert Benchley. Finest humor from early 30s, about pet peeves, child psychologists, post office and others. Mostly unavailable elsewhere. 73 illustrations by Peter Arno and others. 183pp. 5⅜ x 8½. 22410-4 Pa. $6.95

YEKL and THE IMPORTED BRIDEGROOM AND OTHER STORIES OF YIDDISH NEW YORK, Abraham Cahan. Film Hester Street based on Yekl (1896). Novel, other stories among first about Jewish immigrants on N.Y.'s East Side. 240pp. 5⅜ x 8½. 22427-9 Pa. $7.95

SELECTED POEMS, Walt Whitman. Generous sampling from Leaves of Grass. Twenty-four poems include "I Hear America Singing," "Song of the Open Road," "I Sing the Body Electric," "When Lilacs Last in the Dooryard Bloom'd," "O Captain! My Captain!"—all reprinted from an authoritative edition. Lists of titles and first lines. 128pp. 5³⁄₁₆ x 8¼. 26878-0 Pa. $1.00

THE BEST TALES OF HOFFMANN, E. T. A. Hoffmann. 10 of Hoffmann's most important stories: "Nutcracker and the King of Mice," "The Golden Flowerpot," etc. 458pp. 5⅜ x 8½. 21793-0 Pa. $9.95

FROM FETISH TO GOD IN ANCIENT EGYPT, E. A. Wallis Budge. Rich detailed survey of Egyptian conception of "God" and gods, magic, cult of animals, Osiris, more. Also, superb English translations of hymns and legends. 240 illustrations. 545pp. 5⅜ x 8½. 25803-3 Pa. $13.95

FRENCH STORIES/CONTES FRANÇAIS: A Dual-Language Book, Wallace Fowlie. Ten stories by French masters, Voltaire to Camus: "Micromegas" by Voltaire; "The Atheist's Mass" by Balzac; "Minuet" by de Maupassant; "The Guest" by Camus, six more. Excellent English translations on facing pages. Also French-English vocabulary list, exercises, more. 352pp. 5⅜ x 8½. 26443-2 Pa. $9.95

CHICAGO AT THE TURN OF THE CENTURY IN PHOTOGRAPHS: 122 Historic Views from the Collections of the Chicago Historical Society, Larry A. Viskochil. Rare large-format prints offer detailed views of City Hall, State Street, the Loop, Hull House, Union Station, many other landmarks, circa 1904-1913. Introduction. Captions. Maps. 144pp. 9⅜ x 12¼. 24656-6 Pa. $12.95

OLD BROOKLYN IN EARLY PHOTOGRAPHS, 1865-1929, William Lee Younger. Luna Park, Gravesend race track, construction of Grand Army Plaza, moving of Hotel Brighton, etc. 157 previously unpublished photographs. 165pp. 8⅞ x 11¾. 23587-4 Pa. $13.95

THE MYTHS OF THE NORTH AMERICAN INDIANS, Lewis Spence. Rich anthology of the myths and legends of the Algonquins, Iroquois, Pawnees and Sioux, prefaced by an extensive historical and ethnological commentary. 36 illustrations. 480pp. 5⅜ x 8½. 25967-6 Pa. $10.95

AN ENCYCLOPEDIA OF BATTLES: Accounts of Over 1,560 Battles from 1479 B.C. to the Present, David Eggenberger. Essential details of every major battle in recorded history from the first battle of Megiddo in 1479 B.C. to Grenada in 1984. List of Battle Maps. New Appendix covering the years 1967-1984. Index. 99 illustrations. 544pp. 6½ x 9¼. 24913-1 Pa. $16.95

SAILING ALONE AROUND THE WORLD, Captain Joshua Slocum. First man to sail around the world, alone, in small boat. One of great feats of seamanship told in delightful manner. 67 illustrations. 294pp. 5⅜ x 8½. 20326-3 Pa. $6.95

ANARCHISM AND OTHER ESSAYS, Emma Goldman. Powerful, penetrating, prophetic essays on direct action, role of minorities, prison reform, puritan hypocrisy, violence, etc. 271pp. 5⅜ x 8½. 22484-8 Pa. $7.95

MYTHS OF THE HINDUS AND BUDDHISTS, Ananda K. Coomaraswamy and Sister Nivedita. Great stories of the epics; deeds of Krishna, Shiva, taken from puranas, Vedas, folk tales; etc. 32 illustrations. 400pp. 5⅜ x 8½. 21759-0 Pa. $12.95

THE TRAUMA OF BIRTH, Otto Rank. Rank's controversial thesis that anxiety neurosis is caused by profound psychological trauma which occurs at birth. 256pp. 5⅜ x 8½. 27974-X Pa. $7.95

A THEOLOGICO-POLITICAL TREATISE, Benedict Spinoza. Also contains unfinished Political Treatise. Great classic on religious liberty, theory of government on common consent. R. Elwes translation. Total of 421pp. 5⅜ x 8½. 20249-6 Pa. $10.95

CATALOG OF DOVER BOOKS

MY BONDAGE AND MY FREEDOM, Frederick Douglass. Born a slave, Douglass became outspoken force in antislavery movement. The best of Douglass' autobiographies. Graphic description of slave life. 464pp. 5⅜ x 8½. 22457-0 Pa. $8.95

FOLLOWING THE EQUATOR: A Journey Around the World, Mark Twain. Fascinating humorous account of 1897 voyage to Hawaii, Australia, India, New Zealand, etc. Ironic, bemused reports on peoples, customs, climate, flora and fauna, politics, much more. 197 illustrations. 720pp. 5⅜ x 8½. 26113-1 Pa. $15.95

THE PEOPLE CALLED SHAKERS, Edward D. Andrews. Definitive study of Shakers: origins, beliefs, practices, dances, social organization, furniture and crafts, etc. 33 illustrations. 351pp. 5⅜ x 8½. 21081-2 Pa. $10.95

THE MYTHS OF GREECE AND ROME, H. A. Guerber. A classic of mythology, generously illustrated, long prized for its simple, graphic, accurate retelling of the principal myths of Greece and Rome, and for its commentary on their origins and significance. With 64 illustrations by Michelangelo, Raphael, Titian, Rubens, Canova, Bernini and others. 480pp. 5⅜ x 8½. 27584-1 Pa. $9.95

PSYCHOLOGY OF MUSIC, Carl E. Seashore. Classic work discusses music as a medium from psychological viewpoint. Clear treatment of physical acoustics, auditory apparatus, sound perception, development of musical skills, nature of musical feeling, host of other topics. 88 figures. 408pp. 5⅜ x 8½. 21851-1 Pa. $11.95

THE PHILOSOPHY OF HISTORY, Georg W. Hegel. Great classic of Western thought develops concept that history is not chance but rational process, the evolution of freedom. 457pp. 5⅜ x 8½. 20112-0 Pa. $9.95

THE BOOK OF TEA, Kakuzo Okakura. Minor classic of the Orient: entertaining, charming explanation, interpretation of traditional Japanese culture in terms of tea ceremony. 94pp. 5⅜ x 8½. 20070-1 Pa. $3.95

LIFE IN ANCIENT EGYPT, Adolf Erman. Fullest, most thorough, detailed older account with much not in more recent books, domestic life, religion, magic, medicine, commerce, much more. Many illustrations reproduce tomb paintings, carvings, hieroglyphs, etc. 597pp. 5⅜ x 8½. 22632-8 Pa. $12.95

SUNDIALS, Their Theory and Construction, Albert Waugh. Far and away the best, most thorough coverage of ideas, mathematics concerned, types, construction, adjusting anywhere. Simple, nontechnical treatment allows even children to build several of these dials. Over 100 illustrations. 230pp. 5⅜ x 8½. 22947-5 Pa. $8.95

THEORETICAL HYDRODYNAMICS, L. M. Milne-Thomson. Classic exposition of the mathematical theory of fluid motion, applicable to both hydrodynamics and aerodynamics. Over 600 exercises. 768pp. 6⅛ x 9¼. 68970-0 Pa. $20.95

SONGS OF EXPERIENCE: Facsimile Reproduction with 26 Plates in Full Color, William Blake. 26 full-color plates from a rare 1826 edition. Includes "The Tyger," "London," "Holy Thursday," and other poems. Printed text of poems. 48pp. 5¼ x 7. 24636-1 Pa. $4.95

OLD-TIME VIGNETTES IN FULL COLOR, Carol Belanger Grafton (ed.). Over 390 charming, often sentimental illustrations, selected from archives of Victorian graphics—pretty women posing, children playing, food, flowers, kittens and puppies, smiling cherubs, birds and butterflies, much more. All copyright-free. 48pp. 9¼ x 12¼. 27269-9 Pa. $7.95

PERSPECTIVE FOR ARTISTS, Rex Vicat Cole. Depth, perspective of sky and sea, shadows, much more, not usually covered. 391 diagrams, 81 reproductions of drawings and paintings. 279pp. 5⅜ x 8½. 22487-2 Pa. $9.95

DRAWING THE LIVING FIGURE, Joseph Sheppard. Innovative approach to artistic anatomy focuses on specifics of surface anatomy, rather than muscles and bones. Over 170 drawings of live models in front, back and side views, and in widely varying poses. Accompanying diagrams. 177 illustrations. Introduction. Index. 144pp. 8⅜ x11¼. 26723-7 Pa. $9.95

GOTHIC AND OLD ENGLISH ALPHABETS: 100 Complete Fonts, Dan X. Solo. Add power, elegance to posters, signs, other graphics with 100 stunning copyright-free alphabets: Blackstone, Dolbey, Germania, 97 more—including many lower-case, numerals, punctuation marks. 104pp. 8⅛ x 11. 24695-7 Pa. $8.95

HOW TO DO BEADWORK, Mary White. Fundamental book on craft from simple projects to five-bead chains and woven works. 106 illustrations. 142pp. 5⅜ x 8. 20697-1 Pa. $5.95

THE BOOK OF WOOD CARVING, Charles Marshall Sayers. Finest book for beginners discusses fundamentals and offers 34 designs. "Absolutely first rate . . . well thought out and well executed."—E. J. Tangerman. 118pp. 7¾ x 10⅝. 23654-4 Pa. $7.95

ILLUSTRATED CATALOG OF CIVIL WAR MILITARY GOODS: Union Army Weapons, Insignia, Uniform Accessories, and Other Equipment, Schuyler, Hartley, and Graham. Rare, profusely illustrated 1846 catalog includes Union Army uniform and dress regulations, arms and ammunition, coats, insignia, flags, swords, rifles, etc. 226 illustrations. 160pp. 9 x 12. 24939-5 Pa. $10.95

WOMEN'S FASHIONS OF THE EARLY 1900s: An Unabridged Republication of "New York Fashions, 1909," National Cloak & Suit Co. Rare catalog of mail-order fashions documents women's and children's clothing styles shortly after the turn of the century. Captions offer full descriptions, prices. Invaluable resource for fashion, costume historians. Approximately 725 illustrations. 128pp. 8⅜ x 11¼. 27276-1 Pa. $11.95

THE 1912 AND 1915 GUSTAV STICKLEY FURNITURE CATALOGS, Gustav Stickley. With over 200 detailed illustrations and descriptions, these two catalogs are essential reading and reference materials and identification guides for Stickley furniture. Captions cite materials, dimensions and prices. 112pp. 6½ x 9¼. 26676-1 Pa. $9.95

EARLY AMERICAN LOCOMOTIVES, John H. White, Jr. Finest locomotive engravings from early 19th century: historical (1804–74), main-line (after 1870), special, foreign, etc. 147 plates. 142pp. 11⅜ x 8¼. 22772-3 Pa. $12.95

THE TALL SHIPS OF TODAY IN PHOTOGRAPHS, Frank O. Braynard. Lavishly illustrated tribute to nearly 100 majestic contemporary sailing vessels: Amerigo Vespucci, Clearwater, Constitution, Eagle, Mayflower, Sea Cloud, Victory, many more. Authoritative captions provide statistics, background on each ship. 190 black-and-white photographs and illustrations. Introduction. 128pp. 8⅞ x 11¾. 27163-3 Pa. $14.95

LITTLE BOOK OF EARLY AMERICAN CRAFTS AND TRADES, Peter Stockham (ed.). 1807 children's book explains crafts and trades: baker, hatter, cooper, potter, and many others. 23 copperplate illustrations. 140pp. 4⅝ x 6.
23336-7 Pa. $4.95

VICTORIAN FASHIONS AND COSTUMES FROM HARPER'S BAZAR, 1867–1898, Stella Blum (ed.). Day costumes, evening wear, sports clothes, shoes, hats, other accessories in over 1,000 detailed engravings. 320pp. 9⅜ x 12¼.
22990-4 Pa. $16.95

GUSTAV STICKLEY, THE CRAFTSMAN, Mary Ann Smith. Superb study surveys broad scope of Stickley's achievement, especially in architecture. Design philosophy, rise and fall of the Craftsman empire, descriptions and floor plans for many Craftsman houses, more. 86 black-and-white halftones. 31 line illustrations. Introduction 208pp. 6½ x 9¼.
27210-9 Pa. $9.95

THE LONG ISLAND RAIL ROAD IN EARLY PHOTOGRAPHS, Ron Ziel. Over 220 rare photos, informative text document origin (1844) and development of rail service on Long Island. Vintage views of early trains, locomotives, stations, passengers, crews, much more. Captions. 8⅞ x 11¾.
26301-0 Pa. $14.95

VOYAGE OF THE LIBERDADE, Joshua Slocum. Great 19th-century mariner's thrilling, first-hand account of the wreck of his ship off South America, the 35-foot boat he built from the wreckage, and its remarkable voyage home. 128pp. 5⅜ x 8½.
40022 0 Pa. $5.95

TEN BOOKS ON ARCHITECTURE, Vitruvius. The most important book ever written on architecture. Early Roman aesthetics, technology, classical orders, site selection, all other aspects. Morgan translation. 331pp. 5⅜ x 8½.
20645-9 Pa. $8.95

THE HUMAN FIGURE IN MOTION, Eadweard Muybridge. More than 4,500 stopped-action photos, in action series, showing undraped men, women, children jumping, lying down, throwing, sitting, wrestling, carrying, etc. 390pp. 7⅞ x 10⅝.
20204-6 Clothbd. $27.95

TREES OF THE EASTERN AND CENTRAL UNITED STATES AND CANADA, William M. Harlow. Best one-volume guide to 140 trees. Full descriptions, woodlore, range, etc. Over 600 illustrations. Handy size. 288pp. 4½ x 6⅜.
20395-6 Pa. $6.95

SONGS OF WESTERN BIRDS, Dr. Donald J. Borror. Complete song and call repertoire of 60 western species, including flycatchers, juncoes, cactus wrens, many more–includes fully illustrated booklet.
Cassette and manual 99913-0 $8.95

GROWING AND USING HERBS AND SPICES, Milo Miloradovich. Versatile handbook provides all the information needed for cultivation and use of all the herbs and spices available in North America. 4 illustrations. Index. Glossary. 236pp. 5⅜ x 8½.
25058-X Pa. $7.95

BIG BOOK OF MAZES AND LABYRINTHS, Walter Shepherd. 50 mazes and labyrinths in all–classical, solid, ripple, and more–in one great volume. Perfect inexpensive puzzler for clever youngsters. Full solutions. 112pp. 8⅛ x 11.
22951-3 Pa. $5.95

PIANO TUNING, J. Cree Fischer. Clearest, best book for beginner, amateur. Simple repairs, raising dropped notes, tuning by easy method of flattened fifths. No previous skills needed. 4 illustrations. 201pp. 5⅜ x 8½. 23267-0 Pa. $6.95

HINTS TO SINGERS, Lillian Nordica. Selecting the right teacher, developing confidence, overcoming stage fright, and many other important skills receive thoughtful discussion in this indispensible guide, written by a world-famous diva of four decades' experience. 96pp. 5⅜ x 8½. 40094-8 Pa. $4.95

THE COMPLETE NONSENSE OF EDWARD LEAR, Edward Lear. All nonsense limericks, zany alphabets, Owl and Pussycat, songs, nonsense botany, etc., illustrated by Lear. Total of 320pp. 5⅜ x 8½. (AVAILABLE IN U.S. ONLY.) 20167-8 Pa. $7.95

VICTORIAN PARLOUR POETRY: An Annotated Anthology, Michael R. Turner. 117 gems by Longfellow, Tennyson, Browning, many lesser-known poets. "The Village Blacksmith," "Curfew Must Not Ring Tonight," "Only a Baby Small," dozens more, often difficult to find elsewhere. Index of poets, titles, first lines. xxiii + 325pp. 5⅝ x 8¼. 27044-0 Pa. $8.95

DUBLINERS, James Joyce. Fifteen stories offer vivid, tightly focused observations of the lives of Dublin's poorer classes. At least one, "The Dead," is considered a masterpiece. Reprinted complete and unabridged from standard edition. 160pp. 5$\frac{3}{16}$ x 8¼. 26870-5 Pa. $1.00

GREAT WEIRD TALES: 14 Stories by Lovecraft, Blackwood, Machen and Others, S. T. Joshi (ed.). 14 spellbinding tales, including "The Sin Eater," by Fiona McLeod, "The Eye Above the Mantel," by Frank Belknap Long, as well as renowned works by R. H. Barlow, Lord Dunsany, Arthur Machen, W. C. Morrow and eight other masters of the genre. 256pp. 5⅜ x 8½. (Available in U.S. only.) 40436-6 Pa. $8.95

THE BOOK OF THE SACRED MAGIC OF ABRAMELIN THE MAGE, translated by S. MacGregor Mathers. Medieval manuscript of ceremonial magic. Basic document in Aleister Crowley, Golden Dawn groups. 268pp. 5⅜ x 8½. 23211-5 Pa. $9.95

NEW RUSSIAN-ENGLISH AND ENGLISH-RUSSIAN DICTIONARY, M. A. O'Brien. This is a remarkably handy Russian dictionary, containing a surprising amount of information, including over 70,000 entries. 366pp. 4½ x 6⅛. 20208-9 Pa. $10.95

HISTORIC HOMES OF THE AMERICAN PRESIDENTS, Second, Revised Edition, Irvin Haas. A traveler's guide to American Presidential homes, most open to the public, depicting and describing homes occupied by every American President from George Washington to George Bush. With visiting hours, admission charges, travel routes. 175 photographs. Index. 160pp. 8¼ x 11. 26751-2 Pa. $11.95

NEW YORK IN THE FORTIES, Andreas Feininger. 162 brilliant photographs by the well-known photographer, formerly with *Life* magazine. Commuters, shoppers, Times Square at night, much else from city at its peak. Captions by John von Hartz. 181pp. 9¼ x 10¾. 23585-8 Pa. $13.95

INDIAN SIGN LANGUAGE, William Tomkins. Over 525 signs developed by Sioux and other tribes. Written instructions and diagrams. Also 290 pictographs. 111pp. 6⅛ x 9¼. 22029-X Pa. $3.95

ANATOMY: A Complete Guide for Artists, Joseph Sheppard. A master of figure drawing shows artists how to render human anatomy convincingly. Over 460 illustrations. 224pp. 8⅜ x 11¼. 27279-6 Pa. $11.95

MEDIEVAL CALLIGRAPHY: Its History and Technique, Marc Drogin. Spirited history, comprehensive instruction manual covers 13 styles (ca. 4th century through 15th). Excellent photographs; directions for duplicating medieval techniques with modern tools. 224pp. 8⅜ x 11¼. 26142-5 Pa. $12.95

DRIED FLOWERS: How to Prepare Them, Sarah Whitlock and Martha Rankin. Complete instructions on how to use silica gel, meal and borax, perlite aggregate, sand and borax, glycerine and water to create attractive permanent flower arrangements. 12 illustrations. 32pp. 5⅜ x 8½. 21802-3 Pa. $1.00

EASY-TO-MAKE BIRD FEEDERS FOR WOODWORKERS, Scott D. Campbell. Detailed, simple-to-use guide for designing, constructing, caring for and using feeders. Text, illustrations for 12 classic and contemporary designs. 96pp. 5⅜ x 8½. 25847-5 Pa. $3.95

SCOTTISH WONDER TALES FROM MYTH AND LEGEND, Donald A. Mackenzie. 16 lively tales tell of giants rumbling down mountainsides, of a magic wand that turns stone pillars into warriors, of gods and goddesses, evil hags, powerful forces and more. 240pp. 5⅜ x 8½. 29677-6 Pa. $6.95

THE HISTORY OF UNDERCLOTHES, C. Willett Cunnington and Phyllis Cunnington. Fascinating, well-documented survey covering six centuries of English undergarments, enhanced with over 100 illustrations: 12th-century laced-up bodice, footed long drawers (1795), 19th-century bustles, 19th-century corsets for men, Victorian "bust improvers," much more. 272pp. 5⅜ x 8¼. 27124-2 Pa. $9.95

ARTS AND CRAFTS FURNITURE: The Complete Brooks Catalog of 1912, Brooks Manufacturing Co. Photos and detailed descriptions of more than 150 now very collectible furniture designs from the Arts and Crafts movement depict davenports, settees, buffets, desks, tables, chairs, bedsteads, dressers and more, all built of solid, quarter-sawed oak. Invaluable for students and enthusiasts of antiques, Americana and the decorative arts. 80pp. 6½ x 9¼. 27471-3 Pa. $8.95

WILBUR AND ORVILLE: A Biography of the Wright Brothers, Fred Howard. Definitive, crisply written study tells the full story of the brothers' lives and work. A vividly written biography, unparalleled in scope and color, that also captures the spirit of an extraordinary era. 560pp. 6⅛ x 9¼. 40297-5 Pa. $17.95

THE ARTS OF THE SAILOR: Knotting, Splicing and Ropework, Hervey Garrett Smith. Indispensable shipboard reference covers tools, basic knots and useful hitches; handsewing and canvas work, more. Over 100 illustrations. Delightful reading for sea lovers. 256pp. 5⅜ x 8½. 26440-8 Pa. $8.95

FRANK LLOYD WRIGHT'S FALLINGWATER: The House and Its History, Second, Revised Edition, Donald Hoffmann. A total revision–both in text and illustrations–of the standard document on Fallingwater, the boldest, most personal architectural statement of Wright's mature years, updated with valuable new material from the recently opened Frank Lloyd Wright Archives. "Fascinating"–*The New York Times*. 116 illustrations. 128pp. 9¼ x 10¾. 27430-6 Pa. $12.95

CATALOG OF DOVER BOOKS

PHOTOGRAPHIC SKETCHBOOK OF THE CIVIL WAR, Alexander Gardner. 100 photos taken on field during the Civil War. Famous shots of Manassas Harper's Ferry, Lincoln, Richmond, slave pens, etc. 244pp. 10⅝ x 8¼. 22731-6 Pa. $10.95

FIVE ACRES AND INDEPENDENCE, Maurice G. Kains. Great back-to-the-land classic explains basics of self-sufficient farming. The one book to get. 95 illustrations. 397pp. 5⅜ x 8½. 20974-1 Pa. $7.95

SONGS OF EASTERN BIRDS, Dr. Donald J. Borror. Songs and calls of 60 species most common to eastern U.S.: warblers, woodpeckers, flycatchers, thrushes, larks, many more in high-quality recording. Cassette and manual 99912-2 $9.95

A MODERN HERBAL, Margaret Grieve. Much the fullest, most exact, most useful compilation of herbal material. Gigantic alphabetical encyclopedia, from aconite to zedoary, gives botanical information, medical properties, folklore, economic uses, much else. Indispensable to serious reader. 161 illustrations. 888pp. 6½ x 9¼. 2-vol. set. (Available in U.S. only.) Vol. I: 22798-7 Pa. $9.95
Vol. II: 22799-5 Pa. $9.95

HIDDEN TREASURE MAZE BOOK, Dave Phillips. Solve 34 challenging mazes accompanied by heroic tales of adventure. Evil dragons, people-eating plants, blood-thirsty giants, many more dangerous adversaries lurk at every twist and turn. 34 mazes, stories, solutions. 48pp. 8¼ x 11. 24566-7 Pa. $2.95

LETTERS OF W. A. MOZART, Wolfgang A. Mozart. Remarkable letters show bawdy wit, humor, imagination, musical insights, contemporary musical world; includes some letters from Leopold Mozart. 276pp. 5⅜ x 8½. 22859-2 Pa. $7.95

BASIC PRINCIPLES OF CLASSICAL BALLET, Agrippina Vaganova. Great Russian theoretician, teacher explains methods for teaching classical ballet. 118 illustrations. 175pp. 5⅜ x 8½. 22036-2 Pa. $6.95

THE JUMPING FROG, Mark Twain. Revenge edition. The original story of The Celebrated Jumping Frog of Calaveras County, a hapless French translation, and Twain's hilarious "retranslation" from the French. 12 illustrations. 66pp. 5⅜ x 8½. 22686-7 Pa. $3.95

BEST REMEMBERED POEMS, Martin Gardner (ed.). The 126 poems in this superb collection of 19th- and 20th-century British and American verse range from Shelley's "To a Skylark" to the impassioned "Renascence" of Edna St. Vincent Millay and to Edward Lear's whimsical "The Owl and the Pussycat." 224pp. 5⅜ x 8½. 27165-X Pa. $5.95

COMPLETE SONNETS, William Shakespeare. Over 150 exquisite poems deal with love, friendship, the tyranny of time, beauty's evanescence, death and other themes in language of remarkable power, precision and beauty. Glossary of archaic terms. 80pp. 5 3/16 x 8¼. 26686-9 Pa. $1.00

BODIES IN A BOOKSHOP, R. T. Campbell. Challenging mystery of blackmail and murder with ingenious plot and superbly drawn characters. In the best tradition of British suspense fiction. 192pp. 5⅜ x 8½. 24720-1 Pa. $6.95

THE WIT AND HUMOR OF OSCAR WILDE, Alvin Redman (ed.). More than 1,000 ripostes, paradoxes, wisecracks: Work is the curse of the drinking classes; I can resist everything except temptation; etc. 258pp. 5⅜ x 8½. 20602-5 Pa. $6.95

SHAKESPEARE LEXICON AND QUOTATION DICTIONARY, Alexander Schmidt. Full definitions, locations, shades of meaning in every word in plays and poems. More than 50,000 exact quotations. 1,485pp. 6½ x 9¼. 2-vol. set.
Vol. 1: 22726-X Pa. $17.95
Vol. 2: 22727-8 Pa. $17.95

SELECTED POEMS, Emily Dickinson. Over 100 best-known, best-loved poems by one of America's foremost poets, reprinted from authoritative early editions. No comparable edition at this price. Index of first lines. 64pp. $5\frac{3}{16}$ x 8¼.
26466-1 Pa. $1.00

THE INSIDIOUS DR. FU-MANCHU, Sax Rohmer. The first of the popular mystery series introduces a pair of English detectives to their archnemesis, the diabolical Dr. Fu-Manchu. Flavorful atmosphere, fast-paced action, and colorful characters enliven this classic of the genre. 208pp. $5\frac{3}{16}$ x 8¼. 29898-1 Pa. $2.00

THE MALLEUS MALEFICARUM OF KRAMER AND SPRENGER, translated by Montague Summers. Full text of most important witchhunter's "bible," used by both Catholics and Protestants. 278pp. 6⅝ x 10. 22802-9 Pa. $12.95

SPANISH STORIES/CUENTOS ESPAÑOLES: A Dual-Language Book, Angel Flores (ed.). Unique format offers 13 great stories in Spanish by Cervantes, Borges, others. Faithful English translations on facing pages. 352pp. 5⅜ x 8½.
25399-6 Pa. $8.95

GARDEN CITY, LONG ISLAND, IN EARLY PHOTOGRAPHS, 1869–1919, Mildred H. Smith. Handsome treasury of 118 vintage pictures, accompanied by carefully researched captions, document the Garden City Hotel fire (1899), the Vanderbilt Cup Race (1908), the first airmail flight departing from the Nassau Boulevard Aerodrome (1911), and much more. 96pp. 8⅞ x 11¾. 40669-5 Pa. $12.95

OLD QUEENS, N.Y., IN EARLY PHOTOGRAPHS, Vincent F. Seyfried and William Asadorian. Over 160 rare photographs of Maspeth, Jamaica, Jackson Heights, and other areas. Vintage views of DeWitt Clinton mansion, 1939 World's Fair and more. Captions. 192pp. 8⅞ x 11. 26358-4 Pa. $12.95

CAPTURED BY THE INDIANS: 15 Firsthand Accounts, 1750-1870, Frederick Drimmer. Astounding true historical accounts of grisly torture, bloody conflicts, relentless pursuits, miraculous escapes and more, by people who lived to tell the tale. 384pp. 5⅜ x 8½. 24901-8 Pa. $8.95

THE WORLD'S GREAT SPEECHES (Fourth Enlarged Edition), Lewis Copeland, Lawrence W. Lamm, and Stephen J. McKenna. Nearly 300 speeches provide public speakers with a wealth of updated quotes and inspiration–from Pericles' funeral oration and William Jennings Bryan's "Cross of Gold Speech" to Malcolm X's powerful words on the Black Revolution and Earl of Spenser's tribute to his sister, Diana, Princess of Wales. 944pp. 5⅜ x 8⅜. 40903-1 Pa. $15.95

THE BOOK OF THE SWORD, Sir Richard F. Burton. Great Victorian scholar/adventurer's eloquent, erudite history of the "queen of weapons"–from prehistory to early Roman Empire. Evolution and development of early swords, variations (sabre, broadsword, cutlass, scimitar, etc.), much more. 336pp. 6⅛ x 9¼.
25434-8 Pa. $9.95

AUTOBIOGRAPHY: The Story of My Experiments with Truth, Mohandas K. Gandhi. Boyhood, legal studies, purification, the growth of the Satyagraha (nonviolent protest) movement. Critical, inspiring work of the man responsible for the freedom of India. 480pp. 5⅜ x 8½. (Available in U.S. only.) 24593-4 Pa. $8.95

CELTIC MYTHS AND LEGENDS, T. W. Rolleston. Masterful retelling of Irish and Welsh stories and tales. Cuchulain, King Arthur, Deirdre, the Grail, many more. First paperback edition. 58 full-page illustrations. 512pp. 5⅜ x 8½. 26507-2 Pa. $9.95

THE PRINCIPLES OF PSYCHOLOGY, William James. Famous long course complete, unabridged. Stream of thought, time perception, memory, experimental methods; great work decades ahead of its time. 94 figures. 1,391pp. 5⅜ x 8½. 2-vol. set.
Vol. I: 20381-6 Pa. $14.95
Vol. II: 20382-4 Pa. $14.95

THE WORLD AS WILL AND REPRESENTATION, Arthur Schopenhauer. Definitive English translation of Schopenhauer's life work, correcting more than 1,000 errors, omissions in earlier translations. Translated by E. F. J. Payne. Total of 1,269pp. 5⅜ x 8½. 2-vol. set. Vol. 1: 21761-2 Pa. $12.95
Vol. 2: 21762-0 Pa. $12.95

MAGIC AND MYSTERY IN TIBET, Madame Alexandra David-Neel. Experiences among lamas, magicians, sages, sorcerers, Bonpa wizards. A true psychic discovery. 32 illustrations. 321pp. 5⅜ x 8½. (Available in U.S. only.) 22682-4 Pa. $9.95

THE EGYPTIAN BOOK OF THE DEAD, E. A. Wallis Budge. Complete reproduction of Ani's papyrus, finest ever found. Full hieroglyphic text, interlinear transliteration, word-for-word translation, smooth translation. 533pp. 6½ x 9¼.
21866-X Pa. $12.95

MATHEMATICS FOR THE NONMATHEMATICIAN, Morris Kline. Detailed, college-level treatment of mathematics in cultural and historical context, with numerous exercises. Recommended Reading Lists. Tables. Numerous figures. 641pp. 5⅜ x 8½.
24823-2 Pa. $11.95

PROBABILISTIC METHODS IN THE THEORY OF STRUCTURES, Isaac Elishakoff. Well-written introduction covers the elements of the theory of probability from two or more random variables, the reliability of such multivariable structures, the theory of random function, Monte Carlo methods of treating problems incapable of exact solution, and more. Examples. 502pp. 5³/₈ x 8¹/₂. 40691-1 Pa. $16.95

THE RIME OF THE ANCIENT MARINER, Gustave Doré, S. T. Coleridge. Doré's finest work; 34 plates capture moods, subtleties of poem. Flawless full-size reproductions printed on facing pages with authoritative text of poem. "Beautiful. Simply beautiful."–*Publisher's Weekly*. 77pp. 9¼ x 12. 22305-1 Pa. $7.95

NORTH AMERICAN INDIAN DESIGNS FOR ARTISTS AND CRAFTSPEOPLE, Eva Wilson. Over 360 authentic copyright-free designs adapted from Navajo blankets, Hopi pottery, Sioux buffalo hides, more. Geometrics, symbolic figures, plant and animal motifs, etc. 128pp. 8⅜ x 11. (Not for sale in the United Kingdom.) 25341-4 Pa. $9.95

SCULPTURE: Principles and Practice, Louis Slobodkin. Step-by-step approach to clay, plaster, metals, stone; classical and modern. 253 drawings, photos. 255pp. 8⅛ x 11.
22960-2 Pa. $11.95

THE INFLUENCE OF SEA POWER UPON HISTORY, 1660–1783, A. T. Mahan. Influential classic of naval history and tactics still used as text in war colleges. First paperback edition. 4 maps. 24 battle plans. 640pp. 5⅜ x 8½. 25509-3 Pa. $14.95

THE STORY OF THE TITANIC AS TOLD BY ITS SURVIVORS, Jack Winocour (ed.). What it was really like. Panic, despair, shocking inefficiency, and a little heroism. More thrilling than any fictional account. 26 illustrations. 320pp. 5⅜ x 8½. 20610-6 Pa. $8.95

FAIRY AND FOLK TALES OF THE IRISH PEASANTRY, William Butler Yeats (ed.). Treasury of 64 tales from the twilight world of Celtic myth and legend: "The Soul Cages," "The Kildare Pooka," "King O'Toole and his Goose," many more. Introduction and Notes by W. B. Yeats. 352pp. 5⅜ x 8½. 26941-8 Pa. $8.95

BUDDHIST MAHAYANA TEXTS, E. B. Cowell and others (eds.). Superb, accurate translations of basic documents in Mahayana Buddhism, highly important in history of religions. The Buddha-karita of Asvaghosha, Larger Sukhavativyuha, more. 448pp. 5⅜ x 8½. 25552-2 Pa. $12.95

ONE TWO THREE . . . INFINITY: Facts and Speculations of Science, George Gamow. Great physicist's fascinating, readable overview of contemporary science: number theory, relativity, fourth dimension, entropy, genes, atomic structure, much more. 128 illustrations. Index. 352pp. 5⅜ x 8½. 25664-2 Pa. $9.95

EXPERIMENTATION AND MEASUREMENT, W. J. Youden. Introductory manual explains laws of measurement in simple terms and offers tips for achieving accuracy and minimizing errors. Mathematics of measurement, use of instruments, experimenting with machines. 1994 edition. Foreword. Preface. Introduction. Epilogue. Selected Readings. Glossary. Index. Tables and figures. 128pp. 5⅜ x 8½. 40451-X Pa. $6.95

DALÍ ON MODERN ART: The Cuckolds of Antiquated Modern Art, Salvador Dalí. Influential painter skewers modern art and its practitioners. Outrageous evaluations of Picasso, Cézanne, Turner, more. 15 renderings of paintings discussed. 44 calligraphic decorations by Dalí. 96pp. 5⅜ x 8½. (Available in U.S. only.) 29220-7 Pa. $5.95

ANTIQUE PLAYING CARDS: A Pictorial History, Henry René D'Allemagne. Over 900 elaborate, decorative images from rare playing cards (14th–20th centuries): Bacchus, death, dancing dogs, hunting scenes, royal coats of arms, players cheating, much more. 96pp. 9¼ x 12¼. 29265-7 Pa. $12.95

MAKING FURNITURE MASTERPIECES: 30 Projects with Measured Drawings, Franklin H. Gottshall. Step-by-step instructions, illustrations for constructing handsome, useful pieces, among them a Sheraton desk, Chippendale chair, Spanish desk, Queen Anne table and a William and Mary dressing mirror. 224pp. 8⅛ x 11¼. 29338-6 Pa. $13.95

THE FOSSIL BOOK: A Record of Prehistoric Life, Patricia V. Rich et al. Profusely illustrated definitive guide covers everything from single-celled organisms and dinosaurs to birds and mammals and the interplay between climate and man. Over 1,500 illustrations. 760pp. 7½ x 10⅛. 29371-8 Pa. $29.95

Prices subject to change without notice.

Available at your book dealer or write for free catalog to Dept. GI, Dover Publications, Inc., 31 East 2nd St., Mineola, N.Y. 11501. Dover publishes more than 500 books each year on science, elementary and advanced mathematics, biology, music, art, literary history, social sciences and other areas.